W9-AFG-569

DANIELLE WALKER'S
healthy in a hurry

DANIELLE WALKER'S healthy in a hurry

Real Life. Real Food. Real Fast.

Gluten-Free, Grain-Free & Dairy-Free Recipes

Photography by
AUBRIE PICK

TEN SPEED PRESS
California | New York

Contents

Introduction

When I wrote my first cookbook in 2013, I wasn't sure I would have reason to write another. But as the years passed, more and more readers shared with me their stories of finding health through food, and my passion to provide recipes for those on a similar journey only intensified. Now, five books later, it seems that more than ever people realize the value of feeding themselves and their loved ones healthy, nutritious meals over highly processed foods.

I have been trying to recover from the autoimmune disease ulcerative colitis for twelve years. While food has saved me in so many ways over the years, it hasn't been a perfect process and there have been a lot of bumps in the road. Even while eating a healthy diet, I have run myself into the ground or bumped up against unavoidable trauma and life's daily stresses, causing me to experience setbacks. After going through that cycle many times, I've come to realize that while food is a very powerful device in the overall toolbox, it is just one of many ways to maintain my health. I've learned so much about how taking care of my body with nourishing food can be less impactful if I don't take care of my emotional, physical, and spiritual needs, too. For my body to be at its healthiest, I must also prioritize rest, exercise, mindfulness, counseling or therapy, and journaling. But the time I devote to preparing food also goes into the equation. Spending hours in the kitchen in an attempt to eat healthy can sometimes just add to the stress. I wrote this book to achieve the former (healthy eating!) and avoid the latter (kitchen stress).

"I'm too sick." "I don't have time to cook." "My kids or spouse won't like this dish." "The ingredients are too expensive." "I don't know how to cook." At one time or another, I've said all of these things about cooking. And they are also what I hear most frequently from people who are afraid to start cooking healthy foods.

After I released *Eat What You Love*, my cookbook filled with recipes for comfort foods and child-hood favorites, I received so many requests from readers asking for easy meals for beginning cooks. Some wrote of being intimidated by my use of ingredients like arrowroot powder (it looks a lot like cornstarch), coconut aminos (it tastes a lot like soy sauce), and coconut milk (you can use it like cream). Many chronically ill people sought a book that would teach them or their loved ones who care for them how to nourish their bodies with homemade, healthy food. Others told me of simply wanting to cook healthily to nourish their family but of not always having the time to do it. (Isn't that all of us?) Well, this is the book that does all of that! And although you may occasionally see an ingre-dient that you aren't familiar with, the majority of the ingredients are staples in a grain-free kitchen and each will be used multiple times throughout the book, allowing you to purchase them with the confidence they won't go to waste.

I also drew upon my love of different cuisines from all over the world to create these recipes. Having lived in California nearly all of my life, I've had the pleasure of experiencing many different food styles. My dad also traveled internationally for work when I was younger, which meant we frequently had overseas guests who would share some of their culture through food. In addition to inheriting a love of Italian cuisine from my dad's side of the family, I came to appreciate many other food traditions during my childhood. From Thai, Korean, and Moroccan to Greek and traditional California cuisine, there's a lot to love in this book.

I wanted to keep the flavors and approaches fresh and exciting for those of you who, like me, have been eating grain-free and gluten-free for more than a decade. I also tried to ensure that each recipe is approachable enough for those of you who are just venturing into this lifestyle, perhaps feeling afraid that things won't taste as good as the foods you're losing. Nothing should ever, ever taste like cardboard! That's not a sustainable approach. And this way of eating is a lifestyle, not a diet.

eat well, feel great friend!

Danielle

WHY *HEALTHY IN A HURRY*?

I wrote this book in 2020 during a time when people were in their kitchens more often than ever. While it was a difficult year in so many ways, it also showed me how much community matters, and reminded me that food has the power to bring people together despite our differences and distances apart. Food is universal and unifying. It nourishes our bodies and encourages a space for commonality and conversation.

Yet after a few months of ordering far too much takeout and making food decisions based on stress and emotions, my health started to show the effects. Even though I had more time than ever at home, I seemed to have less time to cook—or at least I wanted to spend less time cooking. After realizing just how much the five of us could eat when we're at home nonstop, I understood that I needed not only to simplify some of our meals but also to keep them interesting so I wouldn't be tempted to order takeout four nights of the week.

These recipes are designed to help you spend less time in the kitchen and more time with your people, less time cleaning up and more time snuggling on the couch watching a show or reading an extra book to your children at bedtime. That doesn't mean compromising on quality or eating bland food in the interest of time. Rather, I share ideas for organizing, prepping in advance, cooking once and using twice, and other shortcuts to get healthy meals on the table during busy times. When it's easier and more time efficient to prep as you go instead of prepping everything in advance to have your station ready, I'll let you know. For instance, if something has to cook on the stove for ten minutes, you have time to chop the remaining vegetables, make a quick sauce, or whip up a healthy side salad.

My recipes and techniques will change the way you think about healthy food. It truly can be prepared without a lot of stress, and everything is so tasty that you'll want to serve these dishes to your family—or whole community—whether they eat a standard diet or one that's gluten-free, dairy-free, or otherwise allergy-free.

Cooking everything from scratch definitely takes more time, but the process can be very rewarding. And with the help of all the wonderful store-bought products now available for grain- and gluten-free eating, most of these recipes can be made in about the same amount of time it takes to order and pick up takeout. Of course, convenience often comes with a higher price, so I've included recipes for items like dairy-free heavy cream, almond milk, or cashew milk to make all of those items from scratch if you choose to do so.

I also love to keep loads of spice mixes and sauces in my pantry and refrigerator to jazz up an otherwise mundane plate of protein and vegetables when I really need to put dinner together quickly. And I am a lover of leftovers. I firmly believe in making a double batch one night and repurposing the second batch into something new for lunch or dinner the following day. As a busy, full-time business owner and mother of three, I rely on these tactics week after week to keep fresh food on the table for my family.

HOW TO USE THIS BOOK

When I was creating this book, I frequently polled my readers and social media friends to find out how they cook, what they look for in a recipe, and what they loved most about my past cookbooks. It's true that you can't please everyone, but I think I've come close here. The top priorities I heard were minimal prep times, recipes categorized by cooking method, meal plans, photo indexes to find a recipe easily, and quick dietary reference guides like Whole30, nut-free, or egg-free for each dish.

The prep time listed for each recipe assumes that any sauce or seasoning mix it calls for was made in advance on prep day and stored for later use. All of the recipes were tested by home cooks like you, but everyone works at their own pace, so prep time will vary from kitchen to kitchen. If you choose to prep your vegetables and proteins earlier in the week, you'll save more time. And if you want to cut even more time, I've included some of my store-bought recommendations for homemade pantry staples.

Some of the chapters are by course or meal-type, such as Breakfast (page 47) or Salads and Sides (page 251), but the majority of the book is organized by cooking method. If you want to make dinner using one pan in the oven, see Sheet Pans (page 138). If you need to throw everything together and set it and forget it, turn to One-Pot Meals (page 208) or Soups and Stews (page 232) for pressure cooker, slow cooker, and Dutch oven recipes. And if you're in a heat wave and don't want to fire up your stove, check out On the Grill (page 280) or No-Cook Lunches (page 67).

Each chapter introduction includes a recipe list organized by protein type. So if you're craving grilled chicken or seafood, this simplifies the search.

The following symbols will help you browse and find suitable recipes more efficiently—that means less time flipping through the pages, more time enjoying a meal with your loved ones.

Can be prepped and cooked in 30 minutes or less.

Has fewer than ten ingredients, not including basic staples like oil and seasoning.

Can be made in an electric pressure cooker or slow cooker and often includes stove-top instructions as well.

In addition, I've included handy dietary guidelines for each recipe so you can easily find what meets your needs. As a reminder, everything in this book is free of gluten, grains, legumes, refined sugar, and dairy (with the exception of lactose-free and casein-free ghee).

SCD Specific carbohydrate diet; also GAPS friendly (gut and psychology syndrome diet)
W30 Whole30*
NF Tree nut–free, not including coconut
EF Egg-free
V Vegetarian

*This program has nuanced guidelines about ingredients and quality, so read your labels carefully to ensure all ingredients in the recipe are compatible. Dijon mustard, broths, pickles, bacon or sausage, bottled sauces, jarred vegetables, and mayo often include added sugar, added sulfites, alcohol, or other sub-ingredients that are not compatible, so be sure you choose products that fit the Whole30 guidelines. For more information, head to whole30.com/program-rules.

There are a handful of QR codes throughout the book for extra information and video tutorials. Open your smartphone's camera app and position the lens over the code. Tap the pop-up banner that appears and you'll be taken to a page with links to bonus content!

MY DEFINITION OF HEALTHY

There are so many different food lifestyles out there; it can get really confusing. In fact, at one point or another throughout my decade-plus span of trying to heal my body, I've eaten whole-grain, gluten-free, grain-free, paleo, Whole30, SCD, and GAPS. Today, my definition of healthy is whatever makes my body feel the most vibrant and free of symptoms and ailments. Healthy may look different for you, and that's a great thing to recognize. It's a nuanced process, and your body likely reacts differently than mine does to certain foods.

The easiest way to describe the way I eat is the paleo diet. It focuses on nutrient-dense meals that are high in vegetables, fruits, and good-quality proteins. When you eat a paleo diet, you learn to be aware of the ingredients in the foods you are consuming, and you try to avoid chemicals, fillers, and additives. That means choosing whole, real foods over packaged and processed whenever possible.

The foods that I avoid are those that cause inflammation and digestive issues for me and for many other people. Because good health and a healthy immune system originate in the gut, eliminating these foods has the potential to cause a major positive effect on your overall health and well-being. Every body is different, which means there's no one-size-fits-all diet. If you're not yet sure what foods are problematic for you, my rule of thumb is to first do a strict elimination diet for thirty days to see if your symptoms improve. From there, add back one food group at a time to try to pinpoint what your problem foods may be. You'll find many online guides to elimination diets, including the Whole30 program, which has loads of resources and advice for both the elimination and reintroduction phases. Working with a functional medicine practitioner who can help evaluate your progress and guide your reintroduction is also a really great option.

Foods I Avoid

Grains and pseudograins: Amaranth, buckwheat, corn, kamut, millet, oats, quinoa, rice, sorghum, spelt, teff, wheat (all varieties, including durum, einkorn, and semolina), and wild rice.

Dairy: Milk products from cows, sheep, and goats, such as yogurt, cheese, cream, and ice cream. I do use ghee in this book, as it is 99 percent free of lactose and casein, the two main proteins that cause digestive problems, but there are substitutes given for those with dairy allergies.

Legumes: Beans, lentils, peanuts, and soy.

Processed additives: Xanthan gum, carrageenan, soy lecithin, modified food starch, monosodium glutamate, and so on.

Processed seed oils: Canola, sunflower seed, grapeseed, and rapeseed.

Processed sugars: High-fructose corn syrup, cane sugar or juice, maltose, dextrose, maltrodextrin, agave nectar, and so on.

STOCK YOUR KITCHEN

Having a well-stocked and organized kitchen is a tremendous help in getting meals on the table quickly. The following list outlines what I keep stocked in mine, and these ingredients are also used frequently in this book. My brand favorites are always changing as more items come into the market, so take a look at shop.daniellewalker.com to see my current favorites.

Baking ingredients and breading: Almond flour (blanched), arrowroot flour, baking powder (grain-free), baking soda, cashew flour, coconut sugar (aka coconut crystals or palm sugar), coconut flour, unsweetened or dark chocolate (at least 85 percent cacao and free of soy and dairy), pure vanilla extract, and raw cacao powder or cocoa powder.

Canned, jarred, and bottled: Coconut aminos, fish sauce (no added sugar), capers, olives packed in olive oil, roasted red peppers, tomato products (free of citric acid or added sugars), wild-caught tuna or salmon, condiments (free of added sugars and preservatives; see pages 22 through 30, sauerkraut, kimchi, dairy-free yogurt, pickled vegetables, and vinegars (apple cider, balsamic, champagne, unseasoned rice, white wine, and red wine).

Dry goods and snacks: Plantain or sweet potato chips (cooked in coconut oil), taro chips, tortilla chips (grain-free), and seaweed (with olive oil and salt).

Fats and oils: Extra-virgin olive oil, unrefined (aka cold-pressed or virgin) coconut oil, avocado oil, ghee, sesame oil (toasted and cold-pressed), and animal fats such as lard, schmaltz, and tallow.

Fruits and vegetables: All fresh fruits and vegetables; dried fruits and fruit juices that contain no added sugars, sulfur, or colorings.

Milk alternatives: Full-fat coconut milk and coconut cream (canned) and unsweetened nut milks, including almond, cashew, and pecan (free of carrageenan and gums).

Nuts and seeds: All nuts and seeds (raw or dry roasted, sprouted, and organic when possible), tahini, and nut butters (free of added sugars and oils).

Proteins: Eggs, beef, pork, lamb, poultry, fish, and shellfish.

When it's accessible and within your budget, opt for 100 percent grass-fed, grass-finished beef and lamb because they contain higher levels of inflammation-fighting omega-3 fatty acids; they aren't fed anything that contains GMOs or has been sprayed with chemical pesticides; and they're not given any growth hormones or unnecessary antibiotics. Look for pasture-raised organic poultry and for deli meats and bacon free of added sugars, carrageenan, nitrates, sulfates, and MSG. Look for pork that is sourced from pigs with heritage-breed lineage, free of antibiotics or added hormones, and raised humanely and on pasture.

While farmed fish can still be healthy, if you can afford it, seek out sustainable and wild-caught seafood. Wild-caught fish, especially salmon, contain more minerals and a healthier balance of omega-3 essential fatty acids versus omega-6. Farmed fish can also contain more potentially harmful contaminants and antibiotics.

Spices and herbs: Himalayan pink salt, black pepper, all spices (whole or ground and preferably organic to avoid pesticides and other chemicals), and spice blends (free of preservatives; see pages 31 through 35).

Sweeteners: Minimally processed or natural sweeteners, such as honey, maple syrup, dates, and coconut sugar.

HEALTHY DOESN'T HAVE TO BREAK THE BANK

One of the most common reasons people think they can't eat healthy is because it's too expensive. Sadly, the marketing and grocery worlds make you feel that way. Fast food and convenience stores are easy to find, and processed foods are often the least expensive.

But I find that what I spend on healthful groceries, I save in doctor visits, medications, and childcare. Eating well and clean is not inexpensive—that is true—but it can be done smartly to save money and redistribute funds from other areas within your budget. When people evaluate the cost of mass-produced, packaged foods—and that definitely includes takeout from restaurants—many families find they end up spending *less* money when they switch to a real-food diet.

The number of new ingredients you need to purchase to eat healthy can be a shock, however. Here are some money-saving tips to help you shop cost efficiently every time you go to the grocery store.

15 Tips for Eating Healthy and Grain-Free on a Budget

1 Choose between your time and your dollar. Often times, the cost of making condiments, sauces, bone broths, seasoning mixes, and even ghee is half the price of store-bought products, especially if you purchase your spices from the bulk bins at your market. For example, you can purchase a raw chicken, cook it in the pressure cooker (see page 41), use the meat all week, and then use the bones to make broth, or you can spend up to three times the amount on a precooked chicken. But if you're a busy person with little time and some extra income, purchasing that precooked bird or other premade items can be a sanity saver and free you up to do other things, like spend time with your family.

2 Buy seasonal local produce, or choose frozen produce for a more economical option for fruits and vegetables currently out of season.

3 Shop at a farmers' market or local farm stand. The produce can be more affordable than buying organic items at your grocery store, which likely had to travel a ways to get there. If you shop toward the end of the market's hours, you can usually find even lower costs.

4 Buy organic when possible, but consult the Environmental Working Group's Dirty Dozen list to know when buying conventional is safe and economical. And when organic doesn't fit into the budget at all, know that incorporating more vegetables and fruits into your diet and cutting out grains and refined oils and sugars are two big steps toward better health.

5 Take an inventory of your fridge and pantry before you shop to avoid buying duplicates. My meal plans (page 19) and accompanying grocery lists (available online) will help you avoid excessive purchasing, which can lead to waste.

6 Grow your own produce, even if it's only fresh herbs on the windowsill of your apartment or one small garden bed in the backyard.

7 Look around for sales and search online for deals before you shop. Even high-end stores put meat on sale from time to time. When you see a sale, stock up on cuts you know you'll use and freeze them. (Keep an empty plastic bin or a large bowl in the fridge and put your frozen meats in it to defrost for a day or two before using.)

8 If grain-fed meat is the most affordable and accessible for you, buy lean cuts. The fat in conventional meats is what holds omega-6 fatty acids, which can be inflammatory. For grass-fed meats, look for cheap cuts (stew meat, roasts, and so on) and bone-in meats. Anytime meat is purchased boneless and/or skinless, the cost of the labor it took to prep it has been added to the price. In the end, though, good-quality red meat, whether grass-fed or conventional, is still better than processed or sugary foods, so buy what you can afford.

9 Go meatless one day a week. Meats are more expensive than vegetables. And while I don't consider myself a master of vegetarian cooking, especially since I cannot use the grains or legumes many vegetable-based dishes call for, I have included a handful of my favorite meat-free dishes in this book: Chilaquiles (page 61), Sweet Chili Noodle Stir-Fry (page 134), Roasted Tomato and Pesto Penne (page 133),Veggie Fried Rice (page 202), Creamy Polenta with Woody Mushroom Sauce (page 205), Wild Mushroom and Zucchini Enchiladas with Mango-Pineapple Salsa (page 206), and Mac and Cheese (page 137).

10 Seek out the most affordable grocery stores. You don't have to purchase everything at a health foods or natural foods store. Places like Trader Joe's, Costco, ALDI, Target, and Walmart frequently carry quality whole foods at a lower cost than other retailers. And the online Thrive Market has the best prices on pantry and shelf-stable items.

11 Buy nuts, seeds, coconut, and even dried fruits from the bulk bins. Bring your own jars or reusable bags and fill them yourself. Many markets offer bulk spices as well. Keep in mind that most of these items will last for only six months or so, so buy accordingly. Bulk bins also make it possible to buy just what you need to cook a single recipe or to test a new ingredient whenever you don't want to invest in a larger quantity.

12 Join a CSA (community-supported agriculture) program for affordable seasonal local produce.

13 Get together with some friends and order a whole butchered animal (called a meat share). Check eatwild.com for a local farmer. You'll need a large freezer for this, but the price per piece ends up being much cheaper than buying individual cuts of meat. Online meat services like butcherbox.com or thrivemarket.com can be a money saver as well, as they allow you to choose smaller quantities.

14 Minimize waste by planning your meals ahead of time (see page 19 for my meal plans) and utilizing the leftovers. Save your pan drippings from cooking bacon or chicken to use in future meals, and buy and use your fresh produce wisely so nothing goes bad before you eat it. When all else fails, make soup with all of the odds and ends in the vegetable crisper drawer of your fridge.

15 Batch cook. Whether you're feeding a large family or a party of two, batch cooking can save so much time and money. Try doubling or even tripling your recipes, then use the leftovers in other dishes, repurpose the proteins into something completely different with a new sauce or added vegetables, or just freeze individual portions for later use. It takes nearly the same amount of time and the same number of dishes to triple a recipe as it does to make one batch, so you may as well get more bang for your buck. Many of the recipes in this book have make-ahead tips, and check out the Freeze It (page 89) chapter for more inspiration.

1

Building Blocks and Meal Plans

Think of this chapter as your foundation of flavor: the building blocks you can use to turn any weeknight meal into a masterpiece in no time. My quick sauces and spice mixes can be made ahead of time and kept on hand to add quick flavor to any meal or to repurpose leftovers. The majority of the sauces will keep in the refrigerator for 2 to 4 weeks and in the freezer for up to 6 months, and the spice mixes will keep at room temperature for up to 6 months. I've also included some quick-and-easy, make-ahead protein and starch options to speed up your mealtime prep. These come in handy when you want to make a healthy lunch but have only a few minutes to throw something together. Precooked chicken and potatoes tossed with one of my spice mixes or sauces can be a nourishing meal within minutes. For the times when you're craving something creamy or cheesy, without the dairy, I've also included a handful of my favorite recipes for substitutes for items like heavy cream or milk.

It's a good idea to set aside some time each month to make your favorites so you can use them in different ways in the weeks ahead. I usually pick one weekend day a month to bang out a bunch of these recipes. Definitely look at your month ahead and make double or triple batches of the things you think you'll use over and over again. I've also listed other uses for the spices, sauces, and meal prep items so you have less waste, and more flavor during your week!

Convenience vs. Cost

Although the most economical option for these flavor bombs is to make everything yourself, you can purchase a lot of these items on my website. My line of Healthy in a Hurry spice blends are all available for purchase in bulk so you can gain back some time with your family! Scan the QR code (see opposite) or head to daniellewalker.com/spices.

For when you need a more convenient alternative, I've also included some of my favorite store-bought brands for sauces and meal-prep items next to the recipes. The good news is that the current grain-free and paleo-friendly marketplace is so much better and bigger than it was when I first started cooking this way in 2009.

Note: These commercial sauces are good substitutes, but the flavors of the finished dish will change a bit.

Meal Plans

When I meal plan, I make sure to incorporate a mix of different proteins and balance more time-intensive recipes with leftover make-ahead recipes, easy soups, or no-cook meals. This meal plan follows that philosophy while also being mindful of utilizing your prep-day recipes to their full potential or incorporating things like herbs or jarred items that you may have opened for one recipe but didn't finish.

We tend to eat leftovers at least one night a week and order-in one night of the weekend, so I've given you five weeknight meals, as well as a prep day for some of the items that are shelf-stable or will last in the refrigerator for the week (or more!). The prep-day lists assume you are following all six meal weeks chronologically, so if you skip around, you may need to modify your prep day to have on hand what you need.

Of course, feel free to substitute for a simple meal of a grilled or pan-fried protein and vegetables with any of the seasoning mixtures from pages 31 through 35 on one or two of these nights to save time and make the week less stressful.

To download the accompanying grocery lists and six more weeks of meal plans, visit daniellewalker.com/mealplans or scan the QR code (see opposite).

Note: Many of the prep-day recipes can be substituted for a convenient store-bought alternative. My favorites are listed under each of the original recipes in this chapter.

Week 1

PREP DAY

- Double batch Creamy Almond-Cauliflower Polenta (page 264)
- Pressure Cooker Chicken (page 41)
- Cajun Seasoning (page 32)

MONDAY

Pork Ragù over Creamy Polenta (page 102)

TUESDAY

Curry Chicken Salad–Stuffed Avocados (page 72)

Note: Use Pressure Cooker Chicken or a rotisserie chicken.

WEDNESDAY

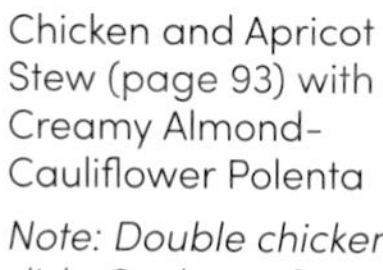

Chicken and Apricot Stew (page 93) with Creamy Almond-Cauliflower Polenta

Note: Double chicken dish. Cook one for dinner; freeze second for another meal.

THURSDAY

Peruvian Steak and French Fries (page 156)

FRIDAY

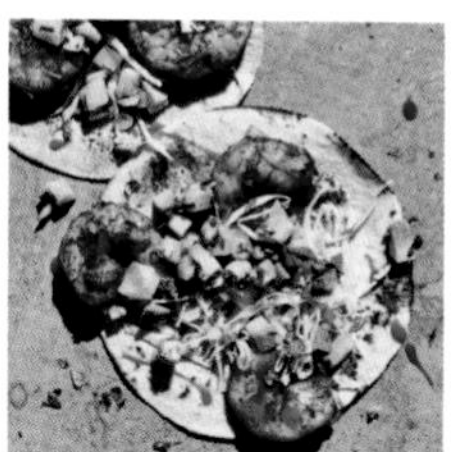

Ancho-Citrus Shrimp Tacos with Roasted Pineapple Salsa (page 160)

Week 2

PREP DAY

- Mango Chutney (page 24)
- Burnt Broccoli Seasoning (page 31)
- Caribbean Seasoning (page 33)

MONDAY

Chicken Cordon Bleu with Creamy Dijon Sauce (page 178)

TUESDAY

Mango and Vanilla–Glazed Pork Tenderloin with Spiced Sweet Potatoes (page 193)

WEDNESDAY

Curry Chicken Burgers with Mango Chutney and Cucumber Raita (page 290)

THURSDAY

Sticky Green Onion Stir-Fried Beef (page 185)

FRIDAY

Jerk Chicken Wings and Burnt Broccoli (page 143)

Week 3

PREP DAY

- Creamy Thai-Style Almond Sauce (page 29)
- Taco Seasoning (page 35)
- Roasted Red Pepper Sauce (page 294)

MONDAY

Chicken Tortilla Soup (page 94)

Note: Double. Cook one for dinner; freeze second for another meal.

TUESDAY

Steak with Roasted Red Pepper Sauce and Lemon-Charred Beans and Tomatoes (page 294)

Note: Save leftover steak for Wednesday.

WEDNESDAY

Chilled Sesame Beef, Mango, and "Noodle" Salad (page 80)

THURSDAY

Salsa Chicken Tacos (page 98)

FRIDAY

Crispy Salmon and Ginger-Garlic Rice with "Peanut" Sauce (page 197)

Week 4

PREP DAY

- Cilantro-Kale Pepita Pesto (page 28)
- Stir-Fry Sauce (page 27)
- Mediterranean Seasoning (page 34)

MONDAY

Grilled Shrimp and Asparagus with Cilantro-Kale Pepita Pesto (page 301)

TUESDAY

Veggie Fried Rice (page 202)

WEDNESDAY

Mediterranean Salmon with Artichokes and Peppers (page 163)

THURSDAY

Crispy Chicken with Pesto, Charred Romanesco, and Potatoes (page 173)

FRIDAY

Asian-Style Chicken Slaw (page 75)

Week 5

PREP DAY			
	Cranberry sauce (see page 286)	Mashed Potatoes (page 266)	Herb Ranch Dressing (page 23)

MONDAY

Swedish Meatballs (page 225)

Note: Double meatballs to use Wednesday.

TUESDAY

Creamy Sun-Dried Tomato Shrimp (page 198)

WEDNESDAY

Mediterranean Meatball Bowl with Spicy Ranch (page 147)

Note: Use meatballs from Monday

THURSDAY

Lemon-Caper Chicken and Rice (page 181)

FRIDAY

Baked Pepperoni Pizza Spaghetti with Ranch (page 106)

Note: Double. Cook one for dinner; freeze the second for another meal.

Week 6

PREP DAY			
	Tagine Seasoning (page 34)	Baked Bacon (page 44)	BBQ Rub (page 32)

MONDAY

Kalua Pork with Pineapple Fried Rice (page 222)

TUESDAY

BBQ Bacon Burger Bowls with Honey-Mustard Vinaigrette (page 298)

WEDNESDAY

Thai Curry Noodle Soup (page 237)

THURSDAY

Spiced Crispy Lamb with Eggplant, Squash, and Hummus (page 194)

FRIDAY

California Sunrise (page 51)

Ketchup

MAKES 3 CUPS - W30, EF, NF, V, SCD

Prep Time: 25 minutes

2 to 4 ounces pitted Deglet Noor dates (12 to 17 small dates; see Note)
3 cups tomato puree
¼ cup plus 2 tablespoons water
¼ cup plus 1 tablespoon white wine vinegar
¼ cup tomato paste
1 clove garlic
1 teaspoon onion powder
¾ teaspoon fine sea salt
¼ teaspoon dry mustard powder
⅛ teaspoon ground cloves
⅛ teaspoon ground allspice

Bring a kettle of water to a boil. Put the dates into a small heatproof bowl, add boiling water to cover, and let soak for 15 minutes. Drain the dates, discarding the water, and transfer them to a blender. Add the tomato puree, water, vinegar, tomato paste, garlic, onion powder, salt, mustard powder, cloves, and allspice and blend on high speed for about 3 minutes, until smooth.

Store in an airtight container in the refrigerator for up to 4 weeks. Or freeze for up to 4 months, then thaw in the refrigerator overnight before using.

Note: **The number of dates you use depends on how sweet you want your ketchup to be. If you're used to store-bought, use 4 ounces.**

Buy It: **True Made Foods**

Use It: **Quick BBQ Sauce (page 22), Sweet-and-Sour Pork (page 152), and Hawaiian BBQ Chicken with Grilled Bok Choy and Pineapple (page 285)**

Quick BBQ Sauce

MAKES 2½ CUPS - EF, NF, V, W30*
*omit maple syrup

Prep Time: 3 minutes

2 cups Ketchup (page 22)
¼ cup BBQ Rub (page 32)
2 tablespoons pure maple syrup or date syrup
2 teaspoons natural liquid smoke

In a glass jar or bottle, combine the ketchup, rub, maple syrup, and liquid smoke. Cap tightly and shake vigorously to mix well. Store in the refrigerator for up to 4 weeks or in the freezer for 6 months. Thaw for 2 days in the refrigerator before using.

Buy It: **Noble Made or Primal Kitchen**

Use It: **Cast-Iron Rib-Eye Steaks with Garlic Mushrooms (page 182), BBQ Bacon Burger Bowls with Honey-Mustard Vinaigrette (page 298), and on grilled or roasted pork, beef, chicken, or turkey**

Herb Ranch Dressing

MAKES 2 CUPS - W30, EF*, NF, V, SCD
*sub egg-free mayo

Prep Time: 8 minutes

1 cup avocado oil mayonnaise
½ cup full-fat coconut milk
¼ cup chopped fresh flat-leaf parsley
2 cloves garlic, minced
2 tablespoons chopped fresh chives
2 tablespoons chopped fresh dill
4 teaspoons freshly squeezed lemon juice
½ teaspoon onion powder
½ teaspoon fine sea salt

In a bowl, whisk together the mayonnaise, coconut milk, parsley, garlic, chives, dill, lemon juice, onion powder, and salt until well mixed. Store in an airtight container in the refrigerator for up to 2 weeks.

Buy It: **Although nothing compares to homemade, Tessemae's is the closest!**

Use It: **Baked Pepperoni Pizza Spaghetti with Ranch (page 106), Mediterranean Meatball Bowl with Spicy Ranch (page 147), Chicken, Bacon, and Ranch Squash Noodles (page 148), and California Chicken Sandwiches with Arugula Pear Salad (page 289)**

Cajun Aioli

MAKES ½ CUP - W30, EF, NF, V, SCD

Prep Time: 5 minutes

⅓ cup avocado oil mayonnaise
1½ teaspoons spicy or Dijon mustard
1 tablespoon Cajun Seasoning (page 32)
1½ teaspoons freshly squeezed lemon juice
1½ teaspoons hot sauce
½ teaspoon dill pickle juice

In a small bowl, gently stir together the mayonnaise, mustard, Cajun seasoning, lemon juice, hot sauce, and pickle juice. Store in an airtight container in the refrigerator for up to 2 weeks.

Buy It: **Primal Kitchen Chipotle Lime Mayo**

Use It: **Cajun Shrimp and Andouille Sausage (page 51)**

Lemon-Dill Aioli

MAKES ½ CUP - W30, EF*, NF, V, SCD
*sub egg-free mayo

Prep Time: 5 minutes

½ cup avocado oil mayonnaise
1 green onion, white and tender green parts, minced
2 tablespoons chopped fresh dill
1 tablespoon freshly squeezed lemon juice
Zest of 1 lemon
½ teaspoon fine sea salt

In a small jar, combine the mayonnaise, green onion, dill, lemon juice and zest, and salt and stir to mix well. Cap tightly and store in the refrigerator for up to 2 weeks.

Buy It: **Stonewall Kitchen Lemon & Avocado Oil Aioli**

Use It: **Roasted Spring Vegetables with Lemon-Dill Aioli (page 263)**

Garlic Aioli

MAKES ½ CUP - W30, EF*, NF, V, SCD
*sub egg-free mayo

Prep Time: 5 minutes

3 cloves garlic
½ cup avocado oil mayonnaise
1 teaspoon freshly squeezed lemon juice
½ teaspoon fine sea salt
¼ teaspoon garlic powder

In a small bowl, gently stir together the garlic, mayonnaise, lemon juice, salt, and garlic powder. Store in an airtight container in the refrigerator for up to 2 weeks.

Buy It: **Primal Kitchen Garlic Aioli Mayo**

Use It: **Smoky Shrimp and Mussels with Crunchy Noodles (page 129), Philly Cheesesteak Skillet (page 186), and Chipotle Cranberry–Sweet Potato Turkey Burgers (page 286)**

Mango Chutney

MAKES ABOUT 2 CUPS - W30, EF, NF, V, SCD

Prep Time: 5 minutes
Cook Time: 35 minutes

5 cups frozen mango cubes
1 cup minced yellow onion
½ cup golden raisins
½ cup unsweetened pineapple juice
½ cup apple cider vinegar
¾ teaspoon ground ginger
½ teaspoon dry mustard powder
½ teaspoon red pepper flakes
½ teaspoon fine sea salt

In a saucepan, combine the mango, onion, raisins, pineapple juice, vinegar, ginger, mustard, pepper flakes, and salt over medium-high heat and bring to a boil. Turn down the heat to medium-low and simmer, stirring occasionally, for 30 minutes, until the mixture is syrupy.

Remove from the heat and let cool to room temperature, then mash the mango pieces with a fork. Store the chutney in the fridge for up to 2 weeks or in the freezer for up to 1 year.

Use It: **Mango and Vanilla–Glazed Tenderloin with Spiced Sweet Potatoes (page 193), Curry Chicken Salad–Stuffed Avocados (page 72), or Kabocha, Sweet Potato, Apple, and Bok Choy Curry (page 230)**

Cucumber Raita

MAKES ABOUT 1½ CUPS - W30*, EF, NF, V, SCD
*use unsweetened and compliant dairy-free yogurt

Prep Time: 10 minutes

2 small Persian or other small seedless cucumbers, finely chopped
1 cup Dairy-Free Yogurt (page 37)
2 tablespoons chopped fresh cilantro
½ teaspoon ground cumin
¼ teaspoon fine sea salt
¼ teaspoon garam masala

In a bowl, combine the cucumbers, yogurt, cilantro, cumin, salt, and garam masala and mix well. Store the raita in the fridge for 1 week.

Buy It: There aren't any dairy-free raita products, but you can purchase your favorite dairy-free yogurt to make this quickly, or substitute in Kite Hill Dairy-Free tzatziki for a bit of a different flavor profile.

Use It: Curry Chicken Burgers with Mango Chutney (page 290), and Cucumber Raita, Mango and Vanilla-Glazed Tenderloin with Spiced Sweet Potatoes (page 193), Curry Chicken Salad-Stuffed Avocados (page 72), and Kabocha, Sweet Potato, Apple, and Bok Choy Curry (page 230); or spoon atop your favorite Indian-inspired dishes

Vinaigrette

MAKES ABOUT 1 CUP - W30, EF, NF, V, SCD

Prep Time: 5 minutes

3 tablespoons freshly squeezed lemon juice
1½ tablespoons champagne, balsamic, or apple cider vinegar
2 teaspoons Dijon mustard
½ teaspoon fine sea salt
Pinch of freshly ground black pepper
½ cup extra-virgin olive oil

In a bowl, whisk together the lemon juice, vinegar, mustard, salt, and pepper. Slowly whisk in the oil. Use immediately, or transfer to a jar, cap tightly, and store in the refrigerator for up to 3 weeks. Shake well before using.

Buy It: Primal Kitchen Balsamic Vinaigrette

Maple-Cider Vinaigrette

MAKES ABOUT ¾ CUP - EF, NF, V, SCD*
*sub honey for maple syrup

Prep Time: 5 minutes

2 tablespoons pure maple syrup
1½ tablespoons apple cider vinegar
½ tablespoon Dijon mustard
Juice of ½ lemon
¼ teaspoon ground coriander
¼ teaspoon ground cinnamon
¼ teaspoon ground cumin
⅛ teaspoon ground turmeric
½ teaspoon fine sea salt
¼ teaspoon freshly ground black pepper
½ cup extra-virgin olive oil

In a bowl, whisk together the maple syrup, vinegar, mustard, lemon juice, coriander, cinnamon, cumin, turmeric, salt, and pepper. Slowly drizzle in the oil while whisking vigorously. Use immediately, or transfer to a jar, cap tightly, and store in the fridge for up to 3 weeks. Shake well before using.

Hoisin Sauce

MAKES ABOUT 1 CUP - **W30, EF, NF, V**

Prep Time: 8 minutes

4 pitted Medjool dates
½ cup coconut aminos
2 tablespoons warm water
1½ tablespoons tahini
2½ teaspoons apple cider vinegar
1 teaspoon garlic powder
¾ teaspoon ground ginger
½ teaspoon five-spice powder
2 teaspoons toasted sesame oil
2 teaspoons tomato paste
1 teaspoon fine sea salt
¼ teaspoon cayenne pepper

In a small blender or food processor, combine the dates, coconut aminos, water, tahini, vinegar, garlic powder, ginger, five-spice powder, sesame oil, tomato paste, salt, and cayenne and puree until smooth. Store in an airtight container in the refrigerator for up to 4 weeks or in the freezer for 6 months.

Buy It: **Coconut Secret Hoisin Sauce or Premier Japan Hoisin Sauce**

Use It: **Moo Shu Pork Pasta (page 124) and Chicken Lettuce Wraps (page 174)**

Stir-Fry Sauce

MAKES 2½ CUPS - **W30, EF, NF, V**

Prep Time: 5 minutes

2 cups coconut aminos
2 tablespoons plus 2 teaspoons fish sauce
2 tablespoons plus 2 teaspoons toasted sesame oil
1 tablespoon unseasoned rice vinegar, or 1½ teaspoons apple cider vinegar
1½ teaspoons fine sea salt
1 teaspoon white pepper

In a large jar, combine the coconut aminos, fish sauce, sesame oil, vinegar, salt, and pepper. Cap tightly and shake vigorously to mix well. Store in the refrigerator for up to 3 months.

Buy It: **Big Tree Farms Teriyaki or Primal Kitchen No Soy Teriyaki; both brands are sweeter and have more of a teriyaki sauce flavor than a stir-fry sauce flavor, but they will work with all of the recipes.**

Use It: **Asian-Style Chicken Slaw (page 75), Curry Noodles with Shrimp (page 126), Teriyaki Salmon Packets (page 167), Chicken Lettuce Wraps (page 174), and Veggie Fried Rice (page 202)**

Cilantro-Kale Pepita Pesto

MAKES 2 CUPS - **W30, EF, NF, V, SCD**

Prep Time: 10 minutes

1 cup pepitas, toasted lightly

½ cup firmly packed cilantro leaves and stems

½ cup firmly packed chopped lacinato (Tuscan) kale (stems and ribs removed)

½ teaspoon ground coriander

2 cloves garlic

6 tablespoons extra-virgin olive oil, plus more for storing

¼ cup water

1 tablespoon freshly squeezed lime juice, plus more if needed

1 tablespoon fine sea salt

½ teaspoon freshly ground black pepper

In a food processor, combine the pepitas, cilantro, kale, coriander, and garlic and pulse until coarsely chopped. With the machine running, gradually add 4 tablespoons of the oil, the water, and the lime juice and process until a coarse puree forms. With the machine still running, drizzle in the remaining 2 tablespoons oil and continue to process to your desired consistency. Season with the salt and pepper and with more lime juice if needed.

Transfer the pesto to a storage container and gently drizzle a thin layer of oil, about ¼ inch, evenly over the top. The oil prevents air from reaching the pesto, keeping it green. Cover tightly and store in the refrigerator for up to 3 weeks. Replace the thin layer of oil every time you use, and return it to the refrigerator to keep it fresh.

Use It: **Pesto Chicken, Nectarine, and Avocado Salad (page 71), Crispy Chicken with Pesto, Charred Romanesco, and Potatoes (page 173), and Grilled Shrimp and Asparagus with Cilantro-Kale Pepita Pesto (page 301)**

Dairy-Free Basil Pesto

MAKES ⅓ CUP - **W30, EF, NF, V, SCD**

Prep Time: 8 minutes
Cook Time: 2 minutes

⅓ cup pine nuts, toasted lightly

3 cups tightly packed fresh basil leaves

3 cloves garlic

1 teaspoon freshly squeezed lemon juice

½ teaspoon fine sea salt

⅓ cup extra-virgin olive oil, plus more for storing

In a food processor or blender, combine the pine nuts, basil, garlic, lemon juice, and salt and pulse until finely chopped. With the machine running, slowly drizzle in the oil and process until a pourable paste forms. Continue to process for about 15 seconds more, until smooth.

Transfer the pesto to a storage container and gently drizzle a thin layer of oil evenly over the top. The oil prevents air from reaching the pesto, keeping it green. Cover tightly and store in the refrigerator for up to 3 weeks. Replace the thin layer of oil every time you use, and return it to the refrigerator to keep it fresh.

Use It: **Roasted Tomato and Pesto Penne (page 133) or as a substitute for Cilantro-Kale Pepita Pesto (page 28)**

Mediterranean Tahini Dressing

MAKES 1 CUP - W30, EF, NF, V, SCD

Prep Time: 5 minutes

- 2 cloves garlic, crushed
- ¼ cup tahini
- 2 tablespoons freshly squeezed lemon juice
- ½ teaspoon fine sea salt
- ¼ teaspoon ground cumin
- ¼ teaspoon freshly ground black pepper
- ¼ to ⅓ cup water

In a small bowl, whisk together the garlic, tahini, lemon juice, salt, cumin, and pepper. Slowly whisk in the water, adding just enough to achieve the desired consistency. It should be thicker than salad dressing but still pourable. Store in an airtight container in the refrigerator for 2 weeks.

Buy It: Mother Raw Creamy Tahini

Use It: Curried Cauliflower and Mango Salad (page 260) and Spiced Beef and Lamb Kebabs with Tomato-Cucumber Salad (page 297)

Creamy Thai-Style Almond Sauce

MAKES ¾ CUP - W30*, EF, V
*omit coconut sugar

Prep Time: 8 minutes

- 1 clove garlic, crushed
- ¼ cup tahini
- ¼ cup unsweetened almond or cashew butter
- 2 tablespoons freshly squeezed lime juice
- ¼ cup coconut aminos
- 2 tablespoons coconut sugar
- 1 teaspoon peeled and grated fresh ginger
- 1 to 2 tablespoons water
- Fine sea salt and freshly ground black pepper

In a small bowl, whisk together the garlic, tahini, almond butter, lime juice, coconut aminos, coconut sugar, and ginger. Slowly whisk in just enough of the water to create a thick and creamy sauce. Season to taste with salt and pepper. Store in an airtight container in the refrigerator for up to 1 month.

Tidbits: To turn this into a delicious salad dressing, see page 80.

Buy It: Yai's Thai Almond Sauce

Use It: Chilled Sesame Beef, Mango, and "Noodle" Salad (page 80), Thai-Style Shrimp Salad (page 87), Chicken Pad Thai Noodles (page 116), Crispy Salmon and Ginger-Garlic Rice with "Peanut" Sauce (page 197), Meatballs with Creamy Thai-Style Almond Sauce (page 217), and Thai Curry Noodle Soup (page 237)

Enchilada Sauce

Red Sauce

MAKES 2½ CUPS - W30, EF, NF, V, SCD*
*see Tidbits

Prep Time: 3 minutes
Cook Time: 10 minutes

- 3 tablespoons ghee or coconut oil
- 2 tablespoons arrowroot powder
- 3 tablespoons chili powder
- 1 teaspoon dried oregano
- ¾ teaspoon ground cumin
- ½ teaspoon fine sea salt
- ½ teaspoon onion powder
- 1 (7-ounce) jar tomato paste
- 2 cups chicken Bone Broth (page 42)

In a saucepan, melt the ghee over medium heat. Whisk in the arrowroot and cook, stirring, for 30 to 45 seconds, until thickened. Add the chili powder, oregano, cumin, salt, and onion powder and continue to cook, stirring, for 1 to 2 minutes, until fragrant.

Add the tomato paste and broth and whisk until smooth, then simmer for 5 minutes to thicken to a good sauce consistency. Store in an airtight container in the refrigerator for up to 2 weeks.

Note: **If using coconut oil, I suggest using expeller-pressed so it does not impart a coconut flavor.**

Tidbits: **For SCD, omit the arrowroot powder and sauté ¾ cup minced white onion in the ghee for about 8 minutes, until soft. After whisking in the tomato paste and broth, transfer the mixture to a blender or food processor and puree until smooth.**

Buy It: Siete Red Enchilada Sauce

Use It: Chilaquiles (page 61)

Green Sauce

MAKES 2½ CUPS - W30, EF, NF, V, SCD

Prep Time: 15 minutes
Cook Time: 10 minutes

- 1½ pounds tomatillos, husked and rinsed
- 1 to 4 serrano chiles, stemmed and seeded for mild
- 1 small poblano chile, stemmed
- 1 small white onion, halved
- 3 cloves garlic
- 5 sprigs cilantro
- 2 tablespoons ghee or avocado oil
- 2 teaspoons fine sea salt

In a saucepan, combine the tomatillos and the serrano and poblano chiles, adding the larger number of serranos if you like your sauce hot. Add water to cover, bring to a boil over medium-high heat, and cook for about 15 minutes, until the tomatillos turn a dull green. Drain the tomatillos and chiles and transfer them to a blender. Add the onion, garlic, and cilantro and blend on high speed for about 30 seconds, until smooth.

Return the saucepan to medium-high heat and heat the ghee. Quickly add the tomatillo sauce and cook, stirring constantly, until it bubbles. Turn down the heat to low and cook until the sauce starts to thicken, about 5 minutes more. Stir in the salt and remove from the heat. Store in an airtight container in the refrigerator for up to 2 weeks.

Note: **Start with 1 serrano and increase the number depending on the level of heat you prefer. Seeding the peppers will also make the sauce milder.**

Buy It: Siete Green Enchilada Sauce

Use It: Chilaquiles (page 61), Turkey Chili Verde (page 97), and Wild Mushroom and Zucchini Enchiladas with Mango-Pineapple Salsa (page 206)

Adobo Seasoning

MAKES ABOUT 1 CUP - W30, EF, NF, V, SCD

Prep Time: 5 minutes

¼ cup fine sea salt
¼ cup garlic powder
2 tablespoons dried oregano
2 tablespoons onion powder
1½ tablespoons ground cumin
1 tablespoon freshly ground black pepper
2 teaspoons annatto powder or ground turmeric

In a bowl, stir together all of the ingredients, mixing well. Store in an airtight container in the pantry for up to 6 months.

Buy It: daniellewalker.com/spices

Use It: Creamy Sausage, Kale, and Sweet Potato Soup (page 105), Arroz con Pollo (page 214), and Puerto Rican–Style Plantain Rice (page 273); or sprinkle 1 tablespoon on 2 pounds chicken or fish before roasting or grilling

Burnt Broccoli Seasoning

MAKES ABOUT ½ CUP - W30, EF, NF, V, SCD

Prep Time: 5 minutes

3 tablespoons fine sea salt
2 tablespoons garlic powder
1 tablespoon chili powder
1 tablespoon ground cumin
1 tablespoon onion powder
1½ teaspoons ground cinnamon
1½ teaspoons ground coriander
1½ teaspoons freshly ground black pepper

In a bowl, stir together all of the ingredients, mixing well. Store in an airtight container in the pantry for up to 6 months.

Buy It: daniellewalker.com/spices

Use It: Brussels Sprouts, Apple, and Breakfast Sausage Bowl (page 58), Jerk Chicken Wings and Burnt Broccoli (page 143), Crispy Chicken with Pesto, Charred Romanesco, and Potatoes (page 173), and Burnt Broccoli (page 278); or sprinkle 2 teaspoons on 2 pounds vegetables before roasting

BBQ Rub

MAKES ABOUT 1 CUP - W30, EF, NF, V, SCD

Prep Time: 5 minutes

¼ cup sweet paprika
¼ cup chili powder
2 tablespoons fine sea salt
1 tablespoon garlic powder
1 tablespoon dry mustard powder
2 teaspoons dried oregano
2 teaspoons ground cumin
¾ teaspoon freshly ground black pepper
½ teaspoon cayenne pepper

In a bowl, stir together all of the ingredients, mixing well. Store in an airtight container in the pantry for up to 6 months.

Buy It: daniellewalker.com/spices

Use It: Quick BBQ Sauce (page 22) and BBQ Bacon Burger Bowls with Honey-Mustard Vinaigrette (page 298); or sprinkle 1 tablespoon on 2 pounds beef burgers, steaks, or chicken before grilling or roasting and pair with Quick BBQ Sauce

Cajun Seasoning

MAKES ABOUT 1 CUP - W30, EF, NF, V, SCD

Prep Time: 5 minutes

- ¼ cup smoked paprika
- 2 tablespoons onion powder
- 2 tablespoons garlic powder
- 4 teaspoons dried oregano
- 4 teaspoons dried thyme
- 4 teaspoons fine sea salt
- 2 teaspoons freshly ground black pepper
- 1 to 2 teaspoons cayenne pepper (see Note)
- 1 teaspoon dry mustard powder
- 1 teaspoon red pepper flakes

In a bowl, stir together all of the ingredients, mixing well. Store in an airtight container in the pantry for up to 6 months.

Note: Use up to 2 teaspoons cayenne if you want this to be spicy.

Buy It: daniellewalker.com/spices

Use It: Cajun Aioli (page 23), Cajun Shrimp and Andouille Sausage (page 151), and Cajun Chicken Pasta (page 115)

Italian Seasoning

MAKES ABOUT 1¼ CUPS - W30, EF, NF, V, SCD

Prep Time: 5 minutes

- ¼ cup dried oregano
- ¼ cup dried basil
- 2 tablespoons dried marjoram
- 2 tablespoons dried thyme
- 2 tablespoons dried rosemary
- 2 tablespoons dried sage
- 2 tablespoons dried parsley
- 1 tablespoon red pepper flakes

In a bowl, stir together all of the ingredients, mixing well. Store in an airtight container in the pantry for up to 6 months.

Buy It: daniellewalker.com/spices

Use It: Muffuletta Salad with Tapenade Vinaigrette (page 79), Pork Ragù over Creamy Polenta (page 102), Baked Pepperoni Pizza Spaghetti with Ranch (page 106), One-Pot Beef Pasta with Creamy Tomato-Vodka Sauce (page 121), and Creamy Sun-Dried Tomato Shrimp (page 198)

Caribbean Seasoning

MAKES ABOUT ⅓ CUP - W30, EF, NF, V, SCD

Prep Time: 5 minutes

- 4 teaspoons smoked paprika
- 4 teaspoons onion powder
- 2 teaspoons ground allspice
- 2 teaspoons fine sea salt
- 2 teaspoons chili powder
- 2 teaspoons dried thyme
- 1 teaspoon ground cinnamon
- ½ teaspoon white pepper
- ½ teaspoon ground ginger
- ½ teaspoon cayenne pepper

In a bowl, stir together all of the ingredients, mixing well. Store in an airtight container in the pantry for up to 6 months.

Buy It: daniellewalker.com/spices

Use It: Jerk Chicken Wings and Burnt Broccoli (page 143) and Mango and Vanilla–Glazed Tenderloin with Spiced Sweet Potatoes (page 193)

Mediterranean Seasoning

MAKES 1¾ CUPS - W30, EF, NF, V, SCD

Prep Time: 5 minutes

¼ cup garlic powder
¼ cup dried oregano
¼ cup dried marjoram
¼ cup dried rosemary
¼ cup dried thyme
¼ cup freshly ground black pepper
4 teaspoons dried dill
4 teaspoons fine sea salt
1 teaspoon ground nutmeg
1 teaspoon ground cinnamon

In a spice grinder or a clean coffee grinder, combine all of the ingredients and grind to a fine powder. Store in an airtight container in the pantry for up to 6 months.

Buy It: daniellewalker.com/spices

Use It: Mediterranean Meatball Bowl with Spicy Ranch (page 147), Mediterranean Salmon with Artichokes and Peppers (page 163)

Tagine Seasoning

MAKES 1¾ CUPS - W30, EF, NF, V, SCD

Prep Time: 5 minutes

¼ cup ground cumin
¼ cup ground coriander
2½ tablespoons fine sea salt
2 tablespoons ground cinnamon
1 tablespoon plus 1 teaspoon ground ginger
1 tablespoon plus 1 teaspoon ground turmeric
1 tablespoon ground nutmeg
1 tablespoon freshly ground black pepper
2 teaspoons ground allspice
2 teaspoons cayenne pepper

In a bowl, stir together all of the ingredients, mixing well. Store in an airtight container in the pantry for up to 6 months.

Buy It: daniellewalker.com/spices

Use It: Chicken and Apricot Stew (page 93), Spiced Crispy Lamb with Eggplant, Squash, and Hummus (page 194), Meatballs with Creamy Thai-Style Almond Sauce (page 217), and Spiced Beef and Lamb Kebabs with Tomato-Cucumber Salad (page 297)

Fries Seasoning Salt

MAKES ABOUT ⅓ CUP - W30, EF, NF, V, SCD

Prep Time: 5 minutes

2 tablespoons fine sea salt
1 tablespoon smoked paprika
1 tablespoon garlic powder
1½ teaspoons onion powder
1½ teaspoons chili powder
1½ teaspoons dried basil
¾ teaspoon ground cumin
¾ teaspoon ground sage
¾ teaspoon freshly ground black pepper
¼ teaspoon dried oregano

In a bowl, stir together all of the ingredients, mixing well. Store in an airtight container in the pantry for up to 6 months.

Buy It: daniellewalker.com/spices

Use It: Peruvian Steak and French Fries (page 156) or sprinkle ½ teaspoon per pound of roasted potatoes, sweet potatoes, or French fries after roasting or frying

Taco Seasoning

MAKES ABOUT 2 CUPS - W30, EF, NF, V, SCD

Prep Time: 5 minutes

½ cup plus 2 tablespoons chili powder
⅓ cup fine sea salt
⅓ cup ground cumin
¼ cup dried oregano
2½ tablespoons onion powder
2½ tablespoons ground coriander
2½ tablespoons sweet paprika
1 to 3 teaspoons cayenne pepper (see Note)
1 teaspoon freshly ground black pepper

In a bowl, stir together all of the ingredients, mixing well. Store in an airtight container in the pantry for up to 6 months.

Note: Use up to 3 teaspoons cayenne if you want this to be spicy.

Buy It: daniellewalker.com/spices

Use It: Chicken Tortilla Soup (page 94), Salsa Chicken Tacos (page 98), and "Skillet" Queso Dip (page 226)

Dairy Substitutes

After a couple of years of being completely dairy-free, my gut has healed enough for me to be able to tolerate some dairy about once a week without issue. I do not drink or use any milk or cream, however, as they have the highest levels of lactose and casein, which don't sit well with me. I also use ghee, which is 99 percent free of those proteins, as a favorite cooking fat.

From polls I've taken of my readers, it seems that about half of you still eat cheese occasionally, too. Most people find goat's and sheep's milk cheeses easier than cow's milk cheeses to digest because their protein structures are different. These animals are also more likely raised as free grazing and without a heavy diet of processed grains. When I do consume dairy from cows, raw milk cheese from grass-fed cows is easier for me to digest than pasteurized from conventionally raised cows. The longer a cheese is aged, the lower the amount of lactose, so choose hard cheeses over soft and fresh versions.

Here are a few of my favorite dairy cheeses:

- Cypress Grove Lamb Chopper
- Cypress Grove Midnight Moon
- Trader Joe's goat's milk Gouda
- Manchego.

These are three of my favorite dairy-free cheeses:

- Miyoko's Creamery mozzarella
- Violife feta
- Kite Hill ricotta.

For those of you who avoid all dairy due to inflammation or allergies, this section includes some of my tried-and-true dairy substitutes.

Dairy-Free Sour Cream

MAKES 1 CUP - W30, EF, V, SCD

Prep Time: 5 minutes, plus 24 hours for chilling, and 36 hours fermenting

1 cup full-fat coconut cream (see Tidbits)

1 (50 billion CFU) dairy-free and gluten-free probiotic capsule, capsule casing discarded

2 tablespoons Almond Milk (page 38) or Cashew Milk (page 39)

½ teaspoon freshly squeezed lime juice

¼ teaspoon fine sea salt

Place the coconut cream in a bowl, stir in the powder from the probiotic capsule, and cover the bowl with a clean kitchen towel. Let the bowl sit at room temperature for 36 to 48 hours. The longer you leave it, the sourer it will be.

Once fermented to your desired level of sourness, stir in the almond milk, lime juice, and salt. Store in an airtight container in the refrigerator for up to 1 week.

Note: Plan on 24 hours for chilling the coconut milk and 36 to 48 hours for fermenting the sour cream.

Tidbits: You can purchase cans of full-fat coconut cream that will have mostly thick fat. Discard the thin watery liquid at the bottom of the can. You can also refrigerate 2 cans of full-fat coconut milk for 24 hours and only use the thick cream from the top of the can.

Buy It: Forager Project and, if you tolerate lactose-free dairy, Green Valley Creamery

Use It: Huevos Rancheros (page 54), Chilaquiles (page 61), Chicken Tortilla Soup (page 94), Turkey Chili Verde (page 97), and Salsa Chicken Tacos (page 98)

Dairy-Free Yogurt

MAKES SIX ¼-PINT JARS (3 CUPS TOTAL) - EF, V, SCD

Prep Time: 15 minutes, plus 30 minutes hands-off time
Cook Time: 8 minutes, plus 12 hours fermenting
and 4 hours chilling

- 1 cup (about 150 g) whole raw cashews
- 2 cups filtered water
- 1½ teaspoons unflavored powdered gelatin
- 1½ tablespoons pure maple syrup or light-colored raw honey
- 1 (50 billion CFU) dairy-free and gluten-free probiotic capsule, capsule casing discarded

Bring a kettle of water to a boil. Place the cashews in a heatproof bowl and add boiling water to cover. Let soak at room temperature for 30 minutes, then drain, rinse, and drain again.

Put ½ cup of the water into a saucepan and sprinkle the gelatin over the top. Let the gelatin bloom for 10 minutes.

In a blender, combine the cashews and the remaining 1½ cups water and blend on high speed for about 1 minute, until very smooth. Stop to scrape down the sides if needed, then continue blending until very smooth.

Place the saucepan with the gelatin over medium-high heat and bring just to a boil, whisking constantly to dissolve the gelatin. Immediately turn down the heat to medium, add the cashew liquid, and heat, whisking constantly, for about 5 minutes, until the mixture registers 120°F on a thermometer. Do not allow it to boil.

Remove the pan from the heat and let the mixture cool to 110°F, which will take about 15 minutes. Whisk in the maple syrup and the powder from the probiotic capsule. Pour the mixture through a fine-mesh sieve into six ¼-pint (4-ounce) jars and secure the lids. Place the jars in a yogurt maker or in a dehydrator with the trays removed and set to 110°F. Leave to ferment for 12 to 16 hours. The longer you leave the yogurt, the sourer it will become.

Refrigerate the finished yogurt for at least 4 hours or for up to 5 days to allow the gelatin to set and the yogurt to thicken. Just before serving or using, stir well for a creamy consistency.

Variation

For fruit-flavored yogurt, stir 2 tablespoons fresh fruit puree of choice into each jar before chilling in the refrigerator. My family loves strawberry, peach, blueberry, and banana-mango.

Buy It: Culina and COYO

Use It: Curry Chicken Burgers with Mango Chutney and Cucumber Raita (page 290)

Dairy-Free Parmesan Cheese

MAKES 1 CUP - EF, NF, W30

Prep Time: 10 minutes

- ¾ cup (about 105 g) whole raw cashews
- 2½ tablespoons nutritional yeast
- ¾ teaspoon fine sea salt
- ½ teaspoon garlic powder

Place the cashews, nutritional yeast, salt, and garlic powder in a food processor and process until it has the texture of fine sand.

Store in an airtight jar in the refrigerator for 3 months.

Use It: One-Pot Beef Pasta with Creamy Tomato-Vodka Sauce (page 121), Creamy Sun-Dried Tomato Shrimp (page 198), and Creamy Almond-Cauliflower Polenta (page 264)

Almond Milk

MAKES 4 CUPS - W30, EF, V, SCD

Prep Time: 5 minutes, plus 12 hours soaking time

- 1 cup whole raw almonds
- 8 cups filtered water
- ¼ teaspoon fine sea salt

In a bowl, combine the almonds, 4 cups of the water, and ⅛ teaspoon of the salt. Cover and let soak at room temperature for at least 12 hours or for up to 24 hours.

Drain the nuts, rinse well, and drain again. Transfer them to a blender, add the remaining 4 cups water and ⅛ teaspoon salt, and blend on high speed for about 2 minutes, until smooth.

Strain the milk through a fine-mesh sieve, a nut milk bag, or double-layer cheesecloth, pressing against or squeezing the solids to remove all of the liquid. Store in an airtight container in the refrigerator for up to 5 days.

Note: **Plan on 12 to 24 hours for soaking the almonds.**

Tidbits: **If you plan to drink the almond milk on its own or use it for a sweet dish, add 1 to 3 pitted dates to the blender to sweeten the milk naturally. Other nuts can be substituted for the almonds to make a variety of nut milks. Try hazelnuts, walnuts, or pecans for a fresh spin on this dairy-free milk alternative!**

Buy It: **Three Trees, MALK, or other unsweetened original flavor brands with the fewest ingredients and no carrageenan or gums**

Use It: **Dairy-Free Sour Cream (page 36), Lemon Chia Pudding with Berries and Toasted Coconut (page 62), and Açai Bowls (page 109)**

Dairy-Free Heavy Cream

MAKES 1½ CUPS - W30, EF, V, SCD

Prep Time: 5 minutes, plus 4 hours soaking time

- 1¼ cups (about 185 g) whole raw cashews
- ¾ cup water
- 1 tablespoon freshly squeezed lemon juice
- ¼ teaspoon fine sea salt
- ¾ teaspoon apple cider vinegar

In a bowl, combine the cashews with water to cover. Cover and let soak at room temperature for 4 hours.

Drain the nuts, rinse well, and drain again. Transfer them to a high-speed blender, add the water, lemon juice, salt, and vinegar, and blend on high speed for about 1 minute, until very smooth and creamy. There should be no visible bits of cashew. If needed, scrape down the sides with a rubber spatula and blend again for 30 seconds.

Store in an airtight container in the refrigerator for 5 days.

Note: **Plan on 4 hours for soaking the cashews.**

Tidbits: **Use this dairy-free cream in place of heavy cream in creamy soups or casseroles. A high-speed blender is necessary to puree the cashews to a very smooth cream. If you don't have one, substitute 1 cup unsweetened raw cashew butter. In this case, skip the soaking step and reduce the water to ⅓ cup.**

Buy It: **Kite Hill Ricotta or Treeline Plain Cashew Cream Cheese; blend together 1 (8-ounce) container with ¼ cup water until thick and creamy and the consistency of heavy cream**

Use It: **Creamy Sausage, Kale, and Sweet Potato Soup (page 105), One-Pot Beef Pasta with Creamy Tomato-Vodka Sauce (page 121), and Shrimp Chowder (page 246)**

Cashew Milk

MAKES 5 CUPS - W30, EF, V, SCD

Prep Time: 5 minutes, plus 4 hours soaking time

1 cup (about 150 g) whole raw cashews
3 cups water
2 pitted dates (optional)
¼ teaspoon fine sea salt

In a bowl, combine the cashews with water to cover. Cover and let soak at room temperature for 4 hours.

Drain the nuts, rinse well, and drain again. Transfer them to a high-speed blender and add the water, dates, and salt. Blend on low speed for 30 seconds, then blend on high speed for 1 to 2 minutes, until very smooth and creamy. There should be no visible bits of cashew.

Store in an airtight container in the refrigerator for up to 5 days.

Note: Plan on 4 hours for soaking the cashews.

Tidbits: To achieve the proper thickness in cashew milk or in sauces that use cashews as a thickener, measure the nuts using the gram weight provided. If substituting whole blanched almonds or whole raw macadamia nuts for the cashews, weigh them as well, as nuts of different sizes measure differently in cups. If you purchase cashew milk to use in my recipes, be aware that it usually contains additives to keep the milk thin and may not perform as well.

Buy It: I don't use store-bought cashew milk because most brands are strained and not creamy enough to thicken sauces and soups. In a pinch, whisk together ⅓ cup unsweetened raw cashew butter with ½ to ¾ cup warm water until it is the consistency of whole milk.

Use It: Dairy-Free Sour Cream (page 36), Lemon Chia Pudding with Berries and Toasted Coconut (page 62), Açai Bowls (page 109), Cod Florentine (page 201), Creamy Polenta with Woody Mushroom Sauce (page 205), Mashed Potatoes (page 266), and Basic Root Mash (page 267)

Nut-Free Thickening Substitutes

If you have followed my recipes for a long time, you know that pureed raw cashews are my absolute favorite dairy allergy-friendly alternative for heavy cream. The puree has a creamy but mild flavor and can truly stand in for cream undetected in a recipe. It also helps to thicken sauces as they're heated and the cashew puree expands.

Here are two options for nut-free substitutes for ½ cup Dairy-Free Heavy Cream in any recipe:

- In a small saucepan, whisk together ¾ cup full-fat coconut cream, 1 tablespoon arrowroot powder, and ½ teaspoon fine sea salt over medium heat. Bring to a simmer, whisking frequently, and cook for 3 to 5 minutes, until thickened. Omit any water in the recipe that is either blended with the cashews or whisked with the cashew butter.
- Add 2 teaspoons avocado oil or ghee to a pan over medium heat. Add 1 large yellow onion, chopped, and 4 cloves garlic, chopped, and sauté for 7 to 10 minutes, until well browned. Transfer the cooked vegetables to a blender, add 1 tablespoon arrowroot powder and 2 tablespoons water, and blend on high speed until smooth. Pour the mixture back into the pan and simmer, stirring often, for 3 to 5 minutes, until thickened.

Parboiled Potatoes

MAKES ABOUT 4 CUPS - **W30, EF, NF, V**

Prep Time: 5 minutes
Cook Time: 6 minutes

3 pounds baby creamer potatoes or white-fleshed sweet potatoes, unpeeled and cut into 1½-inch cubes

Fill a large pot of water two-thirds full and bring to a boil over high heat. Add the potatoes and boil for 4 to 6 minutes, until just fork-tender. Drain the potatoes and run them under cold running water to stop the cooking. Let cool to room temperature, then store in an airtight container in the refrigerator for up to 7 days.

Tidbits: **Parboiling potatoes saves a lot of time when you're making dinner, and it also helps them get nice and crispy on the outside once baked, while remaining tender inside.**

Use It: **Za'atar Fries (page 275), Rosemary-Garlic Oven Fries (page 277), Salmon Niçoise Potato and Green Bean Salad (page 84), Sweet Chili Sweet Potatoes (page 276), and Brats with Warm Potato Salad and Kraut (page 190)**

Pressure Cooker Sweet Potatoes

MAKES 4 POTATOES - **W30, EF, NF, V**

Prep Time: 5 minutes
Cook Time: 15 minutes

4 sweet potatoes, unpeeled

1 tablespoon avocado oil

1 teaspoon fine sea salt

1 cup water

Rub the sweet potatoes all over with the oil, then sprinkle them all over with the salt, patting the potatoes with your hands so the salt adheres to the skins.

Place a steamer insert on the bottom of an electric pressure cooker and pour in the water. Place the sweet potatoes on the steamer insert. Secure the lid, select the manual button, and cook at high pressure for 15 minutes.

Quick release the pressure, then test the potatoes with a fork for doneness. If the potatoes are on the large side and are still too firm, cook at high pressure for 1 to 3 minutes more.

Store the potatoes in an airtight container in the refrigerator for up to 1 week. To use, reheat in a preheated 400°F oven for about 15 minutes, until heated through.

Tidbits: **A precooked sweet potato, reheated with leftover vegetables, a protein, and a drizzle of one of the prep-day sauces is my favorite quick post-workout or school drop-off meal.**

Use It: **Twice-Baked Breakfast Sweet Potatoes, Three Ways (page 51) and Huevos Rancheros (page 54); or load them up with ghee and salt for an easy side dish or for stuffing with meats and veggies**

Pressure Cooker Chicken

MAKES 6 BONE-IN, SKINNED PIECES
(2 EACH BREASTS, THIGHS, AND DRUMSTICKS);
ABOUT 6 CUPS SHREDDED MEAT - **W30, EF, NF, SCD**

Prep Time: 5 minutes
Cook Time: 1 hour

- 1 (4-pound) frozen whole chicken
- 2 tablespoons avocado oil
- 2 tablespoons Adobo Seasoning, Burnt Broccoli Seasoning, Tagine Seasoning, or other seasoning mix of choice (pages 31 to 35)
- 1 teaspoon coarse sea salt (see Note)
- ½ teaspoon freshly ground black pepper
- 1 cup water

Place a steamer insert on the bottom of a 6-quart electric pressure cooker.

Pat the chicken dry with paper towels. Remove the giblet bag from the cavity.

Rub the chicken all over with the oil. Place the chicken, breast side down, on the steamer rack. Sprinkle about half of the seasoning mix and half each of the salt and pepper all over the exposed area of the bird. Gently press the spices onto the chicken so they adhere to the oil. Flip the chicken over so it is breast side up and sprinkle with the remaining seasoning mix, salt, and pepper and again press to adhere. Carefully add the water to the pot, pouring to the side of the chicken so you don't rinse off the spices.

Secure the lid, select the manual button, and cook at high pressure for 60 minutes (or 45 minutes for an 8-quart machine). It will take the machine about 20 minutes to come to pressure before the timer starts. When the timer sounds, let the pressure release naturally, which will take 18 to 20 minutes. Manually vent any remaining pressure and carefully transfer the chicken to a cutting board.

When the chicken is cool enough to handle, discard the skin and carve the chicken into two breasts, two drumsticks, and two thighs. Or discard the skin, save the bones to make bone broth, and use your hands to shred the chicken. Store in an airtight container in the refrigerator for up to 7 days.

Note: If using a seasoning mixture that includes salt, use only ½ teaspoon coarse sea salt.

Tidbits: My personal favorite seasoning for this chicken is half Adobo Seasoning (page 31) and half Burnt Broccoli Seasoning (page 31). The broth left over in the pot from this combination is divine to sip or to use in soup! If you're planning to make a taco salad, use my Taco Seasoning (page 35). Or you can keep it simple and season the bird with just the salt and pepper. Once you have shredded the chicken, save the bones for making Bone Broth (page 42). If you are not ready to use the bones right away, pack them into a resealable plastic bag and store in the refrigerator for up to 7 days.

I use a frozen chicken in this recipe because I find that I never remember to defrost one when I actually need it. Cooking it from frozen helps keep it tender and helps it to cook evenly, but you can also cook from defrosted or raw for half the time.

Buy It: A rotisserie chicken, or any cooked chicken, will work here. Just check the ingredients and avoid birds prepared with canola oil, modified food starch, potato dextrin, carrageenan, sugar, dextrose, and xanthan gum, all of which are common in rotisserie chickens sold in grocery stores.

Use It: Pesto Chicken, Nectarine, and Avocado Salad (page 71), Curry Chicken Salad–Stuffed Avocados (page 72), Asian-Style Chicken Slaw (page 75), 5 Quick Single-Serving Meals for Leftover Chicken (page 69); or use in salads and sandwiches

Bone Broth

MAKES 8 TO 10 CUPS - W30, EF, NF, SCD

Prep Time: 8 minutes
Cook Time: 80 minutes

- 4 pounds roasted or raw chicken, beef, or turkey bones, or a mixture (see Tidbits)
- 2 tablespoons extra-virgin olive oil, if roasting the bones
- 4 carrots, halved crosswise
- 2 celery stalks (with leaves), halved crosswise
- 1 large yellow onion, quartered
- 1 bunch flat-leaf parsley
- 4 cloves garlic, crushed
- 1 tablespoon apple cider vinegar
- 8 to 10 cups filtered water

If the bones are cooked, put them into an electric pressure cooker or a slow cooker. If the bones are raw, preheat the oven to 400°F. Spread the bones on a large sheet pan, drizzle with the oil, and roast for 20 minutes, until browned. Transfer the bones and any juices to the pressure cooker or slow cooker.

Add the carrots, celery, onion, parsley, garlic, and vinegar to the pot, then add just enough filtered water to barely cover the bones and vegetables. If using a pressure cooker, secure the lid, select the manual setting, and cook on high pressure for 80 minutes. Let the pressure release naturally, which will take about 1 hour. If using a slow cooker, cover and cook on low for 24 hours.

Uncover the pot and skim off the fat from the surface of the broth. Strain the broth through a fine-mesh sieve, discarding the bones and other solids, and let cool to room temperature. Store in an airtight container in the refrigerator for up to 1 week; or freeze in silicone muffin molds, then unmold and store in a resealable bag in the freezer for up to 6 months. To reheat from frozen, place in a saucepan over medium-low heat for about 15 minutes, until heated through.

Tidbits: There are so many good broth brands on the market that contain clean ingredients and have the desired gelatinous quality that comes from slow simmering, but making broth at home is less costly and you can tailor it to your dietary needs. The key to getting a good gel to your broth is to not fill the pot with too much water; add just enough to cover the bones. I use filtered water to avoid the chemicals and metals often present in tap water.

I prefer the flavor of the broth when it is made with roasted bones, but you can skip that step and use raw bones. For beef stock, use a mix of bones with a little meat on them, such as oxtail, short ribs, and/or knucklebones. For poultry, use a mix of backs, legs, and feet. Also see Pressure Cooker Chicken (page 41). If you're sensitive to garlic and/or onion, leave them out.

I make my broth unsalted and then salt to taste with each dish I use it in or add a pinch of salt when drinking it from a mug.

Buy It: Butcher's by Roli Roti, Bonafide Provisions, and Bare Bones; or look for a low- or no-sodium broth

Use It: Soups, stews, sauces, and any recipe that calls for chicken broth or chicken stock!

Mexican Chorizo

MAKES 2 POUNDS - W30, EF, NF, SCD

Prep Time: 10 minutes

2 pounds ground pork

4 cloves garlic, minced

2½ tablespoons ancho chile powder, or 2½ tablespoons smoked paprika plus ½ teaspoon cayenne pepper

2 teaspoons dried Mexican oregano

1¾ teaspoons fine sea salt

1 teaspoon sweet paprika

½ teaspoon freshly ground black pepper

½ teaspoon ground cumin

½ teaspoon ground coriander

½ teaspoon ground cinnamon

½ teaspoon ground cloves

¼ cup apple cider vinegar

In a large bowl, combine the pork, garlic, chile powder, oregano, salt, paprika, black pepper, cumin, coriander, cinnamon, cloves, and vinegar. Use your hands to mix thoroughly. Divide the mixture into eight 4-ounce portions. Slip each portion into a small resealable bag, press out the air, seal closed, and freeze for up to 6 months.

To use the chorizo, thaw in the refrigerator overnight. Alternatively, add it frozen to a pan over medium heat and scrape the cooked bits off the frozen chunk until all of the meat is crumbled and cooked through.

Tidbits: Mexican chorizo is usually sold fresh rather than cured. Spanish chorizo, on the other hand, is a cured dried sausage with highlights of smoked or sweet paprika. I keep my chorizo in 4-ounce packets in the freezer so I can pull them out as needed.

Buy It: Add Siete Chorizo Seasoning to ground pork; each 1.38-ounce seasoning packet will season 1 pound ground pork.

Use It: Huevos Rancheros (page 54), Chilaquiles (page 61), and Clams and Mussels in Creamy Turmeric-Coconut Broth (page 245)

Pressure Cooker Hard-Boiled Eggs

MAKES 6 TO 12 EGGS - W30, NF, V, SCD

Prep Time: 2 minutes
Cook Time: 5 minutes

1½ cups water

6 to 12 eggs

Place a steamer insert on the bottom of an electric pressure cooker and pour in the water. Place as many eggs as will fit in a single layer on the steamer insert. You may need to do this in two batches, depending on the size of your machine. Secure the lid, select the manual setting, and cook on high pressure for 5 minutes. Meanwhile, fill a large bowl with cold water.

Quick release the pressure. Remove the lid and immediately transfer the eggs to the bowl of cold water to halt the cooking and cool them down. If using the eggs right away, when they are cool enough to handle, peel them. To store the eggs, let cool completely in the shell and store in the refrigerator for up to 7 days.

Tidbits: A cook time of 5 minutes yields almost completely cooked yolks. If you like a more jammy, runny yolk, reduce the time to 3 or 4 minutes. If you prefer a firmer yolk, increase the time to 6 or 7 minutes. The size of your eggs can also affect the timing and doneness.

Now that I've perfected hard-boiling eggs in an electric pressure cooker, I will never go back to the stove again! And the shells . . . well, they practically fall off. You will never have mangled egg whites for deviled eggs again with this method.

Buy It: Vital Farms

Use It: Egg Salad with Smoked Salmon (page 83), Salmon Niçoise Potato and Green Bean Salad (page 84), Creamy Almond-Cauliflower Polenta (page 264) with hard-boiled eggs (jammy yolks) and green onions, roasted asparagus with hard-boiled eggs (jammy yolks) and Mediterranean Tahini Dressing (page 29), or pesto deviled eggs by mixing 4 hard-boiled egg yolks (firm yolks) with ¼ cup Dairy-Free Basil Pesto (page 28)

Baked Bacon

SERVES 6 TO 8 - W30, EF, NF, SCD

Prep Time: 2 minutes
Cook Time: 22 minutes

3 (8-ounce) packages bacon

Line two large sheet pans with parchment paper. Arrange the bacon slices in a single layer on the prepared pans. The bacon will shrink as it bakes, so it's alright if the pieces are touching, but don't overlap them.

Position one oven rack in the top ⅓ slot and one in the bottom ⅓ slot of the oven. Place the pans on the two racks in the unheated oven and turn on the oven to 400°F. Bake for 12 minutes, then flip the slices and switch the pans between the racks. Bake for 8 to 10 minutes more for thin slices or 12 to 15 minutes more for thick slices, until the bacon is crisp around the edges and slightly soft in the center.

Line a large plate on another sheet pan with paper towels. Using tongs, transfer the bacon to the prepared pan, blotting off any excess fat. Enjoy hot, or let cool, then transfer to an airtight container and store in the refrigerator for 8 to 10 days. To reheat the bacon, place the desired amount of bacon on a sheet pan under a preheated broiler for 1 to 2 minutes, until warmed through.

Tidbits: I included this recipe in this chapter because I bake two or three packages of bacon at a time. We eat a little for breakfast, and then I use the rest on sandwiches and burgers and in salads and wraps throughout the week.

Buy It: Look for bacon that is free of nitrates and added sugar. Some of my favorite brands are ButcherBox, Applegate, and Wellshire Farms.

Use It: California Sunrise Sweet Potatoes (page 31), Chicken, Bacon, and Ranch Squash Noodles (page 148), Brats with Warm Potato Salad and Kraut (page 190), Creamy Bacon Cheeseburger Soup (page 242), Shrimp Chowder (page 246), California Chicken Sandwiches with Arugula Pear Salad (page 289), and BBQ Bacon Burger Bowls with Honey-Mustard Vinaigrette (page 298)

Mexican-Style Pickled Vegetables

MAKES 5 CUPS - W30, EF, NF, V

Prep Time: 10 minutes, plus 24 hours to pickle
Cook Time: 2 minutes

1 small jicama, peeled and cut into julienne
2 large carrots, peeled and cut into julienne
1 small red onion, halved and thinly sliced into half-moons
2 jalapeño chiles, thinly sliced crosswise
2 cups water
2 teaspoons fine sea salt
¼ cup freshly squeezed lime juice
¼ cup apple cider vinegar
1 teaspoon coriander seeds

Divide the jicama, carrots, onion, and chile slices evenly between two large jars. Using the back of a spoon, gently pack down the vegetables onto the bottom of each jar.

In a small saucepan, bring the water just to a boil over medium-high heat. Add the salt, stir until dissolved, and immediately remove from the heat. Add the lime juice, vinegar, and coriander, stir briefly, and then pour the hot liquid into the jars, dividing it evenly and submerging the vegetables fully. Let cool, then secure the lids on the jars and refrigerate for at least 24 hours before using.

The pickles will continue to build flavor and will keep in the refrigerator for up to 1 month.

Buy It: Sonoma Brinery Jalapeño Escabeche (carrots and onions)

Use It: Wild Mushroom and Zucchini Enchiladas with Mango-Pineapple Salsa (page 206), Huevos Rancheros (page 54), Chilaquiles (page 61), Muffuletta Salad with Tapenade Vinaigrette (page 79), and Skirt Steak Tacos with Sriracha Aioli (page 293); or pair with Cilantro-Kale Pepita Pesto (page 28) and serve over grilled fish, steak, chicken, or shrimp

2

Breakfast

"Breakfast for dinner" is a frequent occurrence around our house. It feels special and my kids are thrilled. More often than not, we have a simple combo of grain-free pancakes, bacon (page 44), and fruit. Most of the recipes in this chapter are the more exciting dishes I love to make on a Saturday when the family isn't running out the door. I've also included a couple of dishes that you can grab and go or make as single servings when you need something quick like a smoked jerky stick. (Yes, my kids eat "meat sticks" for breakfast nearly five days a week!)

In addition to my Lemon Chia Puddings (page 62) and Instant Strawberry and Cream Porridge (page 65), which are both easy to grab and go, the box at right lists a few store-bought options for really quick, healthy breakfasts on the run. I usually pair these with a green smoothie, a couple of hard-boiled eggs (page 43), or a Lara or RX Bar.

Grab-and-Go Breakfasts

Breakfast sausages: I love Applegate Organic's Chicken & Apple and No Sugar Pork varieties! Microwave the sausages for 2 minutes, then wrap 'em up and head out the door. They're small and easy to eat while driving (keep your hands on the wheel!).

Jerky sticks: I keep The New Primal's Lightly Peppered Turkey and Chomps' Original Beef in my purse for a quick snack and along with a piece of fruit or a muffin from the freezer.

Dairy-free yogurt: The Blueberry Lavender and Bourbon Vanilla flavors from coconut-based yogurt brand Culina are delicious when topped with homemade grain-free or Purely Elizabeth granola.

Potato and sausage bake: I always keep roasted sweet potatoes and a few links of chicken and apple sausage in the fridge. Slice the sausages, toss the potatoes in a little ghee, and place everything on a tray. Roast for 5 to 7 minutes, until the potatoes are heated through and the sausage is browned. Eat with a spoonful of sauerkraut to get some healthy morning probiotics and drizzle with your favorite sauce.

Apples and almond butter: Fill a small container with unsweetened almond butter and slice an apple before you head out the door. The protein and fat in the almond butter will give you an energetic jumpstart to your day until you have time to eat a proper meal!

Twice-Baked Breakfast Sweet Potatoes, Three Ways

I've been stuffing sweet potatoes for years. Once I realized that I could tolerate sweet potatoes, they became my go-to option for a starchy carb. Now I'm here to share my sweet potato breakfast secrets.

I first started making these potatoes when I had to omit eggs from my diet for a long period of time. I usually have a few roasted sweet potatoes in my fridge that I can stuff to the brim with dinner leftovers. The egg-free recipes are specially formulated to help you make up for the nutrients you would usually get with eggs: protein, choline, selenium, vitamin D, and folate, to name a few.

Make It Ahead: **For the California Sunrise, bake the filled potatoes and let them cool. Store in the refrigerator for up to 3 days, then reheat in a preheated 400°F for 10 minutes or microwave on low power for 2 minutes. For the others, store the cooked meats, vegetables, and fruits in a separate container from the cooked potatoes in the refrigerator for up to 5 days. Fill and then reheat as directed for California Sunrise.**

California Sunrise

W30, NF

SERVES 4

Prep Time: 8 minutes
Cook Time: 8 minutes

4 Pressure Cooker Sweet Potatoes (page 40) or roasted sweet potatoes

4 eggs

1 cup chopped Baked Bacon (page 44)

¼ cup crumbled dairy-free feta

½ cup cherry tomatoes, halved

Fine sea salt and freshly ground black pepper

2 serrano chiles, seeded (for mild flavor) and sliced

2 avocados, halved, pitted, peeled, and sliced

¼ cup watercress, tough stems discarded

Place the sweet potatoes on a sheet pan and place it in the oven. Preheat the oven to 425°F. When the oven has preheated, remove the tray, carefully cut a lengthwise slit in the top of each potato, and gently push the ends of the potato toward the center to open it up. Fluff the flesh with a fork, being careful to keep the skin intact. Crack an egg into each potato. Sprinkle the bacon, feta, and tomatoes on top of each. Season each potato generously with salt and pepper.

Bake the potatoes for 8 to 10 minutes, until they are heated through and the whites of the eggs are set. Top with the chiles, avocado, and watercress and serve hot.

CONTINUED

Sausage and Blueberries with Creamy Coconut Spinach

SERVES 4

Prep Time: 3 minutes
Cook Time: 8 minutes

4 Pressure Cooker Sweet Potatoes (page 40) or roasted sweet potatoes (see Note)

4 tablespoons ghee or avocado oil

4 chicken apple sausages, thinly sliced

1½ cups firm fresh blueberries

4 cups firmly packed baby spinach leaves

¾ teaspoon fine sea salt

½ teaspoon ground nutmeg

¼ cup full-fat coconut milk

½ teaspoon ground cinnamon

1 teaspoon white chia seeds

Cut a lengthwise slit in the top of each sweet potato and gently push the ends of the potato toward the center to open it up. Fluff the flesh with a fork, being careful to keep the skin intact.

In a large skillet, heat 3 tablespoons of the ghee over medium-high heat. Add the sausages and cook, stirring occasionally, for 1 to 2 minutes, until well browned. Add the blueberries and cook for 2 to 3 minutes more, until the berries begin to burst. Using a spoon or fork, gently crush any berries that failed to burst. Remove from the heat, then divide the sausages, blueberries, and any pan juices evenly among the potatoes.

Return the skillet to medium-high heat and add the remaining 1 tablespoon ghee, the spinach, salt, and nutmeg and cook, stirring and tossing, for about 30 seconds, just until the spinach wilts. Stir in the coconut milk and cook for about 30 seconds, until the liquid has evaporated. Remove the pan from the heat.

Top the sweet potatoes with the cinnamon and chia seeds and serve the spinach on the side.

Note: Try Stokes Purple sweet potatoes for this dish. Not only do they give a beautiful presentation, but they're slightly more starchy and much less sweet than their orange-fleshed sibling.

Tidbits: Be sure to find sausages that do not contain sugar or nitrates. My favorite chicken and apple sausages are from Applegate or Aidells.

Blueberry, Almond Butter, and Banana Sweet Potatoes

SERVES 4

Prep Time: 5 minutes

4 Pressure Cooker Sweet Potatoes (page 40) or roasted sweet potatoes (see Note)

½ cup fresh blueberries

2 bananas, peeled and thinly sliced

4 tablespoons unsweetened almond butter

4 teaspoons pure maple syrup or light-colored raw honey

½ teaspoon ground cinnamon

¼ teaspoon ground nutmeg

¼ cup chopped raw Brazil nuts (see Note), or 2 teaspoons white chia seeds, flaxseeds, or sprouted sunflower seeds

Cut a lengthwise slit in the top of each sweet potato and gently push the ends of the potato toward the center to open it up. Fluff the flesh with a fork, being careful to keep the skin intact.

Divide the blueberries and bananas evenly among the potato cavities, then spoon 1 tablespoon almond butter over each fruit portion. Drizzle the maple syrup on top, sprinkle with the cinnamon and nutmeg, and finish with the nuts. Serve warm.

Note: Try Stokes Purple sweet potatoes for this dish. I use Brazil nuts for their selenium and zinc, but macadamias, almonds, or cashews can be substituted.

W30, NF, SCD*   *sub butternut squash for sweet potatoes

Huevos Rancheros

SERVES 4

Prep Time: 8 minutes
Cook Time: 8 minutes

A traditional rancher's breakfast in Mexico, huevos rancheros has become a favorite of Californians for its ease and incredible flavors. It's usually served over a corn tortilla and often includes beans, but I've skipped the grains and legumes here and instead seasoned a sweet potato puree to give a bit of refried beans flavor and texture. I use my homemade chorizo here, but any breakfast sausage will work, or you can use leftovers from a Mexican-inspired meal, such as Pork Chile Verde (page 229) or Salsa Chicken Tacos (page 98). The jammy yolks of the eggs can easily take the place of cheese, but a sprinkle of Cotija, queso fresco, or dairy-free feta takes this breakfast plate to another level! I love using Stokes Purple sweet potatoes in this dish for the contrast of colors and because they have a slightly nutty flavor and are less sweet and have a drier texture than many other varieties.

3 large Pressure Cooker Sweet Potatoes (page 40), reheated as directed

1½ tablespoons ghee or rendered bacon fat

1½ teaspoons freshly squeezed lime juice

¾ teaspoon ground cumin

1 teaspoon fine sea salt

½ teaspoon freshly ground black pepper

8 ounces Mexican Chorizo (page 43)

1½ cups fresh tomato salsa

4 eggs

2 avocados, halved, pitted, peeled, and sliced

1 serrano chile, seeded (for mild flavor) and thinly sliced

¼ cup loosely packed fresh cilantro leaves and tender stems, chopped

¼ cup Violife feta or any other dairy-free cheese

Scoop the warm flesh from the sweet potato skins into a bowl and discard the skins. Stir in 1 tablespoon of the ghee, the lime juice, cumin, ¾ teaspoon of the salt, and ¼ teaspoon of the pepper. Mash with a fork until smooth, then cover to keep warm.

In a large skillet, cook the chorizo over medium-high heat, breaking it up with a wooden spoon and stirring frequently, for 3 to 5 minutes, until browned and cooked through. Transfer the chorizo to a plate and cover to keep warm.

Return the skillet to medium-high heat, add the salsa, and bring to boil. Turn down the heat to medium and simmer for 1 to 2 minutes, until the liquid has evaporated and the salsa has thickened. Move the salsa to one side of the pan and add the remaining ½ tablespoon ghee to the empty part of the pan. Gently crack the eggs into the pan and fry for 30 seconds, until browned on the edges. Cover the pan and cook for another minute, until the whites are set but the yolks are still runny. Remove the pan from the heat.

Smear the sweet potato puree onto the bottom of four bowls. Top the puree with the salsa, then top each serving with an egg. Divide the chorizo and avocados evenly among the bowls and then top with the chile, cilantro, and feta. Serve immediately.

Tidbits: **Any of your favorite salsas will work here and at whatever heat level you prefer. I prefer the fresh salsa from the refrigerated section for texture and flavor. My favorite is Casa Sanchez Medium Fire Roasted Salsa.**

Savory Polenta with Sausage and Blistered Tomatoes

SERVES 4

Prep Time: 12 minutes
Cook Time: 7 minutes

After a health flare-up a few years ago, I found that I didn't tolerate eggs well unless they were baked into breads or muffins. After avoiding eggs for a year, I was thankfully able to reintroduce them in moderation. I don't typically make this dish from scratch unless we're having a leisurely weekend morning. More often, I make a double batch of the polenta for dinner and save some to use in this recipe or in my Creamy Polenta with Woody Mushroom Sauce (page 205). In fact, if you have any leftover mushrooms from making *that* recipe, add ½ cup of them to the sausage and tomato mixture for a delicious and satisfying spin!

- 1 tablespoon avocado oil
- 12 ounces mild Italian sausages, thinly sliced on the diagonal
- 1 pound cherry tomatoes
- 2 tablespoons extra-virgin olive oil or melted ghee
- 1 bunch chard, stemmed and chopped
- Creamy Almond-Cauliflower Polenta (page 264)
- 2 tablespoons chopped fresh basil or chives

In a large skillet, heat the avocado oil over medium-high heat. Add the sausages and tomatoes and cook, undisturbed, for 2 to 3 minutes, until the sausage is well browned on the first side. Stir and cook for 2 to 3 minutes, until the sausage slices are browned on the second side and the tomatoes begin to blister. Add 1 tablespoon of the olive oil and the chard and stir and toss for 3 to 4 minutes, until the chard is gently wilted.

Divide the polenta among four bowls and spoon the sausage mixture over the top. Drizzle the remaining 1 tablespoon olive oil over the bowls, dividing it evenly, and finish with the basil. Serve immediately.

Tidbits: **Applegate offers both a Sweet Italian Sausage made from chicken and a Classic Pork Italian Sausage that are free of sugar and dairy.**

Make It Ahead: **Make the polenta up to 7 days in advance and store in the fridge. Reheat it in a covered saucepan over medium-low heat, stirring occasionally, while you prepare the sausages. Once cooked, the sausage and tomato mixture can be stored in the fridge for up to 5 days. Reheat it in a dry skillet over medium heat, stirring occasionally, for 3 to 5 minutes.**

W30, EF, NF, SCD  

Brussels Sprouts, Apple, and Breakfast Sausage Bowl

SERVES 4 TO 6

Prep Time: 4 minutes
Cook Time: 8 minutes

This recipe for an egg-free, paleo-friendly breakfast bowl is full of flavor and spice and can be modified with different vegetables depending on what's in season. Sautéed cinnamon-spiced apples are mixed with pork and shredded brussels sprouts, then topped with probiotic-rich sauerkraut for a comforting and satisfying one-bowl meal.

1 tablespoon ghee or avocado oil

2 pounds ground pork or dark-meat turkey

2 tablespoons Burnt Broccoli Seasoning (page 31)

½ teaspoon ground turmeric

½ teaspoon fine sea salt

3 apples, peeled, cored, and thinly sliced

1 pound brussels sprouts, trimmed and shredded

Chopped fresh flat-leaf parsley, for garnish

1 cup sauerkraut, for serving

In a large skillet, heat the ghee over medium-high heat. Add the pork and break it up with a wooden spoon. Sprinkle the broccoli seasoning, turmeric, and ¼ teaspoon of the salt over the top, then cook, stirring frequently, for 3 to 5 minutes, until browned and cooked through. Add the apples and sauté for 3 to 5 minutes more, until tender and browned. Remove the sausage and apples from the skillet with a slotted spoon and set aside in a bowl.

With the skillet still over medium-high heat, add the brussels sprouts and the remaining ¼ teaspoon salt and sauté for 2 to 3 minutes, until the sprouts are crisp-tender. Stir the sausage and apples back into the skillet, mixing well, and then remove the pan from the heat.

Divide among individual bowls and top with the parsley. Serve immediately, with the sauerkraut on the side for adding at the table.

Tidbits: **Primal Palate Breakfast Blend can be substituted for my broccoli seasoning in this dish. Consider purchasing a preseasoned bulk breakfast sausage as well.**

Make It Ahead: **Once the sausage and apple mixture is cooked, it can be stored in an airtight container in the fridge for up to 5 days or in the freezer for up to 3 months. Thaw in the refrigerator overnight. Reheat it in a dry skillet over medium heat for 3 to 5 minutes.**

Chilaquiles

SERVES 4 TO 6

Prep Time: 10 minutes
Cook Time: 5 minutes

Mexico is one of our favorite family vacation destinations. In addition to offering two of my favorite things in the world—margaritas and chips and guacamole—Mexico is close to our home in California and relatively inexpensive to visit. A few years ago, we rented a home there, and our host cooked breakfast for us the last morning of our stay. I'll never forget how incredible her chilaquiles (pronounced Chee-lah-KEE-less) were. She whipped up a homemade sauce in the blender with roasted peppers, tomatoes, and seasonings, but I take a shortcut and use a jar of my own enchilada sauce to speed things up in the morning. If I don't have any homemade enchilada sauce on hand, I love Siete brand, but any of your favorite brands will do! If using store-bought sauce, omit the chicken broth. I like to use Violife feta for crumbling on top.

2 tablespoons avocado oil

2½ cups green or red Enchilada Sauce (page 30)

½ cup chicken Bone Broth (page 42)

1 tablespoon ghee or extra-virgin olive oil

4 eggs

Fine sea salt and freshly ground black pepper

36 large grain-free chips (taro, plantain, or sweet potato)

½ cup crumbled dairy-free feta or queso fresco

2 tablespoons finely chopped white onion

2 tablespoons chopped fresh cilantro leaves and tender stems

1 avocado, halved, pitted, peeled, and sliced

Sliced radishes, Dairy-Free Sour Cream (page 36), and lime wedges, for topping

In a skillet, heat the oil over medium-high heat. Whisk in the sauce and broth and simmer for 3 to 5 minutes, until warmed through.

In a second skillet, melt the ghee over medium-high heat. Crack the eggs into the pan and fry for 2 to 3 minutes, until the edges are crispy and the whites are set. Season with salt and pepper and remove the pan from the heat.

When the eggs are ready, add the chips to the sauce and gently turn with tongs until they are well coated with the sauce but still crispy. Remove the skillet from the heat and gently transfer the fried eggs to the coated chips. Top with the cheese, onion, cilantro, avocado, radishes, sour cream, and a few squeezes of lime and serve immediately.

Tidbits: **This dish traditionally uses up leftovers. I love it with fried eggs, but it is often served with shredded chicken (see Pressure Cooker Chicken, page 41) or black beans. My Mexican Chorizo (page 43) or Pork Chile Verde (page 229) would also be amazing sprinkled on top.**

Make It Ahead: **Make the enchilada sauce up to 2 weeks in advance. Chop or slice any toppings, except the avocado, and store in the fridge for up to 5 days.**

Lemon Chia Pudding with Berries and Toasted Coconut

SERVES 4 TO 6

Prep Time: 5 minutes, plus 4 hours to chill

Chia pudding with fresh berries is one of my favorite grab-and-go breakfasts. The healthy fats from the coconut milk and the fiber and protein in the chia seeds make it a balanced and crave-worthy breakfast. Any fresh fruit works, but my favorite combination is blackberries and strawberries.

1 (13.5-ounce) can full-fat coconut milk

Zest of 1 lemon, plus more for serving

Juice of 2 lemons (about ⅓ cup)

½ cup Almond Milk (page 38) or Cashew Milk (page 39)

¼ cup light-colored raw honey (see Note)

1 teaspoon pure vanilla extract

⅛ teaspoon fine sea salt

½ cup white chia seeds

Fresh berries and toasted unsweetened coconut flakes, for serving

In a bowl, whisk together the coconut milk, lemon zest and juice, almond milk, honey, vanilla, and salt. Stir in the chia seeds.

Divide the pudding among four to six small jars, then cover and refrigerate until set, about 4 hours.

To serve, top the pudding with berries and a sprinkle each of lemon zest and coconut.

Note: **To use dates in place of the honey, puree 4½ ounces pitted dates with the coconut milk, then whisk together the ingredients as directed.**

Make It Ahead: **Make the puddings up to 5 days in advance and store in the fridge. Add the toppings just before serving.**

Strawberries and Cream Porridge

SERVES 1

Prep Time: 10 minutes
Cook Time: 1 minute

This comforting bowl of nut-free porridge reminds me of the Cream of Wheat I grew up eating, but with the addition of dried strawberries for some nice sweetness. I grind the flaxseeds and chia seeds in a clean coffee grinder to access all of their omega-3 fatty acids and fiber and so they will instantly thicken the porridge. You can purchase the seeds already ground and store them in the freezer to preserve their shelf life, but I find freshly ground has a better texture.

- ⅓ cup Instant Porridge Mix (recipe follows)
- ¼ to ⅓ cup full-fat coconut milk or water, boiling
- 2 tablespoons dried strawberries
- 1 tablespoon unflavored, vanilla, or chocolate collagen peptides powder (optional)
- 1 teaspoon pure maple syrup, honey, or full-fat coconut cream (optional)
- Fresh strawberries for serving (optional)

To make a single serving of porridge, put the porridge mix into a bowl and stir in ¼ cup of the hot coconut milk. Continue to stir for 10 to 15 seconds, until the porridge is thick and creamy, adding more coconut milk to reach your desired consistency. Stir in the strawberries and collagen peptides powder and top with a drizzle of maple syrup and fresh strawberries if using. Serve immediately.

Tidbits: **Other possible toppings in place of strawberries include fresh banana slices, raspberries, and blueberries or raisins and sliced nuts.**

Instant Porridge Mix

MAKES 2⅔ CUPS; ENOUGH FOR 8 SERVINGS

- 1 cup unsweetened coconut flakes (toasted or untoasted)
- 1 cup pumpkin seeds (see Note)
- 1 cup hemp hearts (also known as hulled hemp seeds)
- 6 tablespoons freshly ground chia seeds
- ¼ cup freshly ground golden flaxseeds
- Pinch of fine sea salt
- 1 tablespoon maple or coconut sugar (optional)

In a food processor, combine the coconut flakes and pumpkin seeds and process for 10 to 15 seconds, until the mixture resembles coarse sand. Add the hemp hearts, chia seeds, flaxseeds, salt, and maple or coconut sugar if using and pulse seven or eight times, until the mixture is finely ground. Do not overprocess or it will turn to seed butter.

Transfer the mixture to a jar, cap tightly, and store in the refrigerator for up to 1 month.

Note: **For easier digestion, use soaked and sprouted pumpkin seeds. I like Go Raw brand.**

3

No-Cook Lunches

Sometimes you can't wait for something to cook. For me, that time is usually lunch. I'm either between meetings or taking the kids places, and I find myself either skipping lunch or eating something that's not nourishing for my body. So I've taken to what I call *component prepping*. I prepare proteins, vegetables, and sauces and store them separately in the fridge so I can easily pull the components together into a healthy, no-cook lunch.

Some of these no-cook meals use meal-prepped foods from chapter 1, and others use up leftovers from a previous night's dinner. Either way, these recipes provide simple and quick ways to get a nutritious but tasty meal on the table quickly,—no cooking required.

I've crafted these recipes to feed two to four people (instead of four to six) because it's rare that my whole family sits down together for lunch. Also, my kids are creatures of habit and love the lunches and snacks from my book *Eat What You Love*, so I made these recipes a little more adult focused. Just put the extra portions in the fridge for another day.

5 Quick Single-Serving Meals for Leftover Chicken

You can use my Pressure Cooker Chicken (page 41) or purchase a clean-ingredient rotisserie chicken (see Buy It section on page 41). If you seasoned with only salt and pepper, the chicken will work with any of the suggestions. If you used a seasoning mix, make sure it complements the flavors in the suggested meal. Scan the QR code (see opposite) to follow along as I make these five quick and easy meals.

1 Chicken Taco Meat: Combine 1 cup cooked chicken + 1 tablespoon Taco Seasoning (page 35) + 1 teaspoon tomato paste + 2 teaspoons avocado oil and heat in a small pan on the stove or in a microwave. Serve over lettuce or cauliflower rice and top with avocado, salsa, cilantro, sour cream (page 36), and crumbled grain-free chips.

2 Chicken Pesto Bowl: Combine 1 cup cooked chicken + 1 cup cooked broccoli + 1 cup frozen cauliflower rice and heat in a small pan on the stove or in a microwave. Top with ⅓ cup Dairy-Free Basil Pesto (page 28). This bowl is also good with leftover salmon.

3 Greek Chicken–Stuffed Sweet Potatoes: Combine 1 cup cooked chicken + 1 tablespoon Mediterranean Seasoning (page 34) + 1 teaspoon avocado oil and heat in a small pan on the stove or in a microwave. Stuff the mixture into a reheated cooked sweet potato and top with 1 tablespoon each jarred chopped roasted red peppers, peperoncini, and olives. Finish with crumbled dairy-free feta.

4 Cajun Chicken with Roasted Potatoes: Combine 1 cup cooked chicken + 1 cup cubed Parboiled Potatoes (page 40) + 1½ tablespoons Cajun Seasoning (page 32) and heat in a small pan on the stove or in the microwave. Drizzle with 2 tablespoons Herb Ranch Dressing (page 23).

5 Burnt Broccoli and Chicken: Combine 2 cups Burnt Broccoli (page 278) + 1 cup cooked chicken + 1 teaspoon avocado oil + ½ teaspoon Adobo Seasoning (page 31) and heat in a small pan on the stove or in a microwave. Serve topped with greens or fresh herbs.

*omit pecans

W30, EF, NF*, SCD

Pesto Chicken, Nectarine, and Avocado Salad

SERVES 2 TO 4

Prep Time: 8 minutes

The tastes of summer shine through in this salad. Peach or mandarin slices would also work nicely with the bright flavors of this pesto. If you don't have the pesto made up, any Italian pesto will stand in perfectly.

- 2 cups shredded chicken or Pressure Cooker Chicken (page 41), chilled
- 6 tablespoons Cilantro-Kale Pepita Pesto (page 28)
- 3 tablespoons extra-virgin olive oil or avocado oil
- 2 teaspoons freshly squeezed lemon juice
- Fine sea salt and freshly ground black pepper
- 6 cups loosely packed baby spinach leaves
- 2 yellow nectarines, pitted and sliced
- 1 avocado, halved, pitted, peeled, and sliced
- ⅓ cup pecan halves

In a medium bowl, combine the chicken and 4 tablespoons of the pesto and stir to coat the chicken evenly. In a small bowl, whisk together the remaining 2 tablespoons pesto, the oil, and lemon juice. Season to taste with salt and pepper.

In a serving bowl, toss together the spinach, nectarines, avocado, and pecans. Top with the pesto chicken and drizzle with 2 tablespoons of the pesto dressing. Serve with the remaining dressing on the side.

Make It Ahead: **This salad is best when eaten the day it's prepared, but you can store all of the components except the avocado separately in the fridge for up to 5 days from when the chicken was cooked.**

W30*, EF*, NF*, SCD  

*omit honey/maple syrup for W30, sub egg-free mayo for EF, omit cashews for NF

Curry Chicken Salad–Stuffed Avocados

SERVES 2

Prep Time: 10 minutes

I've been making some variation of this chicken salad since my great-grandmother passed down a recipe to me that she titled Exotic Chicken Salad! You could also use canned chicken or tuna here. And if you have leftover Mango Chutney (page 24), 2 to 3 tablespoons stirred into the chicken salad are a delicious addition.

- ½ cup avocado oil mayonnaise
- 2 teaspoons pure maple syrup or raw honey
- 1 tablespoon curry powder
- 1½ cups shredded Pressure Cooker Chicken (page 41), chilled
- ¼ cup golden raisins
- ¼ cup chopped toasted cashews
- ¼ cup chopped celery
- Fine sea salt and freshly ground black pepper
- 2 large avocados, halved, pitted, and peeled
- 1 green onion, white and tender green parts, chopped

In a bowl, whisk together the mayonnaise, maple syrup, and curry powder. Stir in the chicken, raisins, cashews, celery, ¼ teaspoon salt, and ⅛ teaspoon pepper, mixing well.

Lightly season the avocado halves with salt and pepper and arrange hollow side up. Scoop one-fourth of the chicken salad onto each avocado half. Top with the green onion and serve.

Make It Ahead: **The chicken salad will keep in the fridge for up to 5 days from when the chicken was cooked. Cut the avocados just before serving.**

*omit honey and date syrup for W30, omit almonds for NF, omit sesame seeds for SCD

Asian-Style Chicken Slaw

SERVES 2 TO 4

Prep Time: 12 minutes

This cabbage salad holds up well even after it's dressed. The flavors actually get better after a day or two in the fridge, so it really is the perfect make-ahead lunch. It's wonderful on its own or as a side salad, but I usually add leftover chicken, steak, or even shrimp to make it protein rich and more filling.

3 cups thinly sliced Napa cabbage

1 (8-ounce) package slaw mix (see Note)

3 mandarin oranges, peeled and segmented

1 cup trimmed and thinly sliced sugar snap peas

3 green onions, white and tender green parts, thinly sliced on the diagonal

¼ cup Stir-Fry Sauce (page 27)

1½ tablespoons raw honey or date syrup

3 tablespoons avocado oil

¾ teaspoon apple cider vinegar

2 cups shredded Pressure Cooker Chicken (page 41), chopped cooked steak, or grilled shrimp (optional)

¼ cup slivered blanched almonds

2 tablespoons lightly toasted sesame seeds

Fine sea salt and freshly ground black pepper

In a large bowl, toss together the cabbage, slaw mix, mandarins, snap peas, and green onions.

In a small bowl, whisk together the stir-fry sauce, honey, oil, and vinegar. Add the chicken, almonds, and sesame seeds to the cabbage mixture and stir and toss to mix. Drizzle evenly with ⅓ cup of the dressing and toss to combine. Season to taste with salt and pepper and with more dressing if needed. Serve with any remaining dressing on the side.

Note: **You can make your own slaw mixture by combining 1 cup each shredded carrot, green cabbage, and red cabbage.**

Make It Ahead: **The tossed salad will keep in a covered container in the fridge for up to 5 days from when the chicken was cooked.**

W30, EF*, NF, SCD  *sub egg-free mayo

Steak Lettuce Wraps with Horseradish Cream Sauce

SERVES 2 TO 4

Prep Time: 10 minutes

Whenever I'm grilling a flank or skirt steak, I frequently grill an extra steak to have easy leftovers for breakfast or lunch. This lettuce wrap with zesty cream sauce is my family's favorite way to make a flavorful, repurposed lunch. If you don't have leftover steak from making Skirt Steak Tacos (page 293), Steak with Roasted Red Pepper Sauce (page 294), or Cast-Iron Rib-Eye Steak (page 182), then deli roast beef is an easy stand-in.

½ cup avocado oil mayonnaise

¼ cup full-fat coconut milk

3 tablespoons prepared horseradish

1 teaspoon white wine vinegar

½ teaspoon fine sea salt

½ teaspoon freshly ground black pepper

8 to 10 butter lettuce cups

1 pound leftover cooked steak, thinly sliced and at room temperature

1 large bunch watercress, tough stems discarded

1 avocado, halved, pitted, peeled, and sliced

¼ red onion, thinly sliced

2 radishes, thinly sliced

In a small bowl, stir together the mayonnaise, coconut milk, horseradish, vinegar, salt, and pepper.

Fill each lettuce cup with a few slices of steak, 2 tablespoons watercress, and the avocado, onion, and radishes, dividing them evenly. Drizzle each cup with 1 to 2 tablespoons of the horseradish sauce and enjoy.

Make It Ahead: **The horseradish sauce will keep in an airtight container in the refrigerator for up to 7 days. Wash and dry the lettuce, watercress, and radishes, wrap in a clean kitchen towel, and store in a plastic bag in the fridge for up to 7 days.**

Muffuletta Salad with Tapenade Vinaigrette

SERVES 2 TO 4

Prep Time: 12 minutes

I'm historically an indecisive person, so a sandwich that includes multiple types of meats is really up my alley. I've turned the classic cold-cuts sandwich from Louisiana into a hearty salad, and the best part is, there's no cooking! Most of the ingredients are shelf-stable, and the cold cuts can all be purchased from your deli counter (I love Applegate, Wellshire Farms, Gusto, and Principe brands).

¼ cup store-bought olive tapenade

½ cup extra-virgin olive oil

2 tablespoons red wine vinegar

¾ teaspoon Italian Seasoning (page 33)

6 cups shredded romaine lettuce

½ cup Mexican-Style Pickled Vegetables (page 44) or store-bought giardiniera

4 ounces thinly sliced prosciutto, cut into strips

4 ounces thinly sliced salami, cut into strips

4 ounces mortadella or ham, cut into ½-inch cubes

¼ cup pepperoncini, sliced

½ cup crumbled Miyoko's Creamery mozzarella or small mozzarella balls (bocconcini)

¼ cup chopped fresh flat-leaf parsley

In a small bowl, whisk together the tapenade, oil, vinegar, and Italian seasoning.

In a large salad bowl, toss together the romaine, pickled vegetables, prosciutto, salami, mortadella, pepperoncini, and mozzarella. Drizzle ¼ cup of the dressing over the top and toss to coat. Sprinkle with the parsley and serve with any remaining dressing on the side.

Make It Ahead: **The dressing will keep in an airtight container in the refrigerator for up to 12 days. The shredded romaine and chopped parsley can be prepped up to 3 days ahead and the sliced and diced prosciutto, salami, and mortadella can be prepped up to 7 days in advance. Store them all tightly covered in the fridge.**

W30, EF

Chilled Sesame Beef, Mango, and "Noodle" Salad

SERVES 4

Prep Time: 15 minutes

I truly believe that the Thai-style almond sauce on this salad can make any vegetable taste delicious. And these "noodles"—made from beets, cucumber, jicama, and carrots—are no exception. Leftover steak is added to make this salad filling, and sweet and tangy mangoes brighten it up. It's refreshing and such a nice change to your standard green salad.

- ⅓ cup Creamy Thai-Style Almond Sauce (page 29)
- 3 tablespoons extra-virgin olive oil
- 1 large English cucumber
- 1 medium golden beet, peeled
- 2 large carrots, peeled
- 1 small jicama, peeled
- 8 ounces leftover steak, thinly sliced, or shredded cooked chicken
- Fine sea salt and freshly ground black pepper
- 2 mangoes (preferably Ataulfo variety), pitted, peeled, and sliced
- ¼ cup chopped fresh basil
- ¼ cup chopped toasted cashews
- 2 tablespoons sesame seeds
- 1 lime, cut into wedges, for serving

In a small bowl, whisk together the almond sauce and oil. Thin with water as needed until the dressing is pourable but still thick. Cover the bowl and refrigerate the dressing while you prepare the salad.

Using a spiralizer or a julienne slicer, cut the cucumber, beet, carrots, and jicama into noodle-like strips, discarding the cucumber seeds. Transfer the vegetable noodles to a large bowl and top with the steak.

Drizzle half of the dressing over the vegetables and toss to coat. Season to taste with salt and pepper, then top with the mangoes, basil, cashews, and sesame seeds. Serve with the remaining dressing and the lime wedges on the side.

Make It Ahead: **All but the cucumber and fresh basil can be mixed together and stored in an airtight container in the fridge for up to 5 days from when the steak or chicken was cooked. Add the cucumber and basil just before serving.**

Egg Salad with Smoked Salmon

SERVES 2 TO 4

Prep Time: 12 minutes

I grew up eating egg salad sandwiches. I always knew when my dad was making them by the smell of hard-boiled eggs wafting from the kitchen. It's not exactly a pleasant odor, but I have fond memories of those sandwiches. He used an immense amount of mayo and always stirred in black olives.

Egg salads are my favorite way to use extra eggs, and it's always fun to play around with mix-ins and flavors. The dill and smoked salmon are the standouts here! If you make the hard-boiled eggs ahead of time or purchase them precooked, this becomes a no-cook lunch in a matter of minutes.

- 8 Pressure Cooker Hard-Boiled Eggs (page 43), cooked for 5 minutes
- ⅓ cup avocado oil mayonnaise
- 2 tablespoons minced shallots
- 2 teaspoons grainy mustard
- 1 tablespoon minced fresh dill, or 1 teaspoon dried dill
- ¼ teaspoon fine sea salt
- ¼ teaspoon freshly ground black pepper
- 2 ounces smoked salmon, chopped
- 8 to 10 butter lettuce cups
- 2 Persian cucumbers, diced
- 2 teaspoons everything bagel seasoning (such as Trader Joe's Everything But the Bagel)
- 2 tablespoons chopped fresh chives
- Drained capers, chopped large or whole cherry tomatoes, sprouts, and/or diced avocado, for topping (optional)

Peel and quarter the eggs into wedges. Place them in a bowl with the mayonnaise, onion, mustard, dill, salt, and pepper and stir to combine. Gently stir in the salmon. Scoop about 1 cup of the egg salad into each lettuce cup and top with the cucumbers, bagel seasoning, chives, and additional toppings of your choice. Serve immediately.

Make It Ahead: **The salad will keep in an airtight container in the refrigerator for up to 3 days. The flavors become more intense after a day of chilling.**

W30*, NF, SCD (30) *omit honey

Salmon Niçoise Potato and Green Bean Salad

SERVES 4 TO 6

Prep Time: 15 minutes

This salad is a wonderful way to utilize your weekend prep vegetables and any leftover salmon from my Mediterranean Salmon with Artichokes and Peppers (page 163), but you can use any leftover fish or even canned salmon here. You can even change things up by substituting leftover roasted vegetables for the green beans and potatoes.

You do need to cook the green beans, eggs, and potatoes, so this is only a no-cook meal if you prep those ingredients in advance or use leftovers from another meal.

- ¼ cup freshly squeezed lemon juice
- 1 tablespoon Dijon mustard
- 1 teaspoon honey
- ½ teaspoon fine sea salt
- ½ teaspoon freshly ground black pepper
- 2 tablespoons chopped fresh chives
- ½ cup extra-virgin olive oil
- 6 cups loosely packed Little Gem lettuce leaves
- 2 cups cubed Parboiled Potatoes (page 40)
- ½ cup black olives, pepperoncini, or pickles
- ½ cup cherry tomatoes, halved
- 2 Persian cucumbers, julienned
- 8 ounces green beans, trimmed and blanched
- 6 ounces leftover cooked salmon, flaked; drained water-packed canned tuna; or canned smoked trout
- 6 Pressure Cooker Hard-Boiled Eggs (page 43), cooked for 5 minutes
- 2 tablespoons chopped fresh basil
- ½ teaspoon coarse sea salt

In a small bowl, whisk together the lemon juice, mustard, honey, fine salt, pepper, and chives. Slowly whisk in the oil.

Spread the lettuce on a large platter. Toss with the potatoes, olives, tomatoes, cucumbers, green beans, and salmon. Peel the eggs, halve lengthwise, and place them around the platter. Drizzle ¼ cup of the dressing evenly over the salad and then top with the basil. Sprinkle the coarse salt evenly over the salad and serve with the remaining dressing on the side.

Make It Ahead: **I like to make all of the components of this salad and keep them stored in the fridge as follows: eggs in one container; green beans, cucumbers, tomatoes, and potatoes in a second container; and the dressing in a sealed jar. All will keep for up to 7 days. The salmon is best eaten within 2 days of cooking, but the canned tuna or trout will keep in the pantry until needed.**

30 W30, EF

Thai-Style Shrimp Salad

SERVES 4 TO 6

Prep Time: 18 minutes

I know mason jar salads may have gone out of fashion, but I still love making a few in advance to take to my office. This Thai-inspired salad reminds me of pad thai with a thick, salty, and slightly sweet peanut sauce similar to pra ram, the sauce that blankets chicken satay and is found on most American Thai restaurant menus. Be sure to put the dressing on the bottom so it doesn't make the rest of the ingredients soggy. Any roasted nuts or seeds will work as the crunchy salad topper, but I really like Go Raw's Spicy Fiesta Seeds for this one. Or I make up a batch of the spicy almonds featured on my blog.

- ½ cup Creamy Thai-Style Almond Sauce (page 29)
- 1 cup shredded red cabbage
- 4 cups firmly packed arugula
- 4 cups firmly packed mixed baby greens
- 1 cup julienned carrots
- 1 cup julienned cucumber
- 1 cup mung bean sprouts
- 1 pound cooked and chilled whole shrimp, shredded chicken, or diced steak
- ¼ cup chopped fresh basil
- ¼ cup chopped fresh cilantro
- ¼ cup spicy roasted nuts, chopped, or seeds

Divide the almond sauce evenly among four to six (24-ounce) widemouthed jars. Divide evenly and layer the cabbage, greens, carrots, cucumber, sprouts, shrimp, basil, and cilantro on top of the sauce in each jar. Be sure to leave at least 1-inch headspace above the greens and herbs to have room for shaking the salad. Finish each jar with the nuts, again dividing evenly, then cover the jars.

When ready to eat, shake each jar vigorously to mix everything together.

Make It Ahead: **The salad will keep in the sealed jars in the fridge for up to 3 days. If not using shrimp, chicken, or steak, the salad will keep for up to 5 days.**

4

Freeze It

I used to be the type of cook who froze only leftovers, usually because they were about to spoil in the fridge or I wanted a break from eating the same ones. After having kids and getting busier with their extracurricular activities and my own work, I began to purposefully prepare freezer-safe meals that I could pull out in a pinch. When you've had a long week, grabbing a meal out of the freezer that you can pop into a skillet or an electric pressure cooker can be a lifesaver. All of the meals in this chapter can be cooked immediately, of course, but they're my favorite recipes to prep and freeze for later use. Scan the QR code below to see how I prep and organize my freezer meals.

If you use an electric pressure cooker, freezing your meals in a 7-cup round container is the best way to meal prep. It's just the right size to fit into the pot of a 6-quart pressure cooker, so all you have to do is immerse the container in warm water for a few minutes to release the food from the container sides and then you can dump the frozen disk right into the pot and cook from frozen! If using a slow cooker, defrost completely overnight in the refrigerator, then place the contents into the slow cooker.

If you use silicone bags (like Stasher brand; I love the "stand-up mega," and the half-gallon size works well for leftovers), I suggest you leave out the liquid (see tip #3 opposite) because the bags are on the smaller side and they'll lie a little flatter that way.

When I'm prepping recipes that contain vegetables, I sometimes use precut frozen organic vegetables because they save me the time and effort of chopping. Also, since they've already been frozen properly, they hold up better. Frozen out-of-season vegetables can be more affordable than fresh and delivered by long-distance transport.

5 Tips for Freezer Cooking

1 Choose three to five recipes to make at the same time, depending on how much space and how much time you have. I find that assembling five recipes takes about an hour if I'm organized in advance. You could also choose to double up on a recipe. If you're making one recipe, double it and divide it into two containers so you have two ready-to-go meals. You may also save money by buying the ingredients in bulk.

2 Eyeball! Don't spend time measuring all of the spices. Instead, use the measurements as a guide. These recipes are all really forgiving, and an additional pinch here and there won't ruin the meal.

3 Skip the liquids if you're short on space. If you have a small freezer or prefer to use bags or glass containers, you can save space by waiting until you're ready to defrost and cook the dish before adding liquid ingredients, such as broth, wine, tomato puree, and so on.

4 Tack a piece of blue painter's tape to the container or silicone bag with the name of the recipe and the amounts of the missing ingredients, as well as a simplified version of the cooking method, so you don't have to find the recipe again! Here's an example of what I would write on the tape or bag:

Chicken Tortilla Soup
Defrost part.
+ 5 cups broth + 1 jar tomatoes
High pressure 15 min
Quick release

5 Air is freezer burn's best friend. If you're using a resealable bag, be sure to press out any air from the bag before sealing.

Chicken and Apricot Stew

SERVES 6 TO 8

Prep Time: 8 minutes
Cook Time: 16 minutes

A Moroccan-style stew like this would traditionally be cooked in a clay tagine, but I usually use an electric pressure cooker. This recipe also works well in a slow cooker. The seasoning is rich and delicious and has just a hint of spice balanced with creamy almond butter and sweet dried fruits. For a full meal, pair this with my Creamy Almond-Cauliflower Polenta (page 264) or Persian-Style Saffron Cauli-Rice with Dried Fruits (page 270).

- 3 pounds boneless, skinless chicken thighs
- 3 tablespoons Tagine Seasoning (page 34)
- 2 tablespoons avocado oil
- 1 medium yellow onion, thinly sliced
- 4 cloves garlic, thinly sliced
- ¼ cup unsweetened almond butter
- 1 teaspoon fine sea salt
- ½ teaspoon freshly ground black pepper
- ¾ to 1¼ cups unsalted chicken Bone Broth (page 42)
- 6 ounces unsweetened, unsulfured dried apricots
- 1 pound small carrots, trimmed
- Juice of 1 lemon
- Toasted sliced almonds, for serving
- Fresh cilantro leaves and tender stems, for serving

Coat the chicken all over with the tagine seasoning. In a large skillet, heat the oil over medium-high heat. Working in batches to avoid crowding, add the chicken and cook, turning once, for 3 to 5 minutes per batch, until well browned. Transfer to a plate and let cool.

Transfer the browned chicken to a resealable bag or glass container and add the onion, garlic, almond butter, salt, and pepper. Seal tightly and refrigerate for up to 3 days or freeze for up to 6 months.

To Use an Electric Pressure Cooker: To cook from frozen, partially defrost the container in a bowl of warm water for 10 minutes. Place the partially frozen ingredients in the pressure cooker, add ¾ cup of the broth, select the manual button, and cook at high pressure for 15 minutes. To cook from thawed, add the ¾ cup broth and cook for 8 minutes. Add the apricots and carrots, secure the lid again, and cook on high pressure for 1 minute. Quick release the pressure. Stir in the lemon juice and serve with the almonds and cilantro sprinkled on top.

To Use a Slow Cooker: Defrost completely, then place the ingredients in the slow cooker with 1¼ cups of the broth. Cover and cook on low for 6 hours or on high for 3 hours. Add the apricots and carrots and cook on high for 1 hour more, until the carrots are tender. Stir in the lemon juice and serve with the toasted almonds and cilantro sprinkled on top.

W30*, EF, NF, SCD*   

*omit plantain chips for W30,
omit sweet potatoes for SCD

Chicken Tortilla Soup

SERVES 4 TO 6

Prep Time: 15 minutes
Cook Time: 8 minutes

Okay, there are technically no tortillas in this soup. You could easily add some grain-free tortilla chips to make this more authentic, but the flavors I love—the rich tomato broth, all of the vegetables, the slight hint of cumin and coriander in the seasoning mix—shine through here. I use butternut squash and sweet potatoes to give the soup the body usually provided by the tortilla strips melting as they absorb the broth. To speed up this recipe, I use a bag of frozen mirepoix—a mix of carrots, celery, and onions—and frozen butternut squash and sweet potatoes.

- 2 pounds boneless, skinless chicken thighs
- 2 cups peeled and cubed butternut squash (fresh or frozen)
- 2 cups peeled and cubed sweet potatoes (fresh or frozen)
- 1 (10-ounce) bag mirepoix base (fresh or frozen)
- 2 cloves garlic, minced
- 2 tablespoons Taco Seasoning (page 35)
- 1½ teaspoons fine sea salt
- ½ teaspoon freshly ground black pepper
- 5 to 6 cups chicken Bone Broth (page 42)
- 1 (18-ounce) jar diced tomatoes with juice
- 2 teaspoons freshly squeezed lime juice
- Lime wedges, cilantro leaves, avocado slices, Dairy-Free Sour Cream (page 36), and/or plantain chips, for serving

Place the chicken, squash, potatoes, mirepoix, garlic, taco seasoning, salt, and pepper in a resealable bag or glass container. Seal tightly and refrigerate for up to 3 days or freeze for up to 6 months.

To Use an Electric Pressure Cooker: To cook from frozen, partially defrost the container in a bowl of warm water for 10 minutes. Place the partially frozen ingredients in the pressure cooker, add 5 cups of the broth and the tomatoes, select the manual button, and cook at high pressure for 15 minutes. To cook from thawed, add the 5 cups broth and tomatoes and cook for 8 minutes. Quick release the pressure. Remove the chicken from the pot and use two forks to shred it. Return the shredded chicken to the pot and stir in the lime juice. Ladle the soup into bowls and serve with the toppings of your choice.

To Use a Slow Cooker: Defrost completely, then place the ingredients in the slow cooker with the 6 cups broth and the tomatoes. Cover and cook on low for 6 hours or on high for 3 hours. Remove the chicken from the pot and use two forks to shred it. Return the shredded chicken to the pot and stir in the lime juice. Ladle the soup into bowls and serve with the toppings of your choice.

Turkey Chili Verde

SERVES 6 TO 8

Prep Time: 8 minutes
Cook Time: 15 minutes

Traditional red chili made with beef and served with grain-free cornbread will always be a comfort-food favorite. But I also love Mexican dishes that include the slightly acidic and bright salsa verde, or green tomatillo salsa. Here, in this lighter take on chili, I use my green enchilada sauce for ease and to give the chili more body. And the diced sweet potatoes and cauliflower florets make this dish hearty and filling without adding beans. Pile on the toppings: grain-free chips, sour cream, cilantro, and a squeeze of fresh lime juice for brightness are my favorites.

- 2 tablespoons avocado oil
- 2 pounds ground dark-meat turkey
- 1 small head cauliflower, cut into small florets
- 1 pound white-fleshed sweet potatoes or parsnips, peeled and diced
- 4 (4-ounce) cans diced green chiles
- 2 teaspoons ground cumin
- 2 teaspoons dried oregano
- 1½ teaspoons fine sea salt
- ½ teaspoon white pepper
- ¼ teaspoon ground cinnamon
- 4 to 5 cups chicken Bone Broth (page 42)
- 3¾ cups green Enchilada Sauce (page 30)
- Cilantro leaves, lime wedges, grain-free tortilla chips, and/or Dairy-Free Sour Cream (page 36), for serving

In a large Dutch oven, heat the oil over medium-high heat. Add the turkey and cook, breaking it up with a wooden spoon and stirring frequently, for 3 to 5 minutes, until browned. Transfer to a resealable bag or glass container and let cool. Add the cauliflower, sweet potatoes, green chiles, cumin, oregano, salt, pepper, and cinnamon. Seal tightly and refrigerate for up to 3 days or freeze for up 6 months.

To Use an Electric Pressure Cooker: **To cook from frozen, partially defrost the container in a bowl of warm water for 15 minutes. Place the partially frozen ingredients in the pressure cooker, add 4 cups of the broth and the enchilada sauce, select the manual button, and cook at high pressure for 5 minutes. To cook from thawed, add the 4 cups broth and the enchilada sauce and cook for 5 minutes. Quick release the pressure. Ladle the chili into bowls and serve with the toppings of your choice.**

To Use a Slow Cooker: **Defrost completely, then place the ingredients in the slow cooker with the 5 cups broth and the enchilada sauce. Cover and cook on low for 6 hours or on high for 3 hours. Ladle the chili into bowls and serve with the toppings of your choice.**

W30*, EF, NF, SCD   *use butter lettuce cups

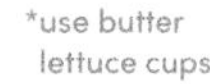

Salsa Chicken Tacos

SERVES 6 TO 8

Prep Time: 5 minutes
Cook Time: 12 minutes

This crazy-easy chicken taco recipe has been one of my family's weekly go-to dinners for years and years. It's a meal I know none of my kids will balk at, and it's my default when I've forgotten to plan and have only frozen chicken ready to go. I can throw it into the electric pressure cooker and have it on the table twenty minutes later. This is also one of those meals that I always double prep. A single portion goes into the slow cooker or pressure cooker for dinner, and the second portion goes straight to the freezer so it's ready for another meal.

2 pounds fresh or frozen boneless, skinless chicken thighs, trimmed of fat

1 pound fresh or frozen boneless, skinless chicken breasts

2 cups mild roasted tomatillo salsa, plus more for serving

¼ cup Taco Seasoning (page 35)

1 cup chicken Bone Broth (page 42)

Butter lettuce cups or grain-free tortillas, for serving

Avocado slices, diced tomatoes, diced red onion, Dairy-Free Sour Cream (page 36), and/or cilantro leaves, for serving

Place the chicken thighs and breasts, salsa, and taco seasoning in a resealable bag or glass container. Seal tightly and refrigerate for up to 3 days or freeze for up to 6 months.

To Use an Electric Pressure Cooker: To cook from frozen, partially defrost the container in a bowl of warm water for 10 minutes. Place the partially frozen ingredients in the pressure cooker with the broth, select the manual button, and cook at high pressure for 20 minutes. To cook from thawed, omit the broth and cook for 12 minutes. Allowing the pressure to release naturally while you prepare the rest of dinner will work well here, but you can also release it manually immediately. Remove the chicken from the pot and use two forks to shred it. Return the shredded chicken to the pot and serve with the lettuce leaves, salsa, and toppings of your choice.

To Use a Slow Cooker: Defrost completely, then place the ingredients in the slow cooker. Omit the broth. Cover and cook on low for 6 hours or on high for 3 hours. Remove the chicken from the pot and use two forks to shred it. Return the shredded chicken to the pot and serve with the lettuce leaves, salsa, and toppings of your choice.

Tidbits: My all-time favorite trick for shredding chicken quickly is to use a handheld electric mixer on low speed. It shreds the chicken perfectly in no time at all! Just cover your hand and the mixer loosely with a towel to avoid splatters.

Coconut Chicken Curry

SERVES 6 TO 8

Prep Time: 8 minutes
Cook Time: 5 minutes

An Indian- or Thai-inspired curry is frequently my go-to recipe when I'm in a pinch for dinner. My kids love a saucy, fall-apart meal of shredded meat, especially if it's served over rice. And I love that I can use coconut milk to keep it naturally dairy-free. This dish is super simple, with no added vegetables because they can get overcooked and mushy in a pressure cooker or slow cooker. But you can bulk this up by adding the vegetables of your choice after the first cook time and letting them cook for an additional minute or so. For a slow cooker on low heat, add the vegetables during the final hour of cooking. This curry can easily be cooked in the moment, but I like to freeze a portion so I don't have to measure out the spices at mealtime. It's also always a nice backup to have in the freezer for those nights when all you have time to do is push a button.

- 3 pounds boneless, skinless chicken thighs
- 1 tablespoon garam masala
- 2½ teaspoons fine sea salt
- 2½ teaspoons ground cumin
- 2½ teaspoons ground turmeric
- 2 teaspoons garlic powder
- 1 teaspoon onion powder
- 1½ teaspoons ground coriander
- 1 (13.5-ounce) can full-fat coconut milk
- Basic Cauli-Rice (page 269) or sautéed vegetables, for serving
- Fresh cilantro leaves, for serving

Put the chicken, garam masala, salt, cumin, turmeric, garlic powder, onion powder, and coriander in a resealable bag or glass container. Seal tightly and refrigerate for up to 3 days or freeze for up to 6 months.

To Use an Electric Pressure Cooker: **To cook from frozen, partially defrost the container in a bowl of warm water for 10 minutes. Place the partially frozen ingredients in the pressure cooker, add the coconut milk, select the manual button, and cook at high pressure for 15 minutes. Let the pressure release naturally. To cook from thawed, add the coconut milk and cook for 5 minutes. Let the pressure release naturally. Remove the lid and turn the machine to sauté on high. Simmer for 2 to 3 minutes to reduce the sauce slightly. Serve over the cauli-rice and top with the cilantro.**

To Use a Slow Cooker: **Defrost completely, then place the ingredients in the slow cooker. Add the coconut milk, cover, and cook on low for 4 hours or on high for 2 hours. Serve over the cauli-rice and top with the cilantro.**

W30*, EF, NF, SCD*

*sub additional bone broth for wine for W30, omit polenta for SCD

Pork Ragù over Creamy Polenta

SERVES 6 TO 8

Prep Time: 15 minutes
Cook Time: 45 minutes

I'm usually in favor of browning meat before adding it to a pressure cooker or slow cooker, but I skip that step in this recipe so everything will come together more quickly. I have also found that even though I don't brown the meat, pressure or slow cooking it with all of the other ingredients creates a savory and super-flavorful topping for my creamy grain-free polenta. If you don't feel like cooking up a batch of polenta, long, wide slices of yellow squash or zucchini that mimic pappardelle are also wonderful with this easy take on a classic ragù. I like to sauté them in a little ghee over medium heat for 2 to 3 minutes until tender.

2 pounds boneless pork butt or lean chuck roast, trimmed of fat and cut into three uniform pieces

1 (10-ounce) bag mirepoix base (fresh or frozen)

6 ounces white button mushrooms, coarsely chopped

4 cloves garlic, chopped

1 (7-ounce) jar tomato paste

1½ tablespoons dried parsley

1 tablespoon fine sea salt

2½ teaspoons Italian Seasoning (page 33)

½ teaspoon freshly ground black pepper

¾ cup to 1¼ cups unsalted beef Bone Broth (page 42)

½ cup full-bodied red wine (such as Zinfandel or Cabernet Sauvignon)

1 (24-ounce) jar tomato puree

Creamy Almond-Cauliflower Polenta (page 264)

Chopped fresh basil, for serving

Dairy-Free Parmesan Cheese (page 37), for serving

Place the pork, mirepoix, mushrooms, garlic, tomato paste, parsley, salt, Italian seasoning, and pepper in a resealable bag or glass container. (If the pork doesn't fit, cut it into smaller, uniform pieces.) Seal tightly and refrigerate for up to 3 days or freeze for up to 6 months.

To Use an Electric Pressure Cooker: **To cook from frozen, partially defrost the container in a bowl of warm water for 10 minutes. Place the partially frozen ingredients in the pressure cooker, add ¾ cup of the broth, the wine, and the tomato puree, select the manual button, and cook at high pressure for 1½ hours. To cook from thawed, add the ¾ cup broth, wine, and tomato puree and cook for 45 minutes. Let the pressure release naturally. Remove the pork from the pot and use two forks to shred it. Return the shredded pork to the pot. Serve over the polenta and top with the basil and Parmesan.**

To Use a Slow Cooker: **Defrost completely, then place the ingredients in the slow cooker with the 1¼ cups broth, the wine, and the tomato puree. Cover and cook on low for 6 hours or on high for 3 hours. Remove the pork from the pot and use two forks to shred it. Return the shredded pork to the pot. Serve over the polenta and top with the basil and Parmesan.**

*sub butternut squash for sweet potato

Creamy Sausage, Kale, and Sweet Potato Soup

SERVES 4 TO 6

Prep Time: 5 minutes
Cook Time: 6 minutes

Nearly every time I cook this soup, I change how I make it—switching from a simple broth to a creamy version that uses my cashew-based heavy cream and cooked sweet potatoes to add body. Either way, it's a delicious comfort soup for those brisk fall and winter days, and even my kids down their bowls! My favorite side for this soup is the arugula pear salad that accompanies my summertime chicken sandwiches (page 289).

2 teaspoons extra-virgin olive oil

1 pound mild Italian sausages, casings removed

1 yellow onion, diced

4 cloves garlic, minced

½ teaspoon apple cider vinegar

2½ teaspoons Adobo Seasoning (page 31)

½ teaspoon fine sea salt

½ teaspoon dried thyme

½ teaspoon freshly ground black pepper

1 sprig rosemary

1 pound orange-fleshed sweet potatoes, peeled and cubed

5 to 6 cups unsalted chicken Bone Broth (page 42)

¾ cup Dairy-Free Heavy Cream (page 38), optional

1 bunch lacinato (Tuscan) kale or Swiss chard, stems and ribs removed and leaves torn (about 2 cups loosely packed)

In a large stockpot, heat the oil over medium-high heat. Add the sausage and cook, breaking it up with a wooden spoon and stirring frequently, for 2 to 3 minutes, until browned. Add the onion and garlic and cook, stirring, for 1 to 2 minutes, until the onion begins to soften. Pour off any excess fat and transfer the ingredients to a resealable bag or glass container. Let cool, then add the vinegar, adobo seasoning, salt, thyme, pepper, rosemary, and sweet potatoes. Seal tightly and refrigerate for up to 3 days or freeze for up to 6 months.

To Use an Electric Pressure Cooker: **To cook from frozen, partially defrost the container in a bowl of warm water for 10 minutes. Place the partially frozen ingredients in the pressure cooker, add 5 cups of the broth, select the manual button, and cook at high pressure for 5 minutes. To cook from thawed, add the 5 cups broth and cook for 3 minutes. Let the pressure release naturally. Remove and discard the rosemary sprig. Scoop out 1 cup of the broth, onion, and sweet potatoes, being careful to avoid the sausage, and transfer to a blender. Add the cream to the blender, blend on high speed until smooth, and return the puree to the pot. Add the kale, turn the machine to sauté on high, bring the soup to a boil, and boil for 1 to 2 minutes, until thickened. Serve immediately.**

To Use a Slow Cooker: **Defrost completely, then place the ingredients in the slow cooker with the 6 cups broth. Cover and cook on low for 6 hours or on high for 3 hours. Remove and discard the rosemary sprig. Scoop out 1 cup of the broth, onion, and sweet potatoes, being careful to avoid the sausage, and transfer to a blender. Add the cream to the blender, blend on high speed until smooth, and return the puree to the pot. Switch the slow cooker to high heat, add the kale, and simmer, uncovered, for 10 to 15 minutes, until thickened. Serve immediately.**

Baked Pepperoni Pizza Spaghetti with Ranch

SERVES 6

Prep Time: 20 minutes
Cook Time: 37 minutes

Pizza dipped in ranch dressing was a common pregnancy craving for me. I don't always have time to make a grain-free crust from scratch, and I rarely have a store-bought one in the freezer, so instead I combine my favorite pizza flavors in a roasted spaghetti squash and drizzle that luscious herby dressing over the top. I frequently double these ingredients and pop one casserole into the oven to have for dinner that night, while the other gets tucked away in the freezer for another meal. Feel free to use boiled and drained gluten-free spaghetti noodles if you'd like, and be sure to purchase a good-quality jar of marinara sauce that does not have additives, soybean oil, sugar, or citric acid.

2 medium spaghetti squash, about 3 pounds each (see Note), or 6 cups noodles of your choice, cooked al dente

2 tablespoons extra-virgin olive oil

1 tablespoon of ghee

Fine sea salt

1 small yellow onion, minced

2 cloves garlic, minced

1 pound mild Italian sausage (chicken or pork), casings removed

1 cup diced pepperoni or salami

2 cups marinara sauce

¾ teaspoon Italian Seasoning (page 33)

¼ teaspoon red pepper flakes

¼ teaspoon freshly ground black pepper

1 cup ricotta (dairy-free Kite Hill brand, or dairy)

1 cup crumbled or shredded cheese (such as Miyoko's Creamery mozzarella or Violife feta)

¼ cup Herb Ranch Dressing (page 23)

Preheat the oven to 425°F. Lightly grease a 9 by 13-inch baking dish with extra-virgin olive oil.

Slice both ends off of each squash, then cut each squash crosswise into four or five rounds. Scoop out the seeds from the center of each round. Coat the rounds on both sides with ghee, sprinkle both sides with salt, and arrange in a single layer in the prepared baking dish. Bake the squash for 15 to 20 minutes, until fork-tender.

Meanwhile, in a large saucepan, heat the ghee over medium-high heat. Add the onion and garlic and sauté for 3 to 5 minutes, until the onion is soft. Crumble the sausage, add it and the pepperoni and cook, stirring occasionally, for 3 to 5 minutes, until the sausage is browned and nearly cooked through. Drain off any excess fat. Add the marinara, Italian seasoning, ½ teaspoon salt, the pepper flakes, and black pepper. Remove the pan from the heat.

When the squash is cool enough to handle, use a fork to pull the flesh into noodle-like strands from the squash rounds, leaving the "noodles" in the baking dish and discarding the skins. Add the ricotta and ½ cup of the crumbled cheese to the squash and stir to combine. Pour the sauce and meat mixture over the top and spread it into an even layer. Top with the remaining ½ cup crumbled cheese. Cover tightly and refrigerate for up to 5 days or freeze for up to 6 months.

To bake from frozen, preheat the oven to 425°F. Bake, uncovered, for 30 to 35 minutes, until the sauce is bubbling on the edges and the center is warmed through. To bake from refrigerated, bake for 15 to 20 minutes. Drizzle the dressing over the top and serve immediately.

Note: **Microwave the uncut squash for 1 minute to make it easier to slice.**

Açai Bowls

SERVES 4

Prep Time: 12 minutes

Açai berries are considered a superfood and contain antioxidants that may protect the body from disease. You can purchase frozen açai puree (look for a brand with no sugar added), or you can buy freeze-dried açai powder like I do. I enjoy using flaxseeds or chia seeds, cacao nibs, grain-free granola, and crispy dried bananas for topping. This is a thick, spoonable smoothie rather than one you drink through a straw, so your blender will need to do some hard work. If you have a machine with a stopper, it comes in handy to keep things moving!

- 2 cups frozen blueberries
- 2 ripe bananas, peeled and sliced
- ½ cup unflavored collagen peptides powder
- 4 tablespoons unsweetened almond butter
- 4 tablespoons açai powder
- 2 cups loosely packed baby spinach
- 4 cups Cashew Milk (page 39) or Almond Milk (page 38), plus more as needed
- Toasted unsweetened coconut flakes, bee pollen, raw honey, chopped nuts, fresh mint leaves, fresh berries, cacao nibs, banana chips, and grain-free granola, for topping

Place ¼ cup of the blueberries, ½ banana, 2 tablespoons of the collagen peptides powder, 1 tablespoon of the almond butter, 1 tablespoon of the açai powder, and ½ cup of the spinach in each of four resealable bags. Seal tightly and freeze for up to 6 months.

To make from frozen, pour 1 cup of the cashew milk into a blender. Add half of the contents of one bag and blend on high speed until smooth. Add the remaining half of the bag and blend again until smooth, stopping to scrape down the sides of the blender or to loosen up the mixture if necessary. Add a bit more milk if needed to reach the desired consistency. Scoop the smoothie base into a bowl and add the toppings of your choice. Repeat with the three remaining bags and enjoy.

5

Pasta

For all of you lovers of Italian food or Asian-inspired noodle dishes like me, get ready to have the joys of a big bowl of pasta reintroduced to your life! When I first started following an SCD diet, there were zero grain-free pastas on the market. Honestly, I've had a lot of fun with spiralized veggies over the years (zucchini noodles were a godsend at the beginning of my journey), but after a decade of eating veggies as a stand-in for pasta, it's nice to indulge occasionally in a store-bought pasta with that real pasta texture and flavor.

It is also such a time-saver! Many of the recipes in this chapter can be on your table in twenty minutes or less using store-bought pasta. That said, I've still provided instructions for using spiralized vegetables for most of these recipes if you want the additional nutrients and a more economical option. Unless the pasta is cooked directly in the sauce, most of these recipes do not include instructions for a particular noodle, so you can choose whatever you like depending on the time you have and what's in your fridge or pantry.

I have tasted and tested every grain-free and gluten-free pasta on the market, as well as "pasta" you can make from veggies. Check out the opposite page for the best options and how to cook them, or scan the QR code below to see all of my favorite noodle brands, how to make the best homemade vegetable noodles, and additional tips on cooking these alternatives perfectly.

Noodles Galore

Shirataki Noodles

These "miracle" noodles work best in Asian cuisine. They're made from the konjac root, which is ground and then shaped into round noodles, flat fettuccine, and even rice kernels. Shirataki noodles have almost zero calories and zero carbs. I don't use them frequently, but they work well in my Sweet Chili Noodle Stir-Fry (page 134).

Kelp Noodles

Made from seaweed, kelp noodles are a great source of iodine. They are crunchy and tend to have a slightly salty and bitter taste that can be lessened with a thorough rinsing. If you prefer a softer noodle texture, more similar to Asian glass noodles, break the noodles apart a bit then soak one 12-ounce package of noodles for 5 to 7 minutes in boiling water mixed with 1 tablespoon baking soda and 2 teaspoons lemon juice. Drain and rinse well before adding them to sauces.

Spiralized Veggies

My favorites are sweet potato, parsnip, zucchini, yellow squash, and butternut squash. Before adding these vegetable noodles to sauces, I sauté them in a dry skillet over medium-high heat for 5 to 7 minutes, until they are crisp-tender and have released some of their moisture.

Grain-Free Favorites

Spaghetti squash (see Shrimp Scampi, page 130, for cooking method) is a popular grain-free option but I also love cassava and chickpea pasta. For these two, add 1 tablespoon extra-virgin olive oil and a pinch of salt to the boiling water before adding the noodles, then stir well to coat the noodles with oil, and cook according to the package instructions.

Jovial cassava pasta (spaghetti, fusilli, penne, elbows): The pastas have only two ingredients, cassava flour and water, and a great texture!

Cassava pasta can get overcooked quickly, so test the texture of the pasta 1 to 2 minutes earlier than the package states and continue cooking to the full time on the package if needed.

Whole Foods Market and Thrive Market chickpea pasta: These two brands also have only two ingredients (chickpea flour and water) and have the best texture of all of the brands of chickpea pastas I've tested.

Gluten-Free Favorites

Brown rice noodles: These are the only grain- or pseudograin-based gluten-free noodles I serve because the ingredients are simple and everyone in our family digests them better than noodles made from corn or quinoa. I like Jovial and Tinkyáda brands. Follow the same instructions for cassava and chickpea pasta.

*omit arrowroot

30 W30, EF, NF, SCD*

Cajun Chicken Pasta

SERVES 4 TO 6

Prep Time: 10 minutes
Cook Time: 17 minutes

Purchasing precut butternut squash noodles is a great time-saver, but you can also cut the noodles yourself the night before and save about half the price. I love the buttery flavor and vibrant color of butternut noodles in this dish, but any vegetable noodle or cooked gluten-free pasta would work. If you prep all of your vegetables ahead and have a jar of the seasoning already made, this meal comes together very quickly.

- 5 tablespoons ghee or avocado oil
- 1½ pounds butternut squash noodles
- 4 tablespoons ghee or avocado oil
- 2½ teaspoons fine sea salt
- 1 small yellow onion, diced
- 2½ tablespoons Cajun Seasoning (page 32)
- 1½ pounds ground dark-meat chicken
- 4 ounces white button mushrooms, sliced
- 1 small red bell pepper, seeded and cut lengthwise into narrow strips
- ½ cup chicken Bone Broth (page 42)
- 3½ teaspoons arrowroot powder
- ¼ cup chopped olive oil–packed sun-dried tomatoes
- Finely grated zest and juice of 1 lemon
- ½ teaspoon freshly ground black pepper
- ¼ cup chopped green onions, white and tender green parts

Preheat the oven to 400°F. Line a large sheet pan with parchment paper.

Melt 2 tablespoons of the ghee. Pile the squash noodles on the prepared pan, top with the melted ghee and 1 teaspoon of the salt, and toss to coat. Spread them in a single layer on the pan. Roast, stirring once halfway through, for 10 to 12 minutes, until crisp-tender.

Meanwhile, in a Dutch oven or large, deep skillet, heat 1 tablespoon of the ghee over medium-high heat. Add the onion and Cajun seasoning and sauté for 1 to 2 minutes, until fragrant. Add the chicken and cook, breaking up the meat with a wooden spoon and stirring frequently, for 2 to 3 minutes, until browned. Add the remaining 1 tablespoon ghee and the mushrooms and bell pepper and sauté for 3 to 5 minutes, until the vegetables are tender and the chicken is cooked through.

In a small bowl, whisk together the broth and arrowroot powder to make a slurry. Add the cooked noodles to the pot and pour in the broth slurry. Stir to combine, bring the sauce to a boil, then turn down the heat to medium-low and simmer for 1 to 2 minutes, until the sauce has thickened and the noodles are fork-tender. Stir in the tomatoes and the lemon zest and juice. Remove the pot from the heat, add the remaining 1½ teaspoons salt and the pepper, and toss to mix.

Serve immediately with the green onions scattered over the top.

Tidbits: I use ground chicken to cut down on prep and cook times, but ground meat is always a bit pricier than cuts of meat. For a more economical option, swap in chicken thighs cut into bite-size pieces or use sliced chicken sausages, such as andouille or roasted red pepper.

Store leftovers in the fridge for up to 3 days. To reheat, sauté in a dry skillet over medium heat for 3 to 5 minutes, or heat in an uncovered baking dish in a preheated 350°F oven for 20 minutes.

Make It Ahead: If spiralizing your own noodles, cut them and store in the fridge for up to 5 days. Cut the other vegetables and store in the fridge for up to 3 days.

W30, EF 30

Chicken Pad Thai Noodles

SERVES 4

Prep Time: 7 minutes
Cook Time: 10 minutes

The pad thai served in American Thai restaurants is typically quite sweet and does not include peanut sauce. But I just love how the velvety sauce combines with the moderate sweetness from coconut aminos and coconut sugar. If you prefer that restaurant-quality sweetness, adding another 1 to 2 tablespoons coconut sugar will help you achieve it.

- ⅓ cup Creamy Thai-Style Almond Sauce (page 29)
- 1 tablespoon tamarind paste (optional)
- 3 medium zucchini, peeled
- 2 large carrots, peeled
- Fine sea salt and freshly ground black pepper
- 1 tablespoon avocado oil
- 1 cup shredded purple cabbage
- 1 cup cauliflower florets, broken into small pieces
- 1 cup mung bean sprouts
- 2 green onions, white and tender green parts, chopped, with white and green parts separated
- 1 pound boneless, skinless chicken breasts, diced
- ½ cup fresh cilantro leaves and tender stems
- ¼ cup chopped toasted cashews

In a small bowl, stir together the almond sauce and tamarind paste. Set aside.

Line a large bowl with a dry, clean kitchen towel. Use a spiralizer or mandoline to create noodles from the zucchini and carrots. Transfer them to the prepared bowl and sprinkle them with salt. Set aside.

In a large skillet, heat the oil over medium-high heat. Add the cabbage, cauliflower, bean sprouts, and white parts of the green onions and sauté for 4 to 5 minutes, until the vegetables are crisp-tender.

Add the carrot and zucchini noodles and stir and cook for about 2 minutes, until the noodles have softened and any liquid has evaporated. Raise the heat to high, stir in the chicken, and sauté for 3 to 5 minutes, until the chicken is cooked through. Remove from the heat.

Pour the sauce into the skillet and toss until all of the ingredients are evenly coated. Season to taste with salt and pepper, then serve garnished with the cilantro, the green parts of the green onions, and the cashews.

Tidbits: I love to sneak veggie noodles into this rendition of pad thai, but you could also use 10 ounces cooked pad Thai rice noodles, cooked according to the package instructions, or two (7-ounce) packages shirataki noodles, rinsed before adding to the skillet.

Store leftovers in the fridge for up to 3 days. To reheat, sauté in a dry skillet over medium heat for 3 to 5 minutes or heat in an uncovered baking dish in a preheated 350°F oven for 15 minutes.

Make It Ahead: Store the sauce in a sealed jar in the fridge for up to 1 month. Spiralize the zucchini and carrots, place in an airtight container lined with a clean kitchen towel to soak up moisture, and store in the refrigerator for up to 2 days.

*use parsnip noodles for W30,
use zucchini noodles for SCD

W30*, EF, NF, SCD*

Creamy Roasted Garlic, Chicken Sausage, and Arugula Pasta

SERVES 4 TO 6

Prep Time: 12 minutes
Cook Time: 25 minutes

You will be using 18 garlic cloves in this pasta. No, that's not a typo. But don't worry, once garlic is roasted, it becomes buttery and any bitterness disappears. In this recipe, those cloves become the base for a super-creamy sauce without needing any dairy or even my beloved cashews to thicken it. Have fun with your choice of sausage to change up these flavors. There are many paleo-friendly brands with clean ingredients, including Applegate, Aidells, and Pederson's Natural Farms. My favorite sausages for this dish are chicken with artichoke and garlic, chicken apple, and chicken and fire-roasted red pepper. Parsnip noodles are my absolute first choice here, but if you prefer a more traditional pasta, both the Whole Foods chickpea pasta shells and the Jovial cassava spaghetti were delicious when I tested them with the sauce.

18 cloves garlic

1 sweet onion, halved and thinly sliced

¼ cup extra-virgin olive oil

2 tablespoons avocado oil

1¼ teaspoons fine sea salt

½ teaspoon freshly ground black pepper

6 chicken sausages

½ cup chicken Bone Broth (page 42), warmed, plus 2 tablespoons if needed

½ teaspoon freshly squeezed lemon juice

¼ teaspoon apple cider vinegar

⅛ teaspoon ground nutmeg

1½ pounds parsnips, peeled and spiralized into noodles, or 1 pound cooked pasta

2 cups firmly packed arugula

Preheat the oven to 450°F. In a small baking dish, toss the garlic and onion with the olive oil, avocado oil, 1 teaspoon of the salt, and the pepper. (The dish should be small enough to nearly submerge the onion and garlic in the oil.) Cover tightly and bake, stirring once halfway through, for 15 to 18 minutes, until the garlic and onion are golden and softened. Remove the baking dish from the oven and use a slotted spoon to transfer the garlic and onion to a blender; leave the oil in the baking dish.

Slice the sausages on the diagonal into ½-inch-thick disks. Heat 2 tablespoons of the reserved garlic-infused oil in a large skillet over medium-high heat. Add the sausage slices and cook, turning once, for 3 to 4 minutes, until browned on both sides. Remove the pan from the heat and use the slotted spoon to transfer the sausage to a bowl; leave the oil in the pan.

Add the ½ cup broth, the lemon juice, vinegar, and nutmeg to the blender with the onion and garlic and blend on high speed for about 30 seconds, until very smooth. If needed, add the remaining 2 tablespoons broth to thin the sauce; it should resemble a thick Alfredo sauce.

Add an additional 1 tablespoon of the garlic-infused oil to the skillet and heat over medium-high heat. Add the parsnip noodles and the remaining ¼ teaspoon salt and sauté for 3 to 5 minutes, until crisp-tender. Remove the skillet from the heat and stir in the sausage, arugula, and mushrooms. Pour the sauce into the skillet and stir to coat all of the ingredients.

CONTINUED

4 ounces cremini, shiitake, or white button mushrooms, stemmed if using shiitake, and sliced

2 tablespoons chopped fresh flat-leaf parsley

Crushed red pepper flakes, optional for serving

Return the skillet to medium-low heat and cook for 3 to 4 minutes, until the sauce has thickened slightly and the mushrooms are tender.

To serve, divide the pasta among individual bowls and sprinkle with the parsley.

Tidbits: If you tolerate dairy, omit the lemon juice and vinegar and add 2 ounces soft goat cheese to the blender when making the sauce.

Save time by purchasing peeled garlic (I prefer to buy organic). Store any leftover cloves in the refrigerator.

Store leftovers in the fridge for up to 3 days. To reheat, sauté in a dry skillet over medium heat for 3 to 5 minutes or heat in an uncovered baking dish in a preheated 350°F oven for 20 minutes.

Make It Ahead: If spiralizing your own noodles, cut them and store in the fridge for up to 5 days. Cut the other vegetables and store in the fridge for up to 3 days. Store the sauce in the fridge for up to 5 days or in the freezer for up to 6 months.

 EF

One-Pot Beef Pasta with Creamy Tomato-Vodka Sauce

SERVES 4 TO 6

Prep Time: 8 minutes
Cook Time: 12 minutes

What is more retro and classic than a one-pot beef and pasta recipe coated in a creamy tomato sauce? The boxed versions of these types of meals were some of my first forays into the kitchen, and I still have a love for them. Check out my Beef Stroganoff (page 221) to see what I mean.

This dish is made with grain-free shells made from chickpeas, but parsnip noodles (see page 123) would contribute nicely to the creaminess of the dish if you want to keep it legume-free. Serve the pasta with a simple green salad for a satisfying meal.

- 1 medium yellow onion, quartered
- 4 cloves garlic, peeled
- 2 teaspoons avocado oil
- 1½ pounds ground beef
- 2 tablespoons Italian Seasoning (page 33)
- 3 teaspoons fine sea salt
- 8 ounces grain-free medium dried pasta shells
- 2 cups beef Bone Broth (page 42)
- ¼ cup grain-free vodka (such as potato or grape)
- 1 (24-ounce) jar strained tomatoes or tomato puree
- ¾ cup Dairy-Free Heavy Cream (page 38)
- 2 tablespoons nutritional yeast
- 2 tablespoons melted ghee or extra-virgin olive oil
- 2 tablespoons chopped fresh flat-leaf parsley
- ¼ cup Dairy-Free Parmesan (page 37), optional for serving

In a blender or food processor, puree the onion and garlic. Alternatively, finely mince them with a knife, then crush to a paste.

On an electric pressure cooker, select the sauté setting on high. Add the avocado oil and onion and garlic puree and cook for 3 to 5 minutes, until bubbling.

Add the beef, Italian seasoning, and 2 teaspoons of the salt and cook, breaking up the meat with a wooden spoon and stirring frequently, for 4 to 6 minutes, until the beef is fully browned and most of the liquid has evaporated. Select the cancel button.

Add the pasta in an even layer on top of the beef mixture, then pour in the broth, vodka, and tomatoes. Do not stir, but make sure the pasta is fully immersed in the liquid. Secure the lid, select the manual button, and cook at high pressure for 3 minutes. Release the pressure manually. If the machine is venting a frothy liquid (from the noodles), turn the valve back to sealing and release the steam a little at a time. The pasta should be al dente but will continue to soften.

Meanwhile, whisk together the cream, yeast, and ghee. Remove the lid from the pressure cooker and switch the mode back to sauté on high. Stir in the cream mixture and simmer for 2 to 3 minutes, until thickened. Add the remaining teaspoon of salt.

To serve, divide the pasta among individual plates and sprinkle with the parsley.

CONTINUED

Tidbits: If you tolerate dairy, omit the dairy-free heavy cream and add ¾ cup dairy cream and top with grated Parmesan or sheep's milk Romano.

Keep in mind that cook times will vary if you use a gluten-free or grain-free pasta not made from chickpeas. Shaped pastas like fusilli, penne, or shells cook more evenly in an electric pressure cooker and don't clump together like spaghetti, fettuccine, or other long noodles typically do. My rule of thumb for cooking dried pasta in a pressure cooker is to cook it for half of the shortest time listed on the package instructions, minus 1 minute. So if the box says 8 to 10 minutes, cook it for 3 minutes. You can always add time if it's not done, but you can't go back once it's overcooked.

Store leftovers in the fridge for up to 5 days. To reheat, sauté in a dry skillet over medium heat for 3 to 5 minutes or heat in an uncovered baking dish in a preheated 350°F oven for 20 minutes.

To Use a Stove Top: Follow the instructions as given, but increase the broth to 2¼ cups and cook, covered, over medium heat for 12 to 14 minutes, until the pasta is al dente. Stir in the cream mixture and simmer over medium-high heat for 2 to 3 minutes, until thickened.

Make It Ahead: Complete the method up until the point of adding the noodles, and store tightly covered in the pressure cooker pot in the refrigerator for 3 days. When ready to cook, add the pot to the machine and select sauté mode on high until simmering. Add the noodles and liquids as instructed, and cook as directed.

Parsnip Noodles Variation

Using the stove-top method, omit the bone broth, add the noodles to the tomato sauce, and reduce the cook time to about 1 minute, until the noodles are done to your taste.

Cheesy-Taco Pasta Variation

Swap out the Italian seasoning for Taco Seasoning (page 34), cilantro for the parsley, and top with chopped fresh tomatoes, sliced black olives, and diced avocado.

Moo Shu Pork Pasta

SERVES 4 TO 6

Prep Time: 10 minutes
Cook Time: 7 minutes

I used to love to order the moo shu pork at the restaurant where I worked in college. However, I did not love having to stand tableside and wrap it up in the warm tortillas using just two forks! This pasta incorporates all of my favorite flavors from that dish—sweet and lightly spiced hoisin sauce, pork, and lots of vegetables—into a one-pot pasta using mildly sweet, white-fleshed Hannah sweet potatoes as the noodles.

- 1 (12-ounce) pork tenderloin, trimmed of fat and cut into ¼-inch-thick slices
- 2 tablespoons plus ⅓ cup Hoisin Sauce (page 27)
- 1 tablespoon coconut aminos
- ¾ teaspoon fine sea salt
- 2 tablespoons avocado oil
- 4 ounces white button mushrooms, thinly sliced
- 2 cups broccoli florets
- 1½ cups snow peas, trimmed and thinly sliced on the diagonal
- 3 medium white-fleshed sweet potatoes (such as Hannah or Japanese), peeled and spiralized
- 3 green onions, white and tender green parts, thinly sliced on the diagonal

Put the pork into a shallow dish, add 2 tablespoons of the hoisin sauce, the coconut aminos, and salt and stir to coat the pork.

In a large skillet, heat 1 tablespoon of the oil over medium-high heat. Add the mushrooms, broccoli, and snow peas and sauté for 3 to 5 minutes, until the broccoli is crisp-tender and bright green. Transfer the vegetables to a plate.

Add the sweet potato noodles to the skillet, cover, and cook for 2 to 3 minutes, until crisp-tender but still holding their shape. Transfer the noodles to the plate with the vegetables.

Heat the remaining 1 tablespoon oil in the skillet over medium-high heat. Add the pork slices in a single layer and cook, without moving the pork, for about 1 minute, until well browned on the bottom. Flip the pork slices and continue to cook for about 1 minute, until the pork is cooked through. Return the noodles and vegetables to the skillet, then add the remaining ⅓ cup hoisin sauce and toss to coat.

To serve, divide the pasta among individual plates and sprinkle with the green onions.

Tidbits: Store leftovers in the fridge for up to 3 days. To reheat, sauté in a dry skillet over medium heat for 3 to 5 minutes or heat in an uncovered baking dish in a preheated 350°F oven for 20 minutes.

Make It Ahead: Marinate the pork in a covered dish in the fridge for up to 24 hours. Cut the noodles, immerse them in a bowl of cold water, and then cover and store in the fridge for up to 2 days. Store the hoisin sauce in a sealed jar in the fridge for up to 4 weeks.

EF, NF 30

Curry Noodles with Shrimp

SERVES 4

Prep Time: 12 minutes
Cook Time: 15 minutes

This dish is my riff on Singapore noodles—a dish that technically has no known connection to Singapore but is said to have originated in Hong Kong. It consists of stir-fried rice noodles, vegetables, curry powder, and sometimes scrambled eggs. Instead of rice noodles, I use kelp noodles, which are softened by simmering them in an acidic mixture of water and baking soda, though they still retain a bit of their crunch. I use a mild curry powder so my entire family can enjoy this noodle dish.

- 1 pound kelp noodles, or 3 cups cooked noodles of your choice
- 1 tablespoon baking soda
- 1 lime, halved, plus wedges for serving
- 2 tablespoons avocado oil
- 3 green onions, white parts thinly sliced and tender green parts sliced on the diagonal into 2-inch pieces, white and green parts separated
- 1½ cups coleslaw mix or a mix of shredded green cabbage, red cabbage, and carrots
- 1 small yellow onion, halved and thinly sliced
- 2¼ teaspoons curry powder
- ¾ teaspoon garlic powder
- ½ teaspoon ground ginger
- ¼ cup Stir-Fry Sauce (page 27)
- 1 cup cherry tomatoes, halved
- 4 ounces mung bean sprouts
- 1 pound large shrimp, peeled and deveined with tails on
- Fine sea salt and white pepper

Break the noodles apart a bit, then soak them in a bowl of boiling water mixed with 1 tablespoon baking soda and 2 teaspoons freshly squeezed lime juice for 5 to 7 minutes.

Meanwhile, in a deep skillet, heat the oil over medium-high heat. Add the white parts of the green onions, the coleslaw mix, and the yellow onion and sauté for 3 to 5 minutes, until the cabbage begins to wilt. Stir in the curry powder, garlic powder, and ginger and sauté for about 30 seconds, until fragrant.

Drain the noodles and rinse them really well. Add them to the skillet. Sauté for 1 minute, then add the sauce and stir vigorously to deglaze the pan. Turn down the heat to medium, stir in the tomatoes, sprouts, and shrimp and cook stirring constantly, for 2 to 3 minutes, until the shrimp are pink and the noodles have softened but still have a little crunch.

Season to taste with salt and white pepper, then remove from the heat. Squeeze the juice from the remaining ½ lime over the top, sprinkle with the green parts of the green onions, and serve with lime wedges on the side.

Tidbits: **Store leftovers in the fridge for up to 3 days. To reheat, sauté in a dry skillet over medium heat for 3 to 5 minutes or heat in an uncovered baking dish in a preheated 350°F oven for 20 minutes.**

Make It Ahead: **Make the stir-fry sauce and cut up the vegetables up to 3 days in advance and store in the fridge.**

W30, EF, NF

Smoky Shrimp and Mussels with Crunchy Noodles

SERVES 6

Prep Time: 7 minutes
Cook Time: 25 minutes

This Spanish-inspired pasta comes together super quickly if you spiralize the noodles in advance or purchase them precut. The noodles are baked and become delightfully crispy before being tossed with the sauce.

- 3 tablespoons extra-virgin olive oil
- 2 teaspoons fine sea salt
- ¼ teaspoon freshly ground black pepper
- 1½ pounds large shrimp, peeled and deveined with tails on
- 1 yellow onion, quartered
- 1 small red bell pepper, seeded and halved
- 4 cloves garlic
- 1 pound white-fleshed sweet potatoes, peeled and spiralized into thin noodles or grated in a food processor
- 1 tablespoon melted ghee
- 1 tablespoon avocado oil
- 1 (18.3-ounce) jar diced tomatoes, drained
- 1½ teaspoons smoked paprika
- 1 pound mussels, scrubbed and debearded
- 2 tablespoons chopped fresh flat-leaf parsley
- 1 tablespoon Garlic Aioli (page 24)
- 1 lemon, cut into 6 wedges

In a bowl, stir together 1 tablespoon of the olive oil, ¼ teaspoon of the salt, and ⅛ teaspoon of the pepper. Add the shrimp and toss to coat evenly. Cover and refrigerate until needed.

Preheat the oven to 450°F. Line a large sheet pan with parchment paper.

In a food processor, combine the onion, bell pepper, and garlic and pulse until finely chopped.

In a large skillet, heat the remaining 2 tablespoons olive oil over medium-high heat until shimmering. Add the onion mixture and ¾ teaspoon of the salt and sauté for 5 to 7 minutes, until the onion begins to soften.

Meanwhile, toss the noodles with 1 tablespoon of the ghee, the avocado oil, and the remaining 1 teaspoon salt. Spread the noodles in a single layer on the prepared sheet pan. (Use two sheet pans if needed to keep the noodles in a single layer so they toast not steam.)

Add the tomatoes and paprika to the skillet, stir well, and simmer over medium-low heat, stirring occasionally, for 15 minutes. While the sauce simmers, place the sheet pan in the oven and roast the noodles, tossing them halfway through, for 14 to 16 minutes, until crispy and browned on the edges. Remove the noodles from the oven and set aside.

Add the shrimp and mussels to the skillet, cover tightly, and continue to simmer for 4 to 5 minutes, until the shrimp turn pink and curl slightly and the mussels have opened (discard any mussels whose shells failed to open during cooking). Remove the skillet from the heat and stir in the crispy noodles just before serving.

Transfer the skillet to the table, add remaining black pepper to taste, and sprinkle the parsley over the top. Dollop the aioli around the pan and serve with the lemon wedges on the side.

Tidbits: **Store leftovers in the fridge for up to 3 days. To reheat, sauté in a dry skillet over medium heat for 3 to 5 minutes or heat in an uncovered baking dish in a preheated 350°F oven for 20 minutes.**

Make It Ahead: **Cut the noodles, immerse them in a bowl of cold water, and then cover and store in the fridge for up to 2 days. Chop the onion, bell pepper, and garlic and store in the fridge for up to 5 days.**

W30*, EF, NF, SCD -10 *sub bone broth for wine

Shrimp Scampi

SERVES 4 TO 6

Prep Time: 10 minutes
Cook Time: 25 minutes

Technically, the name of this dish is redundant, as it means "shrimp shrimp." But this buttery-garlicky, rich shrimp pasta is a classic and is how people often first try shrimp. The shrimp and sauce cook for only 5 minutes, so if you need a super-quick meal, skip the spaghetti squash noodles and serve this on its own with some toasted grain-free bread to soak up the rich sauce or over a roasted potatoes or sweet potatoes (see page 227, Rosemary-Garlic Oven Fries).

- 1 medium spaghetti squash, about 3 pounds (see Note)
- 3 tablespoons extra-virgin olive oil
- Fine sea salt and freshly ground black pepper
- ½ teaspoon garlic powder
- 5 tablespoons chopped fresh flat-leaf parsley
- 3 tablespoons ghee
- 6 cloves garlic, minced
- ¼ cup dry white wine
- ¼ to ½ teaspoon red pepper flakes
- 2 pounds large shrimp, peeled and deveined with tails on
- Finely grated zest and juice of ½ lemon

Preheat the oven to 425°F. Line a sheet pan with parchment paper or a silicon baking mat.

Slice both ends off of the squash, then cut the squash crosswise into four or five rounds. Scoop out the seeds from the center of each round. Coat the rounds on both sides with 1 tablespoon of the oil, sprinkle both sides with ½ teaspoon salt, and arrange in a single layer on the prepared sheet pan. Bake the squash for 20 to 25 minutes, until fork-tender. Let cool, then use a fork to pull the flesh into noodle-like strands away from the squash rounds, leaving the noodles on the sheet pan and discarding the skins.

Toss the squash noodles with any oil remaining on the pan, ½ teaspoon salt, the garlic powder, and 2 tablespoons of the parsley. Turn off the oven, then return the noodles to the oven to keep warm.

In a large skillet, heat the ghee and the remaining 2 tablespoons oil over medium heat. Add the minced garlic and sauté for about 1 minute, until fragrant. Add wine, the remaining 1 teaspoon salt, and the red pepper flakes to taste and increase for more spice. Raise the heat to medium-high. Bring to a simmer and simmer for about 2 minutes, until the wine is reduced by half.

Add the shrimp and sauté for 2 to 3 minutes, until they just turn pink and curl slightly. Stir in the remaining 3 tablespoons parsley and the lemon juice and zest. Season to taste with salt and pepper.

To serve, divide the noodles among individual plates and top with the shrimp.

Note: **Microwave the uncut squash for 1 minute to make it easier to slice.**

Make It Ahead: **Prepare the spaghetti squash noodles with the oil and seasonings and store in the fridge for up to 5 days. Reheat in a dry skillet over medium-high heat, stirring frequently until warmed through, about 5 minutes. The shrimp is best when it's cooked just before serving, but leftovers will keep for up to 2 days. To reheat, sauté the noodles and shrimp in a dry skillet over medium heat for 3 to 5 minutes.**

*use zucchini noodles for W30 and SCD

W30*, EF, V, SCD*

Roasted Tomato and Pesto Penne

SERVES 4 TO 6

Prep Time: 8 minutes
Cook Time: 12 minutes

If you're pressed for time, this recipe is a great option. Roasting the tomatoes brings out their natural sweetness and helps them melt into the noodles. My kids love this dish with or without added protein, but if I have leftover shredded chicken or some fresh shrimp, I'll sauté it in the emptied pasta pot to heat it quickly and then toss it in with the pesto. My favorite noodles to use for my kids are the Jovial cassava penne, but zucchini, spaghetti squash, or even brown rice noodles all work well.

- 2 pints cherry tomatoes
- 3 cloves garlic, minced
- ¼ cup extra-virgin olive oil
- 1 pound grain-free penne pasta
- ⅓ cup Dairy-Free Basil Pesto (page 28)
- ½ teaspoon coarse sea salt
- Finely grated zest of 1 lemon
- ¼ cup loosely packed fresh basil leaves

Preheat the oven to 425°F. Line a large sheet pan with parchment paper or a silicone baking mat. Bring a large pot of water to a boil.

Pile the tomatoes and garlic on the prepared pan, drizzle with the oil, toss to coat, and then spread in a single layer. Roast for 12 to 15 minutes, until the tomatoes have begun to burst and blister.

While the tomatoes roast, add the penne to the boiling water and cook until al dente according to the package instructions. Scoop out 1 tablespoon of the pasta water into a large bowl, then drain the pasta and transfer it to the bowl. Pour the tomatoes and any juices from the pan over the penne and toss to combine. Add the pesto and toss gently to coat. Add the salt and lemon zest and toss gently once more. Sprinkle the basil on top and serve.

Tidbits: **Store leftovers in the fridge for up to 7 days. To reheat, sauté in a dry skillet over medium heat for 3 to 5 minutes or heat in an uncovered baking dish in a preheated 350°F oven for 20 minutes.**

EF, NF*, V

*omit cashews

Sweet Chili Noodle Stir-Fry

SERVES 4 TO 6

Prep Time: 18 minutes
Cook Time: 17 minutes

Since this vegetarian stir-fry is already filled to the brim with veggies, I decided to use shirataki noodles here instead of a spiralized veggie. Shirataki are thin, translucent, gelatinous noodles made from the konjac yam. I love the texture and substance they give the dish and how closely they resemble the rice noodles used in Thai cuisine. You could also use kelp noodles here or, of course, spiralize your favorite veggies like squash or sweet potato.

- ½ cup honey
- ¼ cup coconut sugar
- 3 tablespoons coconut aminos
- 4 teaspoons unseasoned rice vinegar or 2 teaspoons apple cider vinegar
- 4 cloves garlic, minced
- 4 teaspoons peeled and minced fresh ginger
- 1 teaspoon red pepper flakes
- Fine sea salt and freshly ground black pepper
- 2 tablespoons tomato paste
- 14 ounces shirataki noodles
- 1 tablespoon avocado oil
- 2 green onions, white and tender green parts, thinly sliced, with white and green separated
- 8 ounces Napa cabbage, cored and thinly sliced
- 2 cups broccoli florets
- 6 ounces carrots, peeled, halved lengthwise, and cut into thin half-moons
- 4 ounces shiitake mushrooms, stemmed and sliced
- 3 tablespoons toasted cashews, roughly chopped

In a saucepan, stir together the honey, sugar, coconut aminos, vinegar, garlic, ginger, pepper flakes, and 1½ teaspoons salt and set over high heat. Bring the mixture to a boil, turn down the heat to medium-low, and simmer for about 15 minutes, until reduced by half. Remove from the heat, stir in the tomato paste, and set aside.

Meanwhile, fill a large, deep skillet or wok half full with water and bring to a boil over high heat. Add the noodles to the boiling water and cook for 2 minutes. Drain the noodles, rinse them well, and pat them dry.

Return the pan to the stove and heat the oil over medium-high heat. Add the white parts of the green onions, season with salt and pepper, and sauté for 30 seconds, until fragrant and slightly softened. Add the cabbage, broccoli, and carrots and cook, stirring frequently, for 3 to 5 minutes, until the cabbage has softened. Remove the pan from the heat.

Add the noodles to the skillet, toss to combine, then return to medium-high heat and cook, stirring frequently, for 1 to 2 minutes, until most of the liquid has evaporated. Add the mushrooms and half of the sauce and cook, stirring frequently, for 1 to 2 minutes, until the sauce has thickened and coats the noodles.

Garnish with the cashews and green parts of the green onions and serve with the remaining sauce on the side.

Tidbits: **Spiralized vegetable noodles, such as carrot, squash, or sweet potato, would also be great in this dish. Skip the boiling step and sauté the veggie noodles with the other vegetables until crisp-tender.**

Store leftovers in the fridge for up to 3 days. To reheat, sauté in a dry skillet over medium heat for 3 to 5 minutes or heat in an uncovered baking dish in a preheated 350°F oven for 20 minutes.

Make It Ahead: **Cut up the vegetables and make the sauce up to 3 days in advance. Store both in the refrigerator.**

Mac and Cheese

SERVES 8

Prep Time: 10 minutes
Cook Time: 20 minutes

For nearly a decade, my readers pleaded with me to develop a macaroni and cheese recipe, but I never found a good grain-free pasta to use. And I'm sorry, but zucchini noodles (or the stems of cauliflower florets . . . if you read *Food Saved Me*, you know) just don't cut it. But now, many years after starting this food journey, there are a ton of grain-free pastas on the market made with flour from cassava, quinoa, chickpeas, almonds—you name it.

For this nostalgic comfort-food dish, I modified my dairy-free queso recipe (page 226) to work as a creamy, cheese-free sauce. I've also included a dairy cheese option for anyone who eats cheese.

- 2 (8-ounce) boxes grain-free short pasta (such as elbows, shells, or penne; see Tidbits)
- 12 ounces white-fleshed sweet potatoes or russet potatoes, peeled and cubed
- 6 ounces carrots, peeled and halved
- 1⅔ cups chicken Bone Broth (page 42)
- ½ yellow onion, quartered
- 2 cloves garlic
- 3 tablespoons nutritional yeast
- ⅓ cup melted ghee or extra-virgin olive oil
- 2 teaspoons freshly squeezed lemon juice
- ½ teaspoon apple cider vinegar
- ½ teaspoon prepared yellow mustard
- Fine sea salt
- 2 teaspoons arrowroot powder, if needed for thickening
- ¼ teaspoon white pepper

Cook the pasta al dente according to the instructions on the package. While the pasta cooks, prepare the vegetables.

Drain the noodles but do not rinse them and do not wipe the pot clean. Add the potatoes, carrots, broth, onion, garlic, nutritional yeast, ghee, lemon juice, vinegar, mustard, and 3½ teaspoons salt to the pot and set over medium-high heat. Stir to combine, bring the mixture to a boil, then cover and simmer for 10 to 12 minutes, until the vegetables are fork-tender. Remove from the heat.

Let the vegetables and liquid cool slightly, then pour into a blender and blend on high speed for about 1 minute, until very smooth. Alternatively, use an immersion blender directly in the pot to puree until very smooth.

Return the sauce to the pot over medium-high heat, bring to a simmer, and simmer for 2 minutes. If the sauce is too thin, in a small bowl, whisk together the arrowroot and 1 tablespoon water to make a slurry, then whisk the slurry into the sauce and simmer for 3 minutes more, until thickened.

Gently stir the noodles into the sauce until coated. Season to taste with salt and the pepper, then serve immediately.

Tidbits: **Grain-free pastas made from chickpeas are my favorite. They hold up best and have a nice chew to them. All of the grain-free pastas from Jovial, Thrive Market, or Whole Foods will work here. See page 113 for cooking tips.**

Store leftovers in the fridge for up to 7 days. To reheat, cover the container and warm in a preheated 400°F oven for 20 minutes, stirring occasionally.

Cheese Variation

Omit the nutritional yeast and stir in ¼ cup each grated Parmesan and sharp Cheddar just before serving.

6

Sheet Pans

I used to think that cooking an entire meal on a sheet pan would result in overcooked vegetables or soggy proteins. While the easy cleanup was tempting, improperly cooked meals were not. I learned over the years that the sheet pan I was using was too small, so the crowded vegetables were steaming instead of roasting, and the proteins were not cooking at a temperature high enough to create crispy skin.

Some days are made for long simmers and lots of love and effort going into a dish, but more often than not, my days call for a simple prep and an easy cleanup. To avoid my early sheet pan cooking mistakes, see my top five cooking tips at right.

5 Tips to Better Sheet Pan Cooking

1 Use a half sheet pan (13 by 18 inches with a 1-inch rim) so vegetables brown instead of steam from overcrowding. If your oven isn't big enough to accommodate such a large pan, use two smaller sheet pans and rotate them to different racks midway through cooking.

2 Line your sheet pan with parchment paper or a silicone baking mat. This not only prevents heavy metals like aluminum from leaching into your food, but it also makes cleanup a breeze! Stainless-steel sheet pans are wonderful, too, if you can find a large one. The food can be cooked directly on it.

3 Size matters. Large potatoes won't cook at the same rate as a tender piece of salmon or thin asparagus spears, especially if those potatoes are left in large chunks. If you're using ingredients with longer cook times, cut them into small pieces, while leaving quicker-cooking foods in larger pieces. And try to make the pieces of each ingredient relatively uniform in size so they cook evenly.

4 For some of these recipes, I cook the ingredients in stages, starting with longer-cooking foods and adding the quick-cooking ones, such as shrimp or fish, for only the last part of the oven time. You can also speed up the oven time for ingredients like potatoes by blanching them first: Plunge them into boiling water for 1 minute and then drain and rinse in cold water before cooking in the oven. Or use the Parboiled Potatoes from your prep day (page 40).

5 Use a rack for that ultimate crisp. While this technically adds another dish, sometimes setting an oven-safe wire rack on top of the sheet pan is necessary to get a crispy texture. For instance, I use a rack in the Coconut-Crusted Shrimp with Broiled Pineapple–Mint Salad (page 159) and Sweet-and-Sour Pork (page 152) recipes so the proteins don't get soggy. Find a rack that is half the size of your sheet pan so you can roast the vegetables on the other half of the pan.

Jerk Chicken Wings and Burnt Broccoli

SERVES 4 TO 6

Prep Time: 8 minutes
Cook Time: 26 minutes

This dish takes two of Ryan's all-time favorites—wings and burnt broccoli (#burntbroccoliisthebestbroccoli)—and cooks them together on a sheet pan for a super-easy dinner to eat while watching a good baseball game on TV. If you don't know the story behind my popular Burnt Broccoli, which not only makes broccoli lovers swoon but has also won over broccoli haters, see page 278.

Don't crowd the broccoli and chicken on the sheet pan or they will not get crispy. If needed, use two sheet pans. And trust me on this: You will want to triple or quadruple the Burnt Broccoli Seasoning so you can roast up this incredibly flavorful and crispy broccoli multiple times a week. To cut the heat of the dish, make a bowl of my spice-cooling Herb Ranch Dressing (page 23) for dipping the wings.

- 3 heads broccoli, cut into small florets (about 8 cups)
- 2 tablespoons avocado oil
- ¾ teaspoon freshly squeezed lemon juice
- 2½ teaspoons Burnt Broccoli Seasoning (page 31)
- 1 tablespoon ghee or extra-virgin olive oil
- 3 pounds split chicken wings (drumettes and wingettes)
- 3 tablespoons Caribbean Seasoning (page 33)

Position one rack in the top slot and one rack in the middle slot of the oven and preheat the oven to 425°F. Line a large sheet pan with parchment paper or a silicone baking mat.

Pile the broccoli florets on half of the prepared pan. Drizzle with the oil and lemon juice, sprinkle with the broccoli seasoning, and toss the broccoli to coat. Spread the florets in a single layer on half of the pan and drop the ghee onto the center of the broccoli.

Set an oven-safe wire rack on the other half of the sheet pan. In a large bowl, toss the chicken wings with the Caribbean seasoning until evenly coated. Arrange the wings in a single layer on the wire rack.

Roast on the middle rack of the oven for 8 minutes. Toss the broccoli to coat it in the now-melted ghee and flip the chicken wings. Return the pan to the middle rack and roast for 16 to 18 minutes longer, until the chicken and broccoli are browned, crispy, and tender.

Turn the oven to broil. Move the sheet pan to the top oven rack and broil for 1 minute. Flip the broccoli and wings and broil for 1 to 2 minutes more, until the chicken skin is crispy and the broccoli is charred. Serve immediately.

Tidbits: **Triple or quadruple the Caribbean seasoning along with the broccoli seasoning and then store both mixes in tightly capped jars in the pantry for the next time. And the next time. And the time after that. Once you've tasted this recipe, you'll want it on regular rotation.**

W30, EF, NF, SCD* *omit parsnips

Chicken Bruschetta with Tomato Salsa

SERVES 4 TO 6

Prep Time: 18 minutes
Cook Time: 30 minutes

The word *bruschetta* comes from the Italian verb bruscare, or "to toast," and those toasted bread slices are usually brushed with oil and sometimes a little garlic. The toppings can vary wildly! My favorite version has always been the tomato and basil topping many of us know and love. But since I can't eat bread unless it's painstakingly homemade, I use chicken breasts as the vessel here. The fresh tomato topping is really easy to make and will keep in the refrigerator for about a week, but if you want a shortcut, Trader Joe's has a delicious packaged one.

8 ounces small carrots, trimmed

8 ounces parsnips, peeled and cut into thin wedges

1½ teaspoons balsamic vinegar

6 tablespoons extra-virgin olive oil

4 cloves garlic, passed through a garlic press or mashed with the back of a knife

1¼ teaspoons fine sea salt

1½ teaspoons freshly ground black pepper

6 boneless, skinless chicken breasts (about 2½ pounds)

¼ cup chopped fresh sage leaves

6 thin slices prosciutto (about 2 ounces)

Tomato Salsa

12 ounces Roma tomatoes, cored and diced

½ cup loosely packed fresh basil leaves, cut into narrow ribbons

1 tablespoon balsamic vinegar

1 tablespoon extra-virgin olive oil

½ teaspoon fine sea salt

¼ teaspoon freshly ground black pepper

Position one rack in the top slot and one rack in the middle slot of the oven and preheat the oven to 375°F. Line a large sheet pan with parchment paper or a silicone baking mat.

Pile the carrots and parsnips on the prepared pan, top with the vinegar, 2 tablespoons of the oil, 2 of the pressed garlic cloves, and ½ teaspoon each of the salt and pepper, and toss the vegetables to coat. Spread the vegetables in a single layer. Roast on the middle rack of the oven for 10 minutes.

While the vegetables roast, prepare the chicken. Season both sides of the breasts with ½ teaspoon each of the salt and pepper. In a small bowl, stir together the remaining 4 tablespoons oil, the sage, the remaining crushed garlic, and the remaining ¼ teaspoon salt and ½ teaspoon pepper. Rub the mixture on one side of each chicken breast. Lay a slice of prosciutto on seasoned side of each breast.

Remove the sheet pan from the oven and scoot the vegetables to the sides of the pan. Place the chicken breasts, prosciutto side up, in a single layer in the center and return the pan to the oven. Bake the chicken for 18 to 20 minutes, until a thermometer inserted into the thickest part of a breast registers 165°F. Turn the oven to broil and move the pan to the top rack. Broil for 45 to 60 seconds, until the prosciutto crisps.

While the chicken bakes, make the tomato salsa. In a bowl, stir together the tomatoes, basil, vinegar, oil, salt, and pepper. Cover and refrigerate until ready to serve.

Spoon the salsa evenly over the chicken breasts and serve immediately.

Make It Ahead: **Make the salsa and store in the fridge for up to 1 week. Prepare the chicken with the coating and wrap the prosciutto around each breast so it stays intact. Store, tightly wrapped, in the refrigerator for 2 days. Oil and season the vegetables 3 days in advance and store in a separate container. Bring the chicken to room temperature while the vegetables roast, then cook as instructed.**

EF, NF

Mediterranean Meatball Bowl with Spicy Ranch

SERVES 4 TO 6

Prep Time: 15 minutes
Cook Time: 18 minutes

During stay-at-home date nights with Ryan, ordering Greek food from our favorite local spot and eating while watching a movie became a staple. We love gyro meat served over greens without the pita, but a lot of restaurants these days add wheat flour or soy to their meat to keep it tender. Instead of using lamb or beef, I combine ground chicken and Mediterranean spices, then make them into meatballs. If you have leftover or frozen meatballs from my Swedish Meatballs (page 225), those will work here, too. If you tolerate dairy, purchase tzatziki, a yogurt sauce containing herbs and cucumbers, to use in place of the ranch dressing.

- 2 tablespoons extra-virgin olive oil, plus more for coating
- 1 small yellow onion, quartered
- 2 cups plantain chips (about 4 ounces)
- 2 pounds ground dark-meat chicken
- 2 tablespoons Mediterranean Seasoning (page 34)
- 1½ teaspoons fine sea salt
- 1 egg
- Finely grated zest and juice of 1 lemon
- 4 Roma tomatoes, cored and quartered lengthwise
- 1 red bell pepper, seeded and sliced
- 1 tablespoon avocado oil
- ½ cup Herb Ranch Dressing (page 23)
- 1 tablespoon hot sauce
- 1 English cucumber, halved lengthwise and sliced crosswise into half-moons
- 2 tablespoons chopped fresh mint leaves
- 2 tablespoons chopped fresh dill
- Pitted Kalamata olives and whole peperoncini, for serving

Preheat the oven to 450°F. Line a large sheet pan with parchment paper. Brush or spray the parchment generously with olive oil (1 tablespoon).

In a food processor, combine the onion and plantain chips and process until a chunky puree has formed. Remove the blade from the processor, then add the chicken, Mediterranean seasoning, 1 teaspoon of the salt, the egg, and lemon zest to the bowl and mix thoroughly with your hands.

Coat your hands with a bit of olive oil or water and, using about 2 tablespoons for each ball, shape the chicken mixture into about 30 meatballs. As the meatballs are shaped, place them, not touching, on one side of the prepared sheet pan. Spray or brush the tops with 1 tablespoon of the olive oil.

In a bowl, toss together the tomatoes, bell pepper, avocado oil, lemon juice, the remaining 1 tablespoon olive oil, and ½ teaspoon salt. Heap the tomato mixture on the other half of the sheet pan.

Roast for 18 to 20 minutes, until the vegetables are soft, the meatballs are crisp, and a thermometer inserted into the center of a meatball reads 165°F.

Meanwhile, in a small bowl, stir together the ranch dressing and hot sauce.

To serve, divide the meatballs and roasted vegetables evenly among individual bowls. Top each serving with the cucumber, mint, dill, olives, peperoncini, and a drizzle of the sauce. This dish is equally good served hot or room temperature.

Make It Ahead: **Store the uncooked meatballs in the refrigerator for up to 2 days or in the freezer for up to 6 months. To freeze the uncooked meatballs, arrange them in a single layer on a sheet pan lined with parchment paper and place in the freezer. Once frozen, transfer the meatballs to a resealable bag or airtight container. Thaw the frozen meatballs in the refrigerator overnight, or immerse the bag in a bowl of warm water until the meatballs have thawed. Roast as directed in the recipe.**

W30, EF, NF, SCD -10

Chicken, Bacon, and Ranch Squash Noodles

SERVES 4 TO 6

Prep Time: 15 minutes
Cook Time: 22 minutes

I use a mayo-based, dairy-free ranch dressing to coat vegetable noodles in this club sandwich turned pasta! You can easily make this a fifteen-minute meal if you roast your spaghetti squash in advance and use leftover cooked bacon and chicken. It's also easy to bake this all at once on the same sheet pan.

1 medium spaghetti squash (about 3 pounds)

8 ounces thick-cut bacon slices

1½ pounds boneless, skinless chicken breasts

3 tablespoons extra-virgin olive oil

Fine sea salt and freshly ground black pepper

1 pint cherry tomatoes

½ teaspoon garlic powder

½ cup Herb Ranch Dressing (page 23)

Position one rack in the top slot and one rack in the middle slot of the oven. Place the squash directly on the middle rack and turn on the heat to 400°F to soften the skin.

Meanwhile, line a large sheet pan with parchment paper. Arrange the bacon slices and chicken in a single layer on the prepared sheet pan. Drizzle the chicken with 1 tablespoon of the oil and sprinkle with ¾ teaspoon salt and ¼ teaspoon pepper.

Remove the warmed squash from the oven, slice off both ends, and cut crosswise into four or five rounds. Scoop out the seeds from the center of each round. Drizzle both sides of the rounds with 1 tablespoon of the oil, then arrange the rounds in a single layer on the prepared sheet pan.

Place the pan on the middle rack in the oven and bake for 10 minutes. Flip the bacon slices and bake for 10 to 15 minutes more, until the bacon is crisp, the chicken is cooked through, and the squash is fork-tender.

Remove the pan from the oven and transfer the bacon, chicken, and squash to a plate to rest, leaving the rendered bacon fat on the pan. Add the tomatoes to the pan, toss with the bacon fat, season with a pinch each of salt and pepper, and spread in a single layer.

Place on the top rack and turn the oven to broil. Broil for 2 to 3 minutes, until the tomatoes have burst. Meanwhile, dice the chicken and bacon.

Use a fork to pull the flesh into noodle-like strands from the sides of the squash rounds. Discard the skins. Transfer the noodles to a serving bowl, add the remaining 2 tablespoons oil, the garlic powder, ½ teaspoon salt, ¼ teaspoon pepper, and ¼ cup of the ranch dressing, and toss to mix. Gently stir in the bacon, chicken, and tomatoes and drizzle the remaining ranch dressing over the top. Serve immediately.

Make It Ahead: **Bake all of the components and season the noodles. Toss them with the bacon, chicken, and tomatoes and store in the fridge for up to 5 days in advance to shave off a lot of prep time. Spread the mixed pasta on a sheet pan and reheat in a 400°F oven for 10 minutes. Stir in the ranch and serve.**

Cajun Shrimp and Andouille Sausage

SERVES 4 TO 6

Prep Time: 12 minutes
Cook Time: 14 minutes

My favorite way to enjoy this sheet pan meal is to crumble grain-free cornbread onto the bottom of a bowl, spoon the juicy sausage, shrimp, and vegetables on top, and then finish with a drizzle of tangy, spicy aioli for the perfect bite. My Creamy Almond-Cauliflower Polenta (page 264) is a good replacement for cornbread if you have an extra ten minutes to make it. Niman Ranch and Teton Waters Ranch make great sugar-free andouille, or use Pederson's Natural Farms kielbasa.

- 8 ounces andouille sausage, cut crosswise into 2-inch pieces
- 10 ounces cherry tomatoes (about 3 cups)
- 4 medium zucchini, cubed
- 2 poblano chiles, seeded and diced
- 3 cloves garlic, minced
- 4 tablespoons melted ghee or avocado oil
- 3 teaspoons freshly squeezed lemon juice, plus more for serving
- ¾ teaspoon fine sea salt
- 1½ pounds medium shrimp, peeled and deveined with tails on
- 2 to 3 tablespoons Cajun Seasoning (page 32)
- ¼ cup Cajun Aioli (page 23)
- Sliced green onions, white and tender green parts, for serving

Preheat the oven to 425°F. Line a large sheet pan with parchment paper.

In a bowl, toss together the sausage, tomatoes, zucchini, chiles, and garlic with 2 tablespoons of the ghee, 2 teaspoons of the lemon juice, and the salt. Spread the vegetables in a single layer on the prepared sheet pan. Bake for 10 to 12 minutes, until the tomatoes have burst and the sausage starts to brown.

Meanwhile, in the same bowl used for the vegetables, toss the shrimp in the remaining 2 tablespoons ghee and 1 teaspoon lemon juice and the Cajun seasoning.

Remove the pan from the oven and mix in the seasoned shrimp, spreading everything in a single layer. Return the pan to the oven for 4 to 6 minutes more, until the shrimp are pink throughout.

To serve, drizzle the aioli over everything and top with a squeeze of fresh lemon juice and a sprinkle of green onions.

Tidbits: **Chicken thighs, cut into 2-inch cubes, work great in place of the shrimp. Toss with ghee, lemon juice, and Cajun seasoning and cook along with the vegetables and the sausage.**

Make It Ahead: **Cut up the vegetables and sausage and toss them with the seasoning. Store in the refrigerator for 3 days.**

W30, NF

Sweet-and-Sour Pork

SERVES 4 TO 6

Prep Time: 15 minutes
Cook Time: 8 minutes

My kids love this dinner. And who wouldn't like oven-fried pork coated in a sweet and tangy sauce? I prep as I go with this recipe to get dinner on the table in less than twenty minutes, but you can also make a lot of this in advance. Boneless chicken can easily be substituted here; it cooks in the same amount of time. I use a wire rack on the sheet pan to make the pork crispy but tender.

2 pounds boneless pork loin chops or butt, cut into 1-inch pieces
1 egg white
1½ teaspoons fine sea salt
¾ teaspoon garlic powder
¼ cup arrowroot powder
1 green bell pepper, seeded and cut into 1-inch squares
1 red bell pepper, seeded and cut into 1-inch squares
2 tablespoons avocado oil
1 (20-ounce) can pineapple chunks, drained with juices reserved
¼ cup Ketchup (page 22)
½ cup unsweetened apricot jam
2 tablespoons apple cider vinegar
1 tablespoon coconut aminos
¼ teaspoon ground ginger
Basic Cauli-Rice (page 269), for serving

Position an oven rack in the upper quarter of the oven or one slot down from the top. Preheat the oven to 450°F. Line a large sheet pan with parchment paper. Set an oven-safe wire rack half the size of the sheet pan on one side.

In a large bowl, toss the pork with the egg white, 1 teaspoon of the salt, and the garlic powder. Sprinkle the arrowroot over the top and toss to coat the pork evenly. Spread the pork in a single layer on the wire rack and scatter the bell peppers directly on the pan next to the pork. Drizzle everything evenly with the oil. (If you have an oil mister, mist everything with the oil.)

Roast on the top oven rack for 3 to 5 minutes, until the pork is lightly browned and the peppers have begun to soften.

Meanwhile, in the same bowl used for the pork, make a sauce by whisking together ¼ cup of the reserved pineapple juice, the ketchup, apricot jam, vinegar, coconut aminos, ginger, and the remaining ½ teaspoon salt.

Remove the pan from the oven and mix the pineapple with the peppers. Drizzle the sauce over the pineapple and peppers and return the pan to the top oven rack. Bake for 5 to 7 minutes, until the sauce is bubbling and thickened and the peppers are tender.

Toss the pork with the pineapple and peppers and serve immediately over cauli-rice.

Tidbits: **I love St. Dalfour brand for jams because they use natural fruit pectin and have no added sugar. If you like a really thick and sticky sauce, simmer it in a saucepan over medium heat for 10 minutes instead of baking it with the pork and vegetables. Drizzle it over the top just before serving.**

Make It Ahead: **Prepare the pork up to 2 days in advance and the sauce and cut-up vegetables up to 5 days in advance. Store everything in the fridge.**

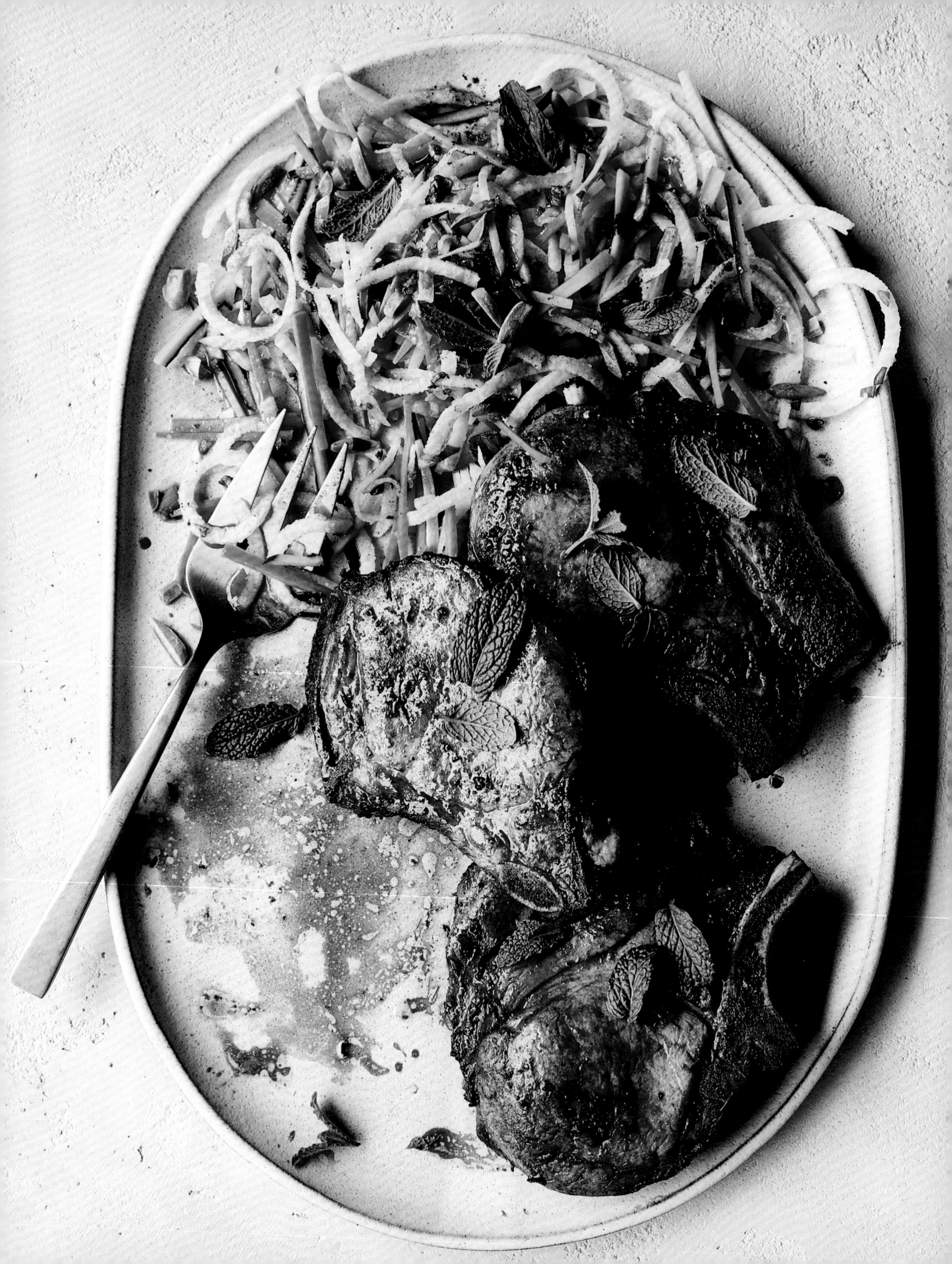

*omit almonds

W30, EF, NF*

Lemongrass-Ginger Pork Chops with Crunchy Jicama and Mint Salad

SERVES 4

Prep Time: 25 minutes, plus 20 minutes marinating time

Cook Time: 5 minutes

Pork chops can overcook and turn out dry if you're not careful, but for this dish, I marinate the chops in a super-aromatic, sweet-and-salty sauce and then quickly cook them under the broiler so the top gets crispy and browned but the inside stays tender. Served with a cooling and crisp salad and lots of fresh herbs, this is a delicious combination of flavors and textures.

Marinade

1 stalk lemongrass

3 pitted Medjool dates (see Note)

½-inch piece fresh ginger, peeled

2 tablespoons fish sauce

¼ cup coconut aminos

1 medium shallot

2 teaspoons unseasoned rice vinegar or apple cider vinegar

⅛ teaspoon red pepper flakes

¼ cup chopped cilantro leaves

4 (1-inch-thick) bone-in pork chops (about 8 ounces each)

Fine sea salt and freshly ground black pepper

Salad

1 small jicama, peeled

2 carrots, peeled and julienned

1 English cucumber, seeded and julienned

4 green onions, white and tender green parts, chopped

¼ cup chopped fresh mint leaves, plus more for garnish

1 tablespoon avocado oil

2 tablespoons freshly squeezed lime juice

Fine sea salt and freshly ground black pepper

¼ cup chopped toasted blanched almonds

Trim the dark green tops and woody base from the lemongrass and remove the tough outer leaves. Cut the stalk into ½-inch pieces. To make the marinade, in a blender, combine the lemongrass, dates, ginger, fish sauce, coconut aminos, shallot, vinegar, and pepper flakes and blend on high speed for 30 to 60 seconds, until smooth. Stir in the cilantro. Reserve 3 tablespoons of the marinade for the salad.

Place the pork chops in a single layer in a shallow dish and use a fork to pierce them all over. Add half of the remaining marinade to the dish and turn the chops to coat. Cover the dish and let the pork chops marinate at room temperature, turning occasionally, for 20 minutes.

Meanwhile, make the salad. Using a spiralizer with the smallest blade, cut the jicama into thin noodles. In a bowl, toss the noodles with the carrots, cucumber, green onions, and mint. Cover and place in the refrigerator to chill.

Position an oven rack in the top slot in the oven and preheat the broiler.

Using tongs, remove the pork chops from the marinade, scraping off any excess marinade, and place them on a large sheet pan. Discard the marinade. Generously season both sides of each chop with salt and pepper. Broil the chops, turning once halfway through, for 5 to 6 minutes total, until they are just cooked through and a thermometer inserted into the thickest part of a chop reads 135°F.

Drizzle the salad with the reserved 3 tablespoons marinade, the oil, and lime juice and toss to coat. Season to taste with salt and pepper.

To serve, arrange the salad and chops on a platter and top the salad with the almonds and the pork chops with the mint. Serve remaining dressing on the side.

Note: **If your dates are dry or hard, soak them in hot water for 10 minutes to soften before blending.**

Make It Ahead: **Make the marinade and store in the fridge for up to 7 days. Marinate the chops in the fridge for up to 3 days for a more intense flavor. Assemble the salad without the dressing and store in the fridge for up to 2 days.**

W30*, EF, NF

*use homemade oven fries

Peruvian Steak and French Fries

SERVES 4 TO 6

Prep Time: 15 minutes
Cook Time: 18 minutes

When Ryan and I were newlyweds, he traveled to Chile and Peru every other month for work and always talked about how much he loved the Peruvian steak and potato dishes. Lomo saltado, a traditional Peruvian dish of steak in a salty and slightly sour sauce with french fries, was his favorite, and lomo a lo pobre (basically, steak, eggs, and potatoes) was the runner-up.

In this version, I make the steak and fries on sheet pans for a match made in heaven. Even though everything would fit on one sheet pan, the meat and fries get crispier when they're separated. If you can't find ají amarillo, I often substitute a habanero, which is much spicier.

- 1 (15-ounce) package frozen french fries (see Note)
- 1 teaspoon Fries Seasoning Salt (page 35), optional
- 1 red onion, halved and thinly sliced
- 1 ají amarillo (yellow chile) or habanero chile, seeded and sliced
- 3½ tablespoons avocado oil
- 1 teaspoon fine sea salt
- 2 pounds top sirloin steak
- ½ teaspoon freshly ground black pepper
- ¾ teaspoon garlic powder
- 3 large Roma tomatoes, cored and cut into wedges
- ¼ cup coconut aminos
- 1 tablespoon apple cider vinegar
- ¼ teaspoon ground ginger
- ¼ cup loosely packed fresh cilantro leaves and tender stems
- Habanero hot sauce, for serving (I like Siete)

Position two oven racks in the top two slots in the oven and preheat the oven to 450°F. Line two sheet pans with parchment paper.

Toss the frozen fries with the seasoning salt and spread in a single layer on one prepared sheet pan, leaving room on one side for the onion and chile. Pile the onion and chile on the empty side of the pan, top with 1½ tablespoons of the oil and ¼ teaspoon of the salt, toss to coat, and then spread in a single layer. Place the pan on the top oven rack and bake for 14 minutes.

Meanwhile, slice the steak against the grain on the diagonal into ¼-inch-thick slices. Transfer to a large bowl, add the remaining 2 tablespoons oil and ¾ teaspoon salt, the black pepper, and garlic powder, and toss to coat. Arrange in a single layer on the second prepared pan.

Remove the pan with the fries from the oven and turn the oven to broil on high. Add the tomatoes to the onion and chile and return the fries to the second oven rack.

Place the steak on the top rack and broil, tossing once halfway through, for 4 to 6 minutes, until the steak is browned.

Meanwhile, in a bowl, whisk together the coconut aminos, vinegar, and ginger.

Remove both pans from the oven and pour off any juices from the steak. Combine the steak with the onion mixture, drizzle with the vinegar sauce, and toss to coat. Sprinkle everything with the cilantro and serve immediately with the hot sauce on the side.

Note: **Although most store-bought french fries contain canola oil, I use frozen fries as a shortcut here. Alexia organic Yukon fries are my favorite. Of course, you can make homemade oven fries (page 277) too!**

Coconut-Crusted Shrimp with Broiled Pineapple–Mint Salad

SERVES 4 TO 6

Prep Time: 20 minutes
Cook Time: 7 minutes

Coconut-breaded shrimp with a tangy, sweet sauce used to be my favorite order at Outback Steakhouse, where Ryan and I frequently went on dates in high school.

I make this a meal by adding a crisp salad of sugar snap peas, pineapple, and watercress. The tropical flavors of shredded coconut and a bright and slightly spicy sauce pair so well with broiled pineapple, which develops a delicious caramelized flavor when exposed to the intense heat of a broiler.

Shrimp

- 1 cup unsweetened finely shredded coconut
- Finely grated zest of 1 lime
- ¾ teaspoon fine sea salt
- ¼ teaspoon freshly ground black pepper
- 2 pounds large shrimp, peeled and deveined with tails on
- 2 egg whites, whisked

Salad

- 1 ripe pineapple
- 8 ounces sugar snap peas
- 1 bunch watercress
- ¼ cup loosely packed fresh mint leaves

Sauce

- ½ cup loosely packed fresh cilantro leaves and tender stems
- ½ cup sugar-free apricot jam (such as St. Dalfour)
- 2 tablespoons freshly squeezed lime juice
- 2 tablespoons avocado oil
- ¼ teaspoon crushed red pepper flakes
- ¼ teaspoon ground ginger
- ¼ teaspoon fine sea salt

Position an oven rack in the top slot in the oven and preheat the broiler. Place an oven-safe wire rack on a large sheet pan.

To make the shrimp, in a shallow bowl, mix together the coconut, lime zest, salt, and pepper. Brush the shrimp with the egg whites, then press each shrimp in the coconut mixture, coating it completely and shaking off the excess. Arrange the breaded shrimp in a single layer on the wire rack. Place the pan on the top oven rack and broil the shrimp, flipping them halfway through, for 3 to 4 minutes, until the coconut is crispy and golden brown and the shrimp are pink and curl slightly. Transfer the shrimp to a plate and set aside to cool.

To make the salad, peel and core the pineapple, then cut it into ½-inch cubes. Trim the sugar snap peas and halve each one on the diagonal. Remove and discard the tough stems of the watercress.

Arrange the pineapple in a single layer on the rack you used for the shrimp. Broil the pineapple, flipping the pieces halfway through, for 4 to 5 minutes, until toasted. Transfer the pineapple to a plate and set aside to cool.

Meanwhile, make the sauce. In a blender, combine the cilantro, jam, lime juice, oil, pepper flakes, ginger, and salt and blend on high speed for 30 to 60 seconds, until smooth and vibrant green.

To assemble the salad, place the broiled pineapple and snap peas in a serving bowl. Toss with the watercress and mint and drizzle with ¼ cup of the sauce. Serve the shrimp and salad with the remaining sauce on the side for dipping.

Make It Ahead: **Make the sauce up to 10 days in advance and the salad up to 3 days in advance and store them separately in the fridge. The shrimp is best cooked and eaten immediately, but you can enjoy leftovers chilled from the fridge for up to 2 days.**

W30*, EF, NF, SCD*

*use lettuce cups for W30 and SCD

Ancho-Citrus Shrimp Tacos with Roasted Pineapple Salsa

SERVES 4 TO 6

Prep Time: 10 minutes, plus 15 minutes marinating

Cook Time: 18 minutes

Ancho chile powder, made by drying ripened poblano chiles and then grinding them to a powder, lends a mildly spicy, smoky flavor to these shrimp tacos. It has a bit more heat than regular chili powder (a blend of ground chile and other spices), so if you cannot find it, use chili powder with a pinch of red pepper flakes. I top each taco with crispy cabbage and fresh cilantro, and the caramelized sweetness of the roasted pineapple salsa balances the spice and citrus of the shrimp. Although it's not required, Siete hot sauce is wonderful drizzled on top.

1½ pounds large shrimp, peeled and deveined

2 tablespoons freshly squeezed orange juice

1 lime, halved

Fine sea salt

2 teaspoons ancho chile powder

1 teaspoon garlic powder

¾ teaspoon onion powder

¼ teaspoon ground cumin

1 small, ripe pineapple, peeled, cored, and cut into 6 long spears

2 teaspoons avocado oil

2 avocados, halved, pitted, peeled, and diced

1 small jalapeño chile, seeded and minced

2 tablespoons minced red onion

1 small head green cabbage

¼ cup chopped fresh cilantro leaves and tender stems

10 butter lettuce cups or grain-free tortillas

Cilantro-Kale Pepita Pesto (page 28), Siete Hot Sauce, or Dairy-Free Sour Cream (page 36), for topping

Position an oven rack in the top slot in the oven and preheat the oven to 450°F. Line a large sheet pan with parchment paper.

In a large bowl, toss the shrimp with the orange juice, juice of ½ lime, 1¼ teaspoons salt, the chile powder, garlic powder, onion powder, and cumin. Cover and set aside to marinate for 15 minutes.

Meanwhile, rub the pineapple spears with the oil and arrange them in a single layer on the prepared sheet pan. Roast the pineapple on the top oven rack for 15 minutes, until golden.

Meanwhile, in a bowl, stir together the avocados, jalapeño, and onion. Core the cabbage, shred into thin strips, and place in a second bowl.

Remove the pan from the oven, move the pineapple to one side of the pan and use tongs to add the shrimp in a single layer to the empty side of the pan (discard the marinade). Return the pan to the top oven rack and roast the shrimp for 2 to 3 minutes, until are they are pink.

Remove the pan from the oven and dice the pineapple. Add it to the bowl with the avocados, squeeze in the juice from the remaining ½ lime, season to taste with salt, and then mix gently.

To serve, place the cilantro and shrimp in separate bowls. Set the lettuce cups on a large cutting board and surround the board with the bowls of shrimp, salsa, cabbage, and cilantro and with your topping of choice. Invite diners to build their own tacos.

Tidbits: **If you're using Siete brand tortillas, try throwing them directly on the grate of a gas range for a few seconds per side! They become pliable and toasty!**

Make It Ahead: **Make the salsa 3 days in advance and store in the fridge. The shrimp is best cooked and eaten immediately, but you can enjoy leftovers chilled from the fridge for up to 2 days.**

Mediterranean Salmon with Artichokes and Peppers

SERVES 6 TO 8

Prep Time: 15 minutes
Cook Time: 15 minutes

As with most of my sheet pan meals, I love to cut up the vegetables for this recipe the night before or during a lunch or nap break. I slice and dice the veggies, drain any jarred products, and mix everything together in a bowl or resealable bag. At dinnertime, I can just empty the bag and add the seasonings. Doing this advance prep work helps me get this meal into the oven in about five minutes. Divina and Native Forest brands make clean and delicious jarred Mediterranean products like roasted red peppers, artichoke hearts, and olives.

- 1 (2½-pound) skin-on salmon fillet, pin bones removed
- 3 tablespoons extra-virgin olive oil
- 1 tablespoon Mediterranean Seasoning (page 34)
- 2 lemons
- 2 cups cherry tomatoes, halved
- 1 cup drained artichoke hearts
- 1 cup drained roasted red peppers, thinly sliced
- ½ cup mixed pitted olives
- 2 shallots, thinly sliced
- ½ teaspoon fine sea salt
- ½ teaspoon freshly ground black pepper
- ¼ cup loosely packed fresh oregano leaves
- 2 sprigs thyme, leaves stripped

Preheat the oven to 425°F. Line a large sheet pan with parchment paper.

Place the salmon fillet along the center of the sheet pan and tuck the thin tail end under itself to even out the thickness. Drizzle the fish with 1 tablespoon of the oil and sprinkle the Mediterranean seasoning over the top. Thinly slice one of the lemons and arrange the slices on and around the fish. Scatter the tomatoes, artichoke hearts, peppers, olive, and shallots around the edges of the pan. Drizzle the remaining 2 tablespoons oil over the vegetables and sprinkle the salt and pepper over the fish and vegetables.

Bake for 15 to 17 minutes, until the fish is cooked through and flakes easily with a fork and the tomatoes have burst.

Cut the remaining lemon into wedges. Garnish the fish with the oregano and thyme and serve immediately with the lemon wedges on the side.

Tidbits: **Store any leftover salmon in the fridge for up to 2 days. Use in my Salmon Niçoise Potato and Green Bean Salad (page 84).**

Variation

To shake things up a little, swap in my Tagine Seasoning (page 34), Cajun Seasoning (page 32), or Adobo Seasoning (page 31). All would taste great on this salmon.

W30, EF, SCD 

Herb-Crusted Black Cod with Harissa Cauliflower

SERVES 4 TO 6

Prep Time: 12 minutes
Cook Time: 18 minutes

This recipe was inspired by my favorite cauliflower appetizer at the restaurant True Food Kitchen. Harissa, a popular North African hot chile paste, quickly adds spice and flavor to vegetables and to fish and other proteins. There are many recipes online for making it yourself, but you can also find it in stores. Grab one with simple ingredients and steer clear of those that add starch or citric acid. My favorite brand is the organic harissa from Les Moulins Mahjoub.

- 1 head cauliflower (about 2 pounds), cut into bite-size florets
- 2 tablespoons avocado oil
- Fine sea salt and freshly ground black pepper
- ¼ cup almond flour
- 3 tablespoons chopped fresh mint leaves
- 3 tablespoons chopped fresh dill leaves
- 6 (6-ounce) pieces skinless cod fillet
- 3 tablespoons melted ghee or extra-virgin olive oil
- 2 tablespoons freshly squeezed lemon juice
- ¼ cup tahini
- 1 clove garlic, crushed
- 2 tablespoons harissa paste
- 3 tablespoons chicken Bone Broth (page 42)
- 3 pitted dates, chopped
- 2 tablespoons toasted pistachios

Position an oven rack in the upper third of the oven and a rack in the middle of the oven and preheat the boiler. Line a large sheet pan with parchment paper.

In a large bowl, toss the cauliflower with the oil, ½ teaspoon salt, and ¼ teaspoon pepper to coat. Spread the florets in a single layer on the prepared sheet pan, place on the upper rack in the oven, and broil for 8 minutes, until browned.

Meanwhile, in a small bowl, stir together the almond flour and 1 tablespoon each of the mint and dill.

Remove the pan from the oven, flip the florets over, and push them to one side of the pan. Reset the oven to bake at 425°F.

Sprinkle the cod pieces on both sides with ¼ teaspoon each salt and pepper and place them on the empty side of the sheet pan. Drizzle the cod evenly with 1½ tablespoons of the ghee and 1 tablespoon of the lemon juice. Sprinkle the almond flour–herb mixture evenly over the cod, then press gently with your fingers to help it adhere. Drizzle the fish evenly with the remaining 1½ tablespoons ghee.

Place the pan on the center oven rack and bake the cod for 10 to 12 minutes, just until the almond flour–herb mixture is browned and the fish flakes easily with a fork.

Meanwhile, make a sauce. In a bowl, stir together the tahini, garlic, harissa paste, broth, the remaining 1 tablespoon lemon juice, and ¼ teaspoon salt.

When the fish and cauliflower are ready, remove the pan from the oven and drizzle 3 tablespoons of the sauce over the cauliflower and sprinkle on the dates and pistachios. Toss to combine and season to taste with salt and pepper.

Serve the fish with the roasted cauliflower and garnish with the remaining 2 tablespoons each mint and dill. Serve the remaining sauce on the side.

Make It Ahead: **Make the sauce up to 1 week in advance and the almond flour–herb mixture up to 3 days in advance. Store them both in the fridge.**

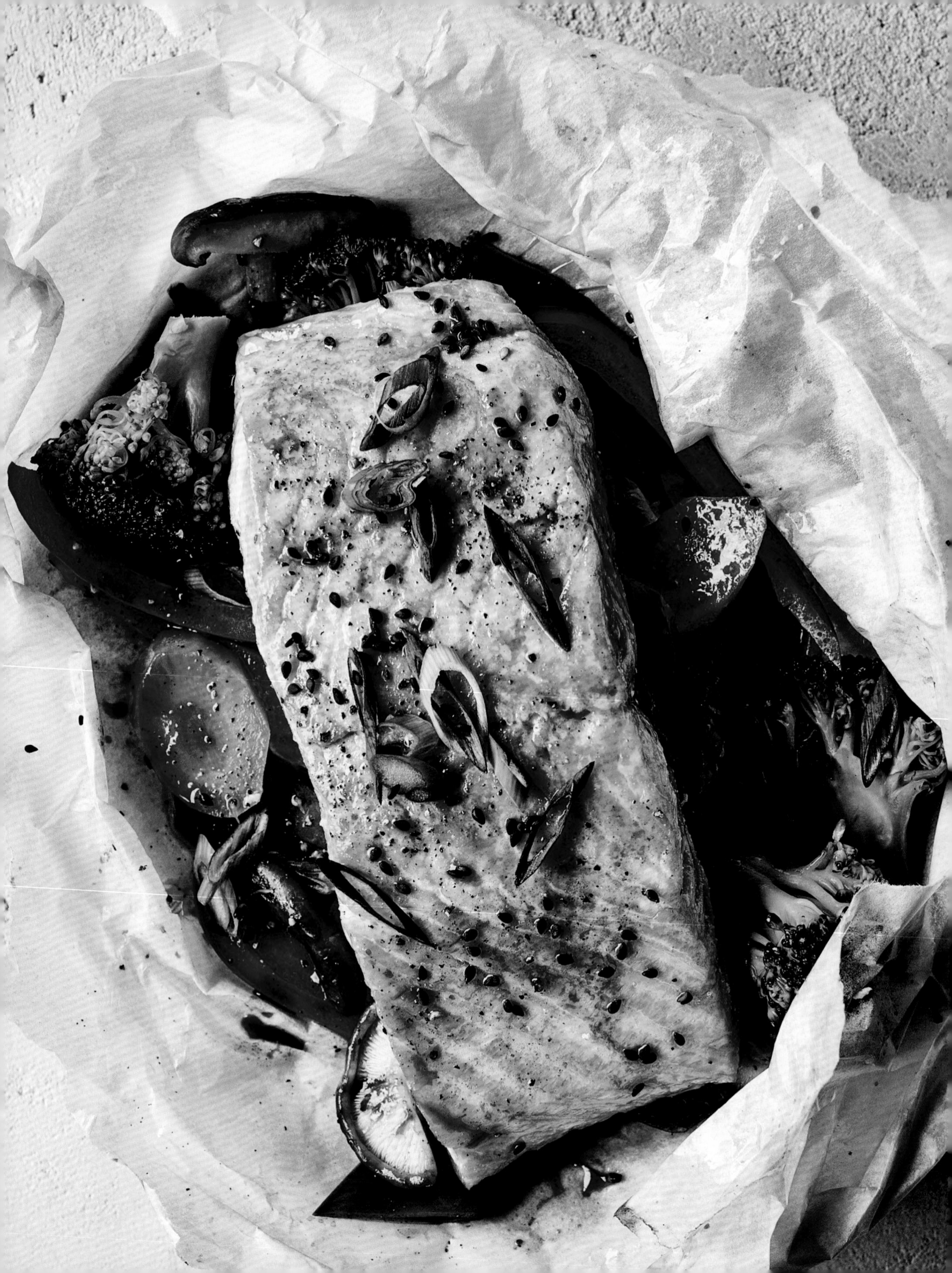

Teriyaki Salmon Packets

SERVES 4 TO 6

Prep Time: 15 minutes
Cook Time: 18 minutes

Poaching salmon in parchment paper packets is a wonderful way to cook the fish and vegetables at the same time without drying out or overcooking either one. Other firm fish, such as ahi (yellowfin tuna), would work here, too. These teriyaki-flavored fish packets are stuffed full of vegetables that soak up the sweet and salty sesame sauce. My kids love to fill their own packets with their favorite vegetables.

3 medium carrots, peeled and thinly sliced

2 cups broccoli florets

1 cup snow peas, trimmed

1 red bell pepper, seeded and thinly sliced

8 shiitake mushrooms, sliced and stems trimmed

3 tablespoons avocado oil

3 tablespoons toasted sesame oil

¾ teaspoon fine sea salt

¼ teaspoon freshly ground black pepper

½ cup Stir-Fry Sauce (page 27)

2 tablespoons honey

¾ teaspoon ground ginger

¾ teaspoon garlic powder

6 (6-ounce) pieces skinless salmon fillet

Sliced green onions, white and tender green parts, and black sesame seeds, for garnish

Preheat the oven to 350°F. Cut six large pieces parchment paper (each about 18 by 13 inches).

In a bowl, toss together the carrots, broccoli, snow peas, bell pepper, mushrooms, avocado oil, sesame oil, salt, and pepper.

In a small bowl, whisk together the stir-fry sauce, honey, ginger, and garlic powder to make a teriyaki sauce.

Fold each piece of parchment paper in half crosswise to create a crease, then unfold to lie flat. Divide the vegetables evenly among the parchment pieces, piling them high on one half of each piece, positioning them just beyond the crease line and leaving a 2-inch border around the edges. Lay a piece of salmon on top of each vegetable portion and then drizzle the teriyaki sauce on the salmon, dividing it evenly among the packets.

Fold the uncovered half of each parchment packet over the salmon, then, beginning at one end of the open edges, fold over the edges, making small, tight pleats as you go. Continue to fold and pleat until you reach the opposite open end and the packet is a half-moon shape. Check your folds to make sure the packet is well sealed so no steam will escape. Place the sealed packets in a single layer on a large sheet pan. If necessary, divide the packets between two pans.

Bake for 18 to 20 minutes, until the fish feels semifirm to the touch through the paper and the paper is browned.

Open the packets, sprinkle the salmon with the green onions and sesame seeds, and serve immediately.

Tidbits: **While there's a handful of great recipes in this book that use up the Stir-Fry Sauce, it's also become my favorite condiment for an easy lunch of a leftover protein with cauliflower rice! Salmon and roast chicken are my favorite.**

Make It Ahead: **Fill and seal the packets and place them on a sheet pan in the refrigerator for up to 24 hours. Remove the pan from the fridge and let the packets sit at room temperature for 30 minutes before baking.**

7

Stir-Fries and Skillets

This is the most robust chapter of this book because one-pan, stove-top meals are my real life. They're my jam. Quick to prepare and quick to cook, they can be plopped down on the table in the skillet for everyone to dish up, and they are quick to clean up. Nearly all of these meals can be on the table in a half hour or less. And they can be easily modified here and there based on what proteins and vegetables you need to use up at the end of the week.

All of these recipes were tested in a 14-inch cast-iron skillet with enamel coating. It's my pan of choice for stove-top cooking because it heats evenly, retains that heat, and gives meats a nice sear. I also love that it can go from stove to oven if needed. Enameled cast-iron pans are also free of the toxic chemicals that can be found in some nonstick pans.

If you prefer a pan with a more nonstick surface, you can purchase nontoxic ceramic skillets. But I've found they don't perform as well, and they aren't good over the higher heat many of these dishes require to get on the table quickly. My favorite skillet brands are Le Creuset and Staub, but Lodge has some more affordable pans. If you don't have a 14-inch skillet, a Dutch oven with a wide, flat bottom can be used.

Swap This for That

Don't eat beef, trying to eat more seafood, or prefer turkey? Here are a few easy swaps for some of the recipes in this chapter.

Chicken Lettuce Wraps (page 174)
Use ground dark turkey meat or ground pork instead of the ground chicken. For vegetarian, substitute 3 cups riced cauliflower and 1 cup finely chopped mushrooms for the ground chicken.

Lemon-Caper Chicken and Rice (page 181)
Make this dish pescatarian by substituting chunks of white cod or salmon for the chicken. Nestle the fish into the rice at the very end of cooking, then cover and steam for 2 minutes, until flaky.

Thai Basil Beef (page 189)
Swap in ground dark meat chicken or turkey to make this red meat free. For vegetarian, substitute 3 cups riced cauliflower and 1 cup finely chopped mushrooms for the ground beef.

Mango and Vanilla–Glazed Tenderloin with Spiced Sweet Potatoes (page 193)
Swap the beef for bone-in, skin-on chicken thighs and cook as directed.

Spiced Crispy Lamb with Eggplant, Squash, and Hummus (page 194)
You can substitute ground beef, turkey, or chicken one-to-one in this recipe. For vegetarian, substitute 1 pound finely chopped cremini mushrooms and for the ground meat.

*omit potatoes 

Crispy Chicken with Pesto, Charred Romanesco, and Potatoes

SERVES 4 TO 6

Prep Time: 10 minutes
Cook Time: 18 minutes

If I'm honest, this recipe was solely created in an effort to find other ways to use my Burnt Broccoli Seasoning and my Cilantro-Kale Pepita Pesto. I would put those two on anything and everything if my family allowed it. Plus, as you now know, I'm not a fan of making something like a sauce or spice mix from scratch and then not maximizing its use. Crispy chicken thighs are always a winner in our household—especially when paired with lightly charred potatoes and a bright, limey sauce.

- 8 boneless, skin-on chicken thighs
- 4 tablespoons avocado oil
- 2¼ teaspoons Burnt Broccoli Seasoning (page 31)
- 1 head romanesco, cut into florets
- 2 pounds baby potatoes, left whole if smaller than 1 inch, or white-fleshed sweet potatoes, cut into bite-size pieces
- ½ teaspoon fine sea salt
- ¼ teaspoon freshly ground black pepper
- ¼ cup Cilantro-Kale Pepita Pesto (page 28)
- ½ lime
- 2 tablespoons toasted pepitas
- 2 tablespoons fresh cilantro leaves

Place a large, oven-safe skillet in the oven and preheat the oven to 450°F.

Place the chicken thighs between two sheets of parchment paper and use a meat tenderizer or a heavy pan to pound the thighs into an even thickness of about ¾ inch. Remove the parchment, drizzle the thighs with 1 tablespoon of the oil, and rub with your hands to coat all sides. Sprinkle the thighs on all sides with the broccoli seasoning, dividing it evenly.

In a bowl, toss the romanesco florets and potatoes with the remaining 3 tablespoons oil, the salt, and pepper to coat.

Carefully remove the hot skillet from the oven and add the chicken, skin side down. Scatter the vegetables around the chicken and return the skillet to the oven. Roast for 12 minutes. Flip the chicken, toss the vegetables, return the skillet to the oven, and roast for 6 to 8 minutes more, until the chicken is cooked through, its skin is crispy, and the vegetables are browned.

To serve, smear the pesto on the bottom of a serving platter. Spoon the vegetables on top of the pesto, then place the chicken thighs on top. Squeeze the juice from the lime (about 1 tablespoon) over the entire platter, then sprinkle with the pepitas and cilantro. Serve immediately.

Tidbits: **I love the combination of the Burnt Broccoli Seasoning and Cilantro-Kale Pepita Pesto, but you can substitute in any of my spice mixes here—Taco, Adobo, or Cajun would all be great!**

Make It Ahead: **Prepare everything and store in a resealable container or bag in the refrigerator for 2 days. Bring to room temperature for 15 minutes before placing in the hot skillet.**

W30, EF, NF  

Chicken Lettuce Wraps

SERVES 4 TO 6

Prep Time: 15 minutes
Cook Time: 5 minutes

One of my favorite quick dinners is to sauté ground chicken or ground beef and whatever vegetables I have in the fridge to wrap in lettuce cups. This recipe is so versatile! You can flavor your fillings with an Asian-style stir-fry sauce and hoisin, as I do here, or you can use pesto with tomatoes and broccoli or tahini sauce with ground lamb and bell peppers. These sauces last for quite a few weeks, so make them in advance to lessen your prep time.

- 1 tablespoon plus 1 teaspoon avocado oil
- 1½ pounds ground dark-meat chicken
- 4 green onions, white and tender green parts, thinly sliced, with white and green separated, plus more for serving
- 1 small orange bell pepper, seeded and diced
- 8 ounces white button mushrooms, minced
- ½ teaspoon garlic powder
- 1 (8-ounce) jar water chestnuts, drained and diced
- ¼ cup Stir-Fry Sauce (page 27)
- Fine sea salt and freshly ground black pepper
- 2 tablespoons Hoisin Sauce (page 27), plus more for serving
- 1 head butter or iceberg lettuce, separated into lettuce cups
- Red pepper flakes, for serving

In a large skillet, heat 1 tablespoon of the oil over high heat. Add the chicken and cook, breaking it up with a wooden spoon and stirring frequently, for 2 to 3 minutes, until browned and cooked through.

Push the chicken to one side of the skillet and add the remaining 1 teaspoon oil to the empty side. When the oil is hot, add the white parts of the green onions, the bell pepper, mushrooms, and garlic powder and sauté for 2 to 3 minutes, until the onions and mushrooms have softened and any liquid has evaporated.

Stir the water chestnuts and the green parts of the green onions into the vegetable mixture and sauté for about 30 seconds, until heated through. Stir together the chicken and vegetables, add the stir-fry sauce, and season to taste with salt and pepper. Remove the pan from the heat and stir in the hoisin sauce.

Spoon several tablespoons of the chicken mixture into the center of each lettuce leaf. Top with red pepper flakes and green onions and serve with the hoisin on the side.

Tidbits: **Store leftovers in the fridge for up to 5 days. To reheat, sauté in a dry skillet over medium heat for 3 to 5 minutes or heat in an uncovered baking dish in a preheated 350°F oven for 20 minutes.**

Make It Ahead: **Prepare the entire dish and store in an airtight container in the refrigerator for up to 5 days. Reheat in a dry skillet over medium heat for 5 to 7 minutes, until heated through. Store washed lettuce cups in a clean, gently dampened cloth in the crisper drawer for 3 days.**

*omit cashews 

Kung Pao–Style Chicken

SERVES 4 TO 6

Prep Time: 12 minutes, plus 10 minutes to marinate

Cook Time: 7 minutes

Laced with peppers and a spicy-sweet sauce, kung pao chicken is a favorite at American Chinese restaurants. Unfortunately, most restaurant versions contain gluten, corn, and sugar. I use coconut aminos, arrowroot powder, and coconut sugar in mine. Because this dish cooks fast once you start, it's helpful to have everything prepared and at your fingertips!

Marinade

1 tablespoon dry sherry, hard cider, or dry white wine

1 tablespoon coconut aminos

2 teaspoons arrowroot powder

¾ teaspoon baking soda

2 pounds skinless, boneless chicken thighs or breasts, cut into 1-inch pieces

3 tablespoons unseasoned rice vinegar or 1½ tablespoons apple cider vinegar

2 tablespoons coconut aminos

2 teaspoons coconut sugar

4 tablespoons avocado oil

2 red bell peppers, seeded and diced

8 to 10 dried red chiles, or ½ teaspoon red pepper flakes

4 green onions, white and tender green parts, chopped

2 Fresno chiles, cut into ¼-inch-thick rings

2-inch piece fresh ginger, peeled and finely chopped

4 cloves garlic, thinly sliced

½ teaspoon freshly ground Sichuan pepper or black pepper

Fine sea salt

½ cup roasted chopped cashews

2 teaspoons toasted sesame oil

Basic Cauli-Rice (page 269), for serving

To make the marinade, in a large bowl, stir together the sherry, coconut aminos, arrowroot, and baking soda. Add the chicken and turn to coat. Let sit at room temperature for at least 10 minutes.

Meanwhile, in a small bowl, stir together the vinegar, coconut aminos, and sugar and set aside.

In a large skillet or wok, heat 2 tablespoons of the avocado oil over medium-high heat. Add the chicken and stir-fry for 2 to 3 minutes, until browned all over. Transfer the chicken to a plate.

Add the remaining 2 tablespoons avocado oil to the pan over medium-high heat. Add the bell peppers and cook, tossing occasionally, for about 3 minutes, until browned and crisp-tender. Add the dried chiles, green onions, Fresno chiles, ginger, garlic, and Sichuan pepper and cook, tossing constantly, for about 1 minute, until very aromatic and the dried chiles are lightly toasted. Add the chicken and the vinegar mixture and cook, tossing occasionally, for about 1 minute more, until the liquid coats the chicken and is nearly evaporated. Taste and season lightly with salt if needed.

To finish, sprinkle with the cashews and drizzle with the sesame oil. Serve the chicken from the skillet with cauli-rice on the side.

Tidbits: **Because of the spice, my kids don't like this dish as it is prepared here. For them, I omit the dried and fresh chiles and the Sichuan pepper and serve it mild-style. They love the sauce and practically lick their plates this way!**

Store leftovers in the fridge for up to 5 days. To reheat, sauté in a dry skillet over medium heat for 3 to 5 minutes or heat in an uncovered baking dish in a preheated 350°F oven for 20 minutes.

Make It Ahead: **Marinate the chicken in the fridge for up to 2 days. Because this cooks quickly, it's helpful to have your vegetables and aromatics chopped and ready to go. Do this in advance and store in the refrigerator for 3 days.**

EF, NF* 30 *see Note

Chicken Cordon Bleu with Creamy Dijon Sauce

SERVES 4 TO 6

Prep Time: 15 minutes
Cook Time: 12 minutes

I was raised on frozen food ordered from Schwan's Home Delivery, or as I called it – the Swan Man. Individually wrapped pieces of breaded chicken stuffed with cheese and ham were a regular order, and while I'm almost certain they tasted nothing like authentic Cordon Bleu from France, I know they were delicious. *Cordon bleu* literally means "blue ribbon," and this one-skillet version (which requires no rolling or breading!) earned one from my family and my recipe testers!

Sauce

- 1¼ cups chicken Bone Broth (page 42)
- ⅓ cup unsweetened raw cashew butter (see Note)
- 2 teaspoons Dijon mustard
- 1 tablespoon nutritional yeast
- 1½ teaspoons arrowroot powder
- 1 teaspoon fine sea salt
- ½ teaspoon garlic powder

- 8 ounces plantain chips, or 1 cup gluten-free panko (Japanese bread crumbs)
- 1½ tablespoons ghee or extra-virgin olive oil
- 1 small yellow onion, minced
- 1 teaspoon fine sea salt
- 2 pounds boneless, skinless chicken breasts, cut into 1½-inch chunks
- ¼ teaspoon freshly ground black pepper
- ¼ cup dry white wine or chicken Bone Broth (page 42)
- 6 ounces deli Black Forest ham, cut into long, narrow strips

To make the sauce, in a bowl, whisk together the broth, cashew butter, mustard, nutritional yeast, arrowroot, salt, and garlic powder and set aside.

Put the plantain chips into a food processor and pulse a few times until they are the texture of coarse sand. Alternatively, place them in a resealable bag and crush them with a rolling pin. Set the crumbs aside. If using panko, skip this step.

Position an oven rack in the top slot in the oven and preheat the oven to 450°F.

In a large, oven-safe skillet, heat 1 tablespoon of the ghee over medium heat. Add the onion and ¼ teaspoon of the salt and sauté for 2 to 3 minutes, until the onion is lightly browned and beginning to soften. Meanwhile, sprinkle the chicken with the remaining ¾ teaspoon salt and the pepper.

Push the onion to the sides of the pan and raise the heat to medium-high. Add the chicken to the empty center of the pan and cook, stirring frequently, for 5 to 7 minutes, until browned on all sides. Add the wine and stir to release any browned bits from the bottom of the pan. Stir everything back together, then stir in the ham and the sauce. Bring the mixture to a boil, and then reduce the heat to medium-low. Simmer for 2 to 3 minutes, until the sauce has thickened.

Mix the remaining ½ tablespoon ghee with the plantain chips and sprinkle them over the top of the chicken. Place the skillet on the top rack of the oven and bake for 2 to 3 minutes, until the topping is browned and the sauce is bubbling. Serve straight from the oven.

Note: **See page 241 for a cashew butter substitute.**

Tidbits: **If you want a nut-free sauce option, my Mac and Cheese sauce (page 137) works here, too. Use 1½ cups of the cheese sauce.**

Make It Ahead: **Prepare the dish as directed, stopping before you top with the plantain chip crumble. Transfer to a baking dish, cover, and refrigerate for up to 3 days or freeze for up to 6 months, then thaw in the refrigerator for 24 hours. Top with the plantain chip crumble and bake in a preheated 450°F for 15 to 18 minutes, until bubbling.**

*omit arrowroot

30 W30, EF, NF, SCD*

Lemon-Caper Chicken and Rice

SERVES 4 TO 6

Prep Time: 15 minutes
Cook Time: 10 minutes

I've always loved chicken piccata for its bright lemon and briny caper flavors. This dish takes those flavors and turns them into a complete meal by adding cauliflower rice and lots of fresh greens. It also eliminates the lengthy step of pounding chicken into thin cutlets, and instead uses diced chicken breasts so it can all be cooked at the same time in one skillet.

- 2 tablespoons ghee or avocado oil
- 2 pounds boneless, skinless chicken breasts, diced
- Fine sea salt and freshly ground black pepper
- 4 cloves garlic, diced
- 1 shallot, diced
- 2 teaspoons dried parsley
- 1 teaspoon dried oregano
- 1 (12-ounce) package frozen cauliflower rice
- ¾ cup chicken Bone Broth (page 42)
- ¼ cup full-fat coconut cream
- 1 tablespoon arrowroot powder
- Finely grated zest and juice of 1 lemon
- 1 bunch lacinato (Tuscan) kale, stems and ribs removed and leaves torn into bite-size pieces
- 2 tablespoons drained capers
- 2 tablespoons chopped fresh flat-leaf parsley

In a large skillet, heat the ghee over high heat. Season the chicken generously with salt and pepper, add to the pan, and cook, stirring occasionally, for 2 to 3 minutes, until well browned on all sides.

Turn down the heat to medium-high, add the garlic, shallot, dried parsley, and oregano and cook, stirring occasionally, for 3 to 5 minutes more, until the shallots begin to soften. Add the cauliflower rice and ¾ teaspoon salt and cook, stirring often, for 2 to 3 minutes, until the cauliflower has thawed and is slightly browned. Pour in the broth and stir to release any browned bits from the bottom of the pan.

In a small bowl, whisk together the coconut cream, arrowroot, and lemon juice. Pour the mixture into the skillet and let it come to a boil. Turn down the heat to medium-low and simmer for 3 to 5 minutes, until the rice has soaked up most of the liquid. Stir in the kale and capers and season to taste with salt and pepper.

Remove from the heat and serve immediately, sprinkled with the lemon zest and fresh parsley.

Tidbits: **Although plain cauliflower rice is the most accessible, if you can find pilaf-style cauliflower rice in the freezer section at Whole Foods, it takes the flavor of this dish up a notch. You could even omit the garlic, parsley, and oregano in this recipe if you use it! That cauliflower-rice pilaf is my secret weapon for easy but flavorful weeknight skillet meals.**

Make It Ahead: **This is one of my favorite meals to meal-prep for lunches for the week. If I'm not serving it right away for dinner, I divide it into a few glass containers that can be thrown into the toaster oven and reheated quickly for a working-lunch at my desk. Reheat at 400°F for 7 to 10 minutes.**

Cast-Iron Rib-Eye Steaks with Garlic Mushrooms

SERVES 4 TO 6

Prep Time: 5 minutes, plus 45 minutes hands-off time

Cook Time: 10 minutes

Cooking a steak in a cast-iron pan on the stove top is my favorite way to do an easy weeknight meal. Choose boneless steaks 1 to 1½ inches thick so they will cook evenly and quickly. I top this classic dinner offering with mushrooms infused with garlic and rosemary and accompany it with a side salad, turning a few simple ingredients into a satisfying meal full of flavor.

2 (14- to 16-ounce) boneless rib-eye steaks, 1 to 1½ inches thick

Coarse sea salt and freshly ground black pepper

3 tablespoons ghee or extra-virgin olive oil

10 ounces assorted mushrooms, sliced

2 cloves garlic, thinly sliced

2 sprigs rosemary

Red Pepper Sauce (page 294), Cilantro-Kale Pepita Pesto (page 28), or Quick BBQ Sauce (page 22), for serving (optional)

Let the steaks rest at room temperature for 45 minutes to 1 hour before cooking.

Pat the steaks dry, then season them generously on one side with salt and pepper. Heat a large skillet over medium-high heat. When the pan is hot, add the steaks, seasoned side down, and cook, undisturbed, for 1 minute, until well browned on the underside. Season the tops of the steaks with salt and pepper, then flip with tongs. Cook for another minute, then flip again and cook for 1 to 2 minutes for medium-rare, until a thermometer inserted into the thickest part of a steak reads 120° to 125°F.

Transfer the steaks to a cutting board and spread 1 tablespoon of the ghee over the top. Tent with aluminum foil and let the meat rest for 5 minutes while you prepare the mushrooms.

Return the skillet to the stove over medium heat and add the remaining 2 tablespoons ghee. Add the mushrooms, garlic, and rosemary and cook, without stirring, for 2 minutes, until browned. Stir the mushrooms and cook for 1 to 2 minutes more, until fragrant and tender. Remove pan from the heat and discard the rosemary.

Slice the steaks against the grain on the diagonal, top with the mushrooms, and serve with the sauce of choice on the side.

Tidbits: **Leftover steak can be repurposed in any of the following recipes: Steak Lettuce Wraps with Horseradish Cream Sauce (page 76), Asian-Style Chicken Slaw (page 75), Chilled Sesame Beef, Mango, and "Noodle" Salad (page 80), and Thai-Style Shrimp Salad (page 87); or use the leftovers in a steak-and-eggs breakfast.**

 EF, NF

Sticky Green Onion Stir-Fried Beef

SERVES 4 TO 6

Prep Time: 14 minutes, plus 45 minutes to chill and 10 minutes hands-off time

Cook Time: 12 minutes

My food preferences and choices during high school and college were heavily influenced by the restaurant chain where I spent so many hours waiting tables. I ate my fair share (maybe more than my fair share) of their Mongolian beef, and I still dream of it (though without the stomach ache afterward). Plus, my parents always asked me to bring home dinner (employee discount!) after my shifts, so some days I would eat it for lunch and dinner! While this stir-fried beef dish is definitely more mine than authentic Chinese, what's not to love about crispy beef coated with a sweet and salty sauce and flecked with bright green onions?

- 2 pounds flank or sirloin steak
- ⅓ cup arrowroot powder, plus more if needed
- ⅓ cup avocado oil
- 1-inch piece fresh ginger, peeled and minced
- 4 cloves garlic, minced
- ½ cup coconut aminos
- ¼ cup coconut sugar
- ¼ cup water
- 10 green onions, tender green parts only, cut into 2-inch pieces
- Basic Cauli-Rice (page 269), for serving

Place the steak in the freezer to chill for 45 minutes to make it easier to slice.

Slice the steak against the grain into ¼-inch-thick strips. Place the strips in a bowl and sprinkle the arrowroot on top. Stir to coat the strips evenly. Set aside for 10 minutes, until the arrowroot has absorbed any juices from the beef.

In a large, deep skillet, heat the oil over medium-high heat until hot. Working in batches to avoid crowding, shake off any excess arrowroot powder from the steak strips, add the strips to the pan in a single layer, and fry, turning once, for 1 to 2 minutes per side, until crispy. (It is important not to crowd the pan or the steak strips will steam and not get crispy.) Using tongs or a slotted spoon, transfer the steak to a plate. Repeat until all the strips are cooked, then set aside.

Pour off all but 1 teaspoon of the oil from the pan and return the pan to medium-high heat. Add the ginger and garlic and stir-fry for 30 seconds, until fragrant. Add the coconut aminos, sugar, and water and whisk until the sugar dissolves. Bring to a boil and cook for 30 to 45 seconds.

Return the beef to the pan, leaving any juices on the plate, and simmer for 30 seconds, until the sauce has thickened. If the sauce does not thicken enough to stick to the meat, in a small bowl, mix together 1½ teaspoons arrowroot powder and 2 teaspoons water to make a slurry, then whisk the slurry into the sauce and boil for 30 seconds to thicken.

Remove the pan from the heat and stir in the green onions. Serve immediately over the cauli-rice.

W30, EF, NF, SCD 

Philly Cheesesteak Skillet

SERVES 4 TO 6

Prep Time: 15 minutes, plus 45 minutes to chill

Cook Time: 10 minutes

Serve this breadless version of a classic Philly cheesesteak with oven fries, but it is also delicious stuffed inside a baked russet potato or Hannah sweet potato or simply on its own with a side salad. The garlic aioli drizzled on top gives the dish the same rich finish the blanket of melted cheese does for the real deal. That said, if you tolerate cheese, go for it. I've given you options if you'd like to add it.

2½ pounds flank steak

2 tablespoons avocado oil

1 tablespoon ghee

1 large yellow onion, halved and thinly sliced

2 teaspoons fine sea salt

2 green bell peppers, seeded and thinly sliced

8 ounces white button mushrooms, sliced

½ teaspoon dried oregano

½ teaspoon freshly ground black pepper

3 tablespoons Garlic Aioli (page 24)

2 tablespoons chopped green onions, white and tender green parts

Rosemary-Garlic Oven Fries (page 277), for serving

Place the steak in the freezer to chill for 45 minutes to make it easier to slice. Then slice the steak against the grain on the diagonal into paper-thin strips.

In a large skillet, heat 1 tablespoon of the oil and the ghee over medium heat. Add the onion and ½ teaspoon of the salt and sauté for 2 to 3 minutes, until the onion begins to soften. Add the bell peppers, mushrooms, ½ teaspoon of the salt, and the oregano and sauté for 3 to 4 minutes, until the vegetables are crisp-tender and any liquid has been absorbed.

Season the steak strips all over with the remaining 1 teaspoon salt and the pepper. Raise the heat to high and push the vegetables to one side of the pan. Working in batches to avoid crowding, add the steak in a single layer to the other side of the pan and cook, undisturbed, for 1 minute, until browned on the underside. Using tongs, flip the steak and leave it undisturbed for 1 minute more, until browned on the second side. Pile the cooked steak on top of the vegetables to make room for the next batch.

When all of the steak is browned, stir together the meat and vegetables and continue to cook for 1 to 2 minutes, until the steak is well browned and crispy and no liquid remains in the pan.

Remove the pan from the heat, top with the aioli and green onions and serve immediately with the potatoes.

Cheese Variation

To add a melted cheese blanket, omit the aioli. Sprinkle ½ cup shredded Cypress Grove Lamb Chopper sheep's milk cheese or Midnight Moon goat's milk cheese, goat's milk Gouda, Manchego, queso (see page 226), or Miyoko's Creamery mozzarella evenly over the contents of the skillet. Place the pan on the top oven rack under a preheated broiler and broil for 1 to 2 minutes, until the cheese is melted and bubbly.

omit coconut sugar  W30, EF, NF

Thai Basil Beef

SERVES 4 TO 6

Prep Time: 10 minutes
Cook Time: 6 minutes

This dish is really versatile and tastes great with any protein. Lamb, dark-meat chicken, or even turkey all work wonderfully, so use whatever you have on hand or whatever is on sale at the market. When I make this for my kids, I add only one chile and I seed it so it's not spicy (but I save the extra chiles for Ryan to sprinkle on top after I've dished out the kids' portions). I serve this over Sweet-and-Sour Thai-Style Salad, my citrusy and salty rendition of a green papaya salad. Cauliflower rice (page 269) or zucchini noodles would be an easy side, too.

- ½ cup beef Bone Broth (page 42)
- ½ cup coconut aminos
- 2 tablespoons fish sauce
- 2 tablespoons coconut sugar
- 2 to 5 fresh red chiles, seeded and thinly sliced
- 2 tablespoons avocado oil
- 8 cloves garlic, crushed
- 4 green onions, white and tender green parts, thinly sliced, with white and green separated
- 2½ pounds ground beef
- ¾ teaspoon fine sea salt
- ¼ teaspoon freshly ground black pepper
- 2 cups tightly packed fresh Thai basil leaves
- Sweet-and-Sour Thai-Style Salad (page 256), for serving

In a small bowl, whisk together the broth, coconut aminos, fish sauce, and sugar and set aside.

Seed and thinly slice the chiles. The number of chiles you use depends on how spicy you want the dish to be, and keeping some seeds will make the dish even hotter. In a large skillet, heat the oil over high heat. Add half of the chiles, the garlic, and the white parts of the green onions and stir-fry for 20 seconds, until fragrant. Add the beef, salt, and pepper and press down on the beef with a flat spatula to form a packed disk about 1 inch thick. Cook the beef for 2 to 3 minutes, until browned on the underside. Then flip the disk in pieces and brown the second side for 1 to 2 minutes more. Use a wooden spoon to break apart the pieces and sauté for 1 to 2 minutes more, until the beef is cooked through.

Drain off any liquid from the skillet, then return it to medium-high heat. Add the broth mixture and bring it to a boil. Cook for 1 minute, until the sauce thickens and coats the meat. Stir in half of the basil and the green parts of the green onions and let them wilt for 30 seconds.

Remove the pan from the heat and sprinkle the remaining basil leaves and chile slices over the top. Serve immediately with the salad.

Tidbits: **Thai basil has a distinct, intense flavor with a slight licorice scent and a tiny bite at the end. Regular Italian basil will do just fine if you can't find the Thai variety. Just increase the amount to 3 cups and stir it in after removing the pan from the stove, as it does not hold up to heat as well as the Thai variety. Adding a tiny pinch of ground anise or fennel can also help provide the authentic flavor of Thai basil.**

Make It Ahead: **This beef and salad get even more flavorful after spending a day or two in the refrigerator. Cook the beef and store in an airtight container for up to 5 days. Store the salad separately for the same amount of time. Reheat in a dry skillet over medium heat for 5 to 7 minutes, until heated through.**

W30*, EF, NF

*omit maple syrup and use bone broth

Brats with Warm Potato Salad and Kraut

SERVES 4 TO 6

Prep Time: 10 minutes
Cook Time: 38 minutes

My grandma Bonnie loved to cook German food and it has always been a favorite of mine. In middle school, I traveled to Germany with my family, and we couldn't get enough of the sausages with sauerkraut and mustard. This recipe combines those flavors in one easy skillet meal. I love Organicville stone-ground mustard and Brat Hans or Family Ranch Organics pork bratwursts.

- 1½ pounds small red potatoes, halved or quartered if large, or skin-on white-fleshed sweet potatoes, cubed
- 4 slices thick-cut bacon
- 1 small sweet onion, chopped
- ¼ cup apple cider vinegar
- 2 teaspoons pure maple syrup
- 2 tablespoons water
- 3 tablespoons extra-virgin olive oil
- 1 teaspoon Dijon mustard
- 2 tablespoons chopped fresh flat-leaf parsley
- Fine sea salt and freshly ground black pepper
- 6 bratwursts
- ½ cup dry hard cider, gluten-free beer, or chicken Bone Broth (page 42)
- 1 cup sauerkraut
- Grainy mustard, for serving

Fill a large, deep skillet two-thirds full with water and bring to a boil over high heat. Add the potatoes and boil for 8 to 10 minutes, until just fork-tender. Drain the potatoes into a colander and place under cold running water to stop the cooking, then set aside.

Line a plate with paper towels. Return the skillet to medium-high heat. Add the bacon and cook for 5 minutes, then flip and cook for 3 to 5 minutes more, until crisp-tender. Using tongs, transfer the bacon to the towel-lined plate to drain. Pour all but 2 tablespoons of the rendered bacon fat into a small heatproof bowl and set the bowl aside.

Return the skillet to medium-high heat and add the onion. Cook for 1 to 2 minutes, until it begins to soften. Add the potatoes and cook, stirring occasionally, for 5 minutes more, until the potatoes start to brown on the edges. Add some of the reserved bacon fat to the pan if the potatoes begin to stick. Whisk together the vinegar, maple syrup, water, oil, and Dijon mustard and stir into the pan. Bring to a boil. Toss to coat the potatoes evenly with the sauce, then transfer to a serving bowl. Chop the cooled bacon and stir it and the parsley into the salad.

Return the skillet to medium-high heat and add 2 tablespoons of the reserved bacon fat. With a fork, poke a few holes on both sides of each bratwurst to keep the sausages from bursting while they cook. Add the brats to the skillet and cook, turning once, for about 4 minutes per side, until browned.

Pour the cider into the skillet and stir to release any browned bits from the bottom of the pan, then cover and turn down the heat to medium. Cook for 8 to 10 minutes, until a thermometer inserted into a sausage reads 160°F and the liquid has evaporated.

Arrange the brats in the center of the pan and spoon the potato salad around the sausages. Top with a pile of sauerkraut and a dollop of grainy mustard. Serve immediately with additional mustard and kraut on the side.

Tidbits: **If you run out of rendered bacon fat, use ghee or avocado oil in its place.**

Make It Ahead: **Parboil the potatoes (see page 40) and store them in the fridge for up to 1 week.**

Mango and Vanilla–Glazed Tenderloin with Spiced Sweet Potatoes

SERVES 6 TO 8

Prep Time: 15 minutes
Cook Time: 23 minutes

My Caribbean Seasoning (page 33) is a less spicy version of the classic Jamaican Jerk seasoning but still has my favorites notes from the original of cinnamon, nutmeg, and thyme. Those spices go so well on a roasted pork tenderloin, and the sweet-tangy mango chutney that coats it just makes them stand out more vibrantly. The vanilla in the glaze adds an unexpected and smooth note that balances out the acidity and spice of the tenderloin, and the sweet potatoes absorb all of the delicious flavors as they melt into the pan.

- ½ cup Mango Chutney (page 24), see Note
- 3 tablespoons melted ghee or avocado oil
- 2 tablespoons freshly squeezed lemon juice
- 2 teaspoons pure vanilla extract
- 2 pork tenderloins (about 1½ pounds each)
- 3 tablespoons avocado oil
- 2½ tablespoons Caribbean Seasoning (page 33)
- 1¼ teaspoons fine sea salt
- 3 sweet potatoes (about 2½ pounds), sliced into ¼-inch-thick rounds
- ½ teaspoon ground cumin
- ¼ teaspoon ground cinnamon
- ¼ teaspoon ground coriander
- 1 cup thinly sliced red onion
- ½ cup loosely packed fresh cilantro leaves and stems or fresh mint leaves

Preheat the oven to 350°F.

In a bowl, mix together the chutney, ghee, lemon juice, and vanilla and set aside.

Rub the pork all over with 1 tablespoon of the oil, the Caribbean seasoning, and ¾ teaspoon of the salt. In a large, oven-safe skillet, heat 1 tablespoon of the oil over medium-high heat. Add the pork and sear for about 2 minutes on each side, until browned on all sides.

Meanwhile, in a large bowl, toss the sweet potatoes with the remaining 1 tablespoon oil, the cumin, cinnamon, coriander, and the remaining ½ teaspoon salt. When the pork is browned, scatter the potatoes around the tenderloins in an even layer. Brush the browned tenderloins all over with half of the chutney mixture and move the skillet to the oven.

Roast for 18 to 20 minutes, until the sweet potatoes are tender and a thermometer inserted into the thickest part of a tenderloin reads 145°F. Remove the skillet from the oven and let the pork rest for 5 minutes.

Thinly slice the pork against the grain on the diagonal. Sprinkle the pork and potatoes with the red onion and cilantro and serve the remaining chutney on the side.

Note: **If you don't have time to make the mango chutney, mix together ½ cup sugar-free apricot jam, 1 tablespoon apple cider vinegar, and ¼ teaspoon ground ginger and use to coat the tenderloins and as a table condiment.**

Tidbits: **Any leftover sweet potatoes can be mashed and used in my Huevos Rancheros (page 54). If you have any Cucumber Raita (page 25) on hand, it's delicious spooned on top of this!**

W30*, EF, NF, SCD*  *use cauliflower-based hummus for W30 and SCD

Spiced Crispy Lamb with Eggplant, Squash, and Hummus

SERVES 4 TO 6

Prep Time: 7 minutes
Cook Time: 15 minutes

Lamb is a great source of protein and other nutrients like iron and zinc and omega-3 fatty acids. Of course, if you prefer ground beef, it would work here, too. The Middle Eastern flavors of my tagine spice mix infuse the meat, which joins sautéed veggies atop a rich slather of hummus for a most decadent dish. All three of my kids love hummus, so this dish was a shoo-in for them. I buy organic hummus for the kids and usually make the cauliflower-based hummus in my book *Eat What You Love* for myself.

- 2 pounds ground lamb
- 1½ teaspoons apple cider vinegar
- 1 tablespoon Tagine Seasoning (page 34)
- Fine sea salt and freshly ground black pepper
- 2 tablespoons ghee or extra-virgin olive oil
- 2 Japanese eggplants, cubed
- 2 zucchini, cubed
- ½ small red onion, halved and thinly sliced into half-moons
- 1 red bell pepper, seeded and thinly sliced
- 4 cloves garlic, chopped
- Juice of 1 lemon
- 1 cup hummus
- ¼ cup toasted pine nuts
- Fresh mint leaves, for topping
- 1 tablespoon extra-virgin olive oil

In a bowl, combine the lamb, vinegar, tagine seasoning, and ½ teaspoon salt and mix well with your hands.

In a large cast-iron skillet, heat 1 tablespoon of the ghee over medium-high heat. Add the lamb mixture and press down on the lamb with a flat spatula to form a packed disk about 1 inch thick. Cook, without disturbing, for 2 to 3 minutes, until browned and crisp on the underside. Season the top with a generous pinch of salt, then break the disc apart, flip the pieces over, and cook for 3 to 4 minutes more, until browned and crisp on the second side. Use a wooden spoon to break up the meat until it crumbles and continue to cook, stirring frequently, about 2 minutes more, until the lamb is cooked through. Using a slotted spoon, transfer the lamb to a plate and keep warm.

Return the pan to medium-heat and add the remaining 1 tablespoon ghee. When the ghee is hot, add the eggplants, zucchini, onion, bell pepper, and garlic and sauté for 5 to 7 minutes, until the vegetables are crisp-tender. Season to taste with salt and pepper, stir in the lemon juice, and remove from the heat.

Spread the hummus on the bottom of a platter. Spoon the lamb over the hummus and then spoon the sautéed vegetables over the lamb. Top with the pine nuts, mint, and oil and serve.

Crispy Salmon and Ginger-Garlic Rice with "Peanut" Sauce

SERVES 4

Prep Time: 18 minutes
Cook Time: 10 minutes

Cauliflower rice has been my number-one choice for nearly a decade whenever I want to replace regular rice with a nice bed of something hearty to soak up delicious sauces. But after so many years of using it all the time, I started to rice other vegetables. Riced broccoli is a beautiful fit for this dish, not only for its vibrant color but also because broccoli is my favorite veggie to use in Thai curries or peanut sauces. This version is laced with ginger, garlic, and green onions and supports a super-crispy fillet of salmon. To finish, I blanket it with my favorite velvety "peanut" sauce and top it with crisp cucumbers and cilantro.

4 (6-ounce) center-cut skin-on salmon fillets, each about 1 inch thick

1½ teaspoons coarse sea salt or kosher salt

2 tablespoons avocado oil

6 cloves garlic, finely chopped

1 (2-inch) piece fresh ginger, peeled and grated

2 green onions, tender green parts only, chopped

2 heads broccoli (about 1 pound), riced (about 6 cups; see page 268)

1 tablespoon coconut aminos

½ teaspoon fine sea salt

4 tablespoons Creamy Thai-Style Almond Sauce (page 29)

1 English cucumber, halved lengthwise and thinly sliced on the diagonal

1 cup loosely packed fresh cilantro leaves and tender stems

2 teaspoons toasted sesame oil

Preheat oven to 300°F.

Dry the fillets well with a clean towel and sprinkle both sides with the coarse salt.

Into a large skillet, pour the avocado oil and place the fillets, skin side down, in the skillet. Set the pan on the stove top and turn on the burner to medium-high heat. Cook the salmon, occasionally lifting each piece with a flexible metal spatula to let some of the oil slide under the fish, for 4 to 5 minutes, until the flesh is opaque up the sides of each fillet and only the top of the thickest part looks raw. If the skin is sticking, let the salmon cook a bit longer until it releases naturally from the pan.

Using tongs, carefully turn each fillet skin side up. Turn off the heat and cook for 1 to 2 minutes, until the skin flakes easily. Carefully transfer the salmon to an oven-safe dish and keep warm in the oven. Do not cover the dish or the skin will lose its crispiness.

Return the skillet to medium heat and add the garlic, ginger, and green onions and cook, stirring constantly, for about 2 minutes, until fragrant but not browned. Raise the heat to medium-high and stir in the broccoli. Sauté for 3 to 5 minutes, until tender and any liquid has evaporated. Stir in the coconut aminos and fine salt.

Spoon the broccoli onto individual plates and top with the salmon fillets, skin side up. Top each fillet with 1 tablespoon of the sauce and then scatter the cucumber and cilantro over the sauce. Drizzle with the sesame oil and serve.

Tidbits: **Peel your ginger knobs and store them in a resealable bag in the freezer. They will grate like a dream, plus they'll keep for months.**

For a shortcut, use the Whole Foods brand frozen pilaf-style cauliflower rice in place of the broccoli rice.

W30*, EF, NF, V, SCD* (30)

*use nutritional yeast for W30, omit arrowroot and use Parmesan for SCD

Creamy Sun-Dried Tomato Shrimp

SERVES 4 TO 6

Prep Time: 12 minutes
Cook Time: 5 minutes

This one-pot dish of creamy shrimp and sun-dried tomatoes is always a pleaser in my house. If you have family members who do not like shrimp, like my son Asher, cod, salmon, or chicken cutlets all work really well, too. To keep this light, I use full-fat coconut cream instead of my usual cashew cream. My kids love this with gluten-free pasta, but I usually eat it with a simple salad or, if I'm feeling indulgent, a few slices of toasted grain-free bread to sop up the creamy sauce.

2 tablespoons ghee or extra-virgin olive oil

6 cloves garlic, minced

¾ teaspoon Italian Seasoning (page 33)

6 ounces baby spinach, stemmed

¾ teaspoon fine sea salt

½ teaspoon freshly ground black pepper

¼ cup olive oil–packed sun-dried tomatoes

2 pounds large shrimp, peeled, deveined with tails on

½ cup full-fat coconut cream

¼ cup chicken Bone Broth (page 42)

1 tablespoon nutritional yeast or Dairy-Free Parmesan cheese (page 37)

2 teaspoons arrowroot powder

Juice of ½ lemon

2 tablespoons sliced fresh basil leaves

In a large skillet, heat the ghee over medium heat. Add the garlic and Italian seasoning and sauté for 1 minute, until the garlic is lightly golden. Add the spinach in batches, stirring for 10 to 15 seconds after each addition until the batch is wilted. Season with ¼ teaspoon each of the salt and pepper, then stir in the sun-dried tomatoes and shrimp and cook for 2 to 3 minutes, until the shrimp are pink.

Meanwhile, in a small bowl, whisk together the coconut cream, broth, nutritional yeast, arrowroot, and lemon juice. When the shrimp are ready, pour the coconut cream mixture into the skillet and bring to a boil. Turn down the heat to medium-low and simmer for 1 to 2 minutes, until the liquid has thickened.

Season with the remaining ½ teaspoon salt and ¼ teaspoon pepper and remove from the heat. Scatter the basil over the top and serve.

Tidbits: **If using coconut cream scooped from the top of a can of coconut milk (rather than from a can of coconut cream), be sure to avoid the thin coconut liquid from the bottom of the can to ensure the sauce is luscious and creamy.**

*sub bone broth for white wine for W30, see Note for NF

-10 30 W30*, EF, NF*, SCD

Cod Florentine

SERVES 4 TO 6

Prep Time: 12 minutes
Cook Time: 10 minutes

After the holidays one year, I had a big container of leftover creamed spinach. In trying to use it up, I ended up serving it with fish for a few meals. That combo reminded me a bit of the chicken Florentine dish my mom frequently made to hide spinach in our dinners. All that butter and cream definitely did it! This version uses fish instead of thin chicken cutlets and a creamy and decadent sauce that happens to be dairy-free. Anything served on a bed of sautéed spinach with a creamy sauce is just fine by me.

- 6 (4-ounce) skinless cod fillets
- 1 teaspoon sea salt
- ½ teaspoon freshly ground black pepper
- 2 tablespoons ghee or extra-virgin olive oil
- 1 small yellow onion, minced
- 5 cloves garlic, minced
- ½ cup dry white wine
- 8 ounces baby spinach, stemmed
- 1 cup Cashew Milk (page 39), see Note
- ½ teaspoon freshly squeezed lemon juice
- ½ teaspoon apple cider vinegar
- ¼ teaspoon ground nutmeg
- ¼ cup chopped fresh basil or flat-leaf parsley

Season the cod on both sides with ½ teaspoon of the salt and ¼ teaspoon of the pepper.

In a large skillet, heat 1 tablespoon of the ghee over medium-high heat. Add the fish and sear for 1 to 2 minutes, until it releases easily. Flip the fillets and continue to cook for 1 to 2 minutes more, until mostly cooked through. Transfer the cod to a plate and set aside.

Add the remaining 1 tablespoon ghee to the pan and return it to medium-high heat. Add the onion and garlic and sauté for 3 to 4 minutes, until the onion begins to soften. Pour in the wine and stir to release any browned bits from the bottom of the pan. Add the spinach in batches, stirring for 10 to 15 seconds after each addition until the batch is wilted. Stir in the cashew milk, lemon juice, vinegar, nutmeg, and the remaining ½ teaspoon salt and ¼ teaspoon pepper. Turn down the heat to medium-low and simmer for 3 to 5 minutes, until the sauce has thickened.

Return the fish to the skillet, nestling it into the spinach. Simmer for 1 to 2 minutes more, until the cod is warmed through, then garnish with basil leaves and serve immediately.

Note: **To make a quick cashew milk using unsweetened raw cashew butter, see the Buy It section of the cashew milk recipe.**

To make the sauce nut-free, whisk together 1 cup thick coconut cream with 1 tablespoon arrowroot powder and ½ teaspoon sea salt.

W30, NF (30)

Veggie Fried Rice

SERVES 4 TO 6

Prep Time: 20 minutes
Cook Time: 10 minutes

When my garden (or crisper drawer) is booming, and I need to use everything up, this recipe is my favorite way to do it. It's also a great option for a Meatless Monday. The shiitake mushrooms and eggs add protein and substance, and the bok choy and cabbage melt right into the sauce. It's hearty and filling and so full of flavor that even my pickiest eater doesn't turn up his nose at it. When stir-frying a bunch of different vegetables, I like to cook them in batches to build flavor on flavor and so the quick-cooking vegetables don't get soggy. Rather than cutting all the vegetables before I start cooking, I've found that it's most efficient to cut up the remaining vegetables as the others cook.

2 tablespoons ghee or avocado oil

3 carrots, peeled and julienned

1 bunch broccolini, chopped

Fine sea salt and freshly ground black pepper

4 cloves garlic, minced

1½ teaspoons peeled and minced fresh ginger

5 green onions, white and tender green parts, thinly sliced, with white and green separated

1 small head Napa cabbage, cored and thinly sliced

1 head baby bok choy, end trimmed and chopped

5 cups Basic Cauli-Rice (page 269)

4 ounces shiitake mushrooms, stemmed and sliced

3 eggs, beaten

½ cup Stir-Fry Sauce (page 27)

1 teaspoon arrowroot powder

In a large, deep skillet, heat 2 teaspoons of the ghee over medium-high heat. Add the carrots, broccolini, and a pinch each of salt and pepper and sauté for 4 to 5 minutes, until the carrots have softened and the broccolini is bright green. Transfer to a bowl and set aside.

Return the pan to medium-high heat and add 2 teaspoons of the ghee. Add the garlic, ginger, and white parts of the green onions and cook, stirring constantly, for 30 seconds to 1 minute, until fragrant. Add the cabbage, bok choy, and cauli-rice and cook, stirring occasionally, for 2 to 3 minutes, until the cabbage is wilted and the cauli-rice is crisp-tender. Season with a pinch each of salt and pepper.

Return the cooked broccolini and carrots to the skillet and stir in the mushrooms. Push the vegetables to one side of the pan to create an open spot to scramble the eggs. Add the remaining 2 teaspoons ghee and then the eggs and stir constantly for 1 minute to scramble. Once the eggs are softly scrambled, stir them into the vegetables.

In a small bowl, whisk together the stir-fry sauce and arrowroot until there are no visible clumps. Stir the sauce into the pan and bring to a boil. Cook for 1 to 2 minutes, until thickened. Season to taste with salt and pepper.

To serve, divide the fried rice among individual bowls and garnish with the green parts of the green onions.

Creamy Polenta with Woody Mushroom Sauce

SERVES 4

Prep Time: 8 minutes
Cook Time: 7 minutes

My daughter, Kezia, has loved sautéed mushrooms since she was a toddler. When I tested this recipe on her, she asked for thirds! I'm always on the lookout for satisfying and rich meat-free meals that still have a high amount of protein, fiber, and healthy fats. That can be difficult to achieve without using legumes and grains, so this dish is a huge win in my book. Mushrooms are also full of zinc and selenium and boast anti-inflammatory and immune-boosting benefits. If you don't want to make the polenta, cauliflower rice or even crispy roasted potatoes are wonderful stand-ins.

Creamy Almond-Cauliflower Polenta (page 264)

¼ cup ghee, unsalted butter, or avocado oil

4 tablespoons extra-virgin olive oil

2 cloves garlic, minced

4 ounces shiitake mushrooms, stemmed and sliced

4 ounces cremini mushrooms, sliced

6 ounces king oyster mushrooms, stemmed and sliced

3 sprigs thyme, leaves stripped and chopped

1 small sprig rosemary, leaves stripped and minced

Fine sea salt and freshly ground black pepper

2 tablespoons coconut aminos

2 teaspoons fish sauce

½ cup Cashew Milk (page 39) or full-fat coconut cream (see Tidbits)

Put the polenta into a saucepan and set over low heat to warm.

In a large skillet, heat the ghee and 3 tablespoons of the oil over medium-high heat. Add the garlic and sauté for 30 to 45 seconds, until fragrant. Turn down the heat to medium-low, add all of the mushrooms, and cook, stirring every so often, for 2 to 3 minutes, until they begin to soften. Add half of the thyme, the rosemary, and ¼ teaspoon salt and cook for 2 to 3 minutes more, until fragrant. Add the coconut aminos and fish sauce, turn down the heat to low, and simmer for 2 to 3 minutes, until the mushrooms are tender. Stir in the cashew milk, then remove the pan from the heat. Season to taste with salt and pepper.

To serve, spoon the mushrooms over the polenta, drizzle with the remaining 1 tablespoon oil, and top with the remaining thyme.

Tidbits: **To make a quick cashew milk from unsweetened raw cashew butter, see the Buy It section of the cashew milk recipe.**

Save any leftover polenta and mushrooms for breakfast (see page 57).

EF, NF, V

Wild Mushroom and Zucchini Enchiladas with Mango-Pineapple Salsa

SERVES 4 TO 6

Prep Time: 15 minutes
Cook Time: 25 minutes

I love rolled enchiladas, but these skillet enchiladas are my go-to answer for great enchiladas in record time. These vegetarian enchiladas are wonderfully filling, but you can add 2 cups chopped cooked shrimp or roasted chicken for added protein.

8 grain-free tortillas

3 tablespoons extra-virgin olive oil or ghee

3 cloves garlic, minced

½ cup minced white onion

10 ounces wild mushrooms (such as chanterelle or black trumpet), sliced (see Note)

1 zucchini, diced

4 cups baby spinach, stemmed and coarsely chopped

2 poblano chiles, seeded and diced

1 teaspoon fine sea salt

1 teaspoon ground cumin

½ teaspoon ground coriander

2 cups green Enchilada Sauce (page 30)

1 cup crumbled dairy-free cheese or queso fresco, shredded Oaxaca, or Cotija

Mango-Pineapple Salsa

½ cup diced mango

½ cup diced pineapple

2 tablespoons chopped fresh cilantro leaves

2 teaspoons freshly squeezed lime juice

¼ teaspoon fine sea salt

1 small jalapeño chile, seeded and minced

1 tablespoon minced red onion

Preheat the oven to 450°F. Cut each tortilla into six uniform strips and set aside.

In a large, oven-safe skillet, heat the oil over medium heat. Add the garlic and cook, stirring, for 30 seconds, until fragrant. Add the white onion and cook, stirring occasionally, for about 5 minutes, until translucent and soft. Add the mushrooms, zucchini, spinach, poblanos, salt, cumin, and coriander and sauté for 3 to 5 minutes, until the vegetables are crisp-tender. Add the tortilla strips, enchilada sauce, and ½ cup of the cheese and stir until combined. Sprinkle the remaining ½ cup cheese over the top.

Move the skillet to the oven and bake for 10 to 15 minutes, until bubbling.

Meanwhile, make the salsa. In a bowl, stir together the mango, pineapple, cilantro, lime juice, salt, jalapeño, and red onion.

Remove the skillet from the oven and spoon the salsa over the enchiladas. Serve immediately.

Note: **If you don't have access to wild mushrooms, substitute oyster, cremini, or clamshell mushrooms.**

Tidbits: **Use my homemade grain-free wraps (the recipe is on daniellewalker.com) or save time and purchase grain-free tortillas. (Both Siete and Thrive Market brand coconut wraps work well.) If you don't tolerate dairy, make the homemade ricotta recipe from my books *Eat What You Love* or *Against All Grain* or purchase a clean-ingredient brand, such as Kite Hill ricotta, Miyoko's Creamery mozzarella, or Violife feta.**

8

One-Pot Meals

All of these recipes can be made on the stove top or in an electric pressure cooker or slow cooker. For the stove-top recipes, a 4- to 6-quart Dutch oven is your best bet. I use an enameled cast-iron Dutch oven for easy cleanup and even heating. My electric pressure cooker is a 6-quart Instant Pot. The larger 8-quart pot requires 2 cups liquid to come to pressure, so you will need to adjust accordingly. If the Instant Pot intimidates you, allow me to help you get acquainted with it! Scan the QR code below for my top five Instant Pot tips and tricks. Using a wide (rather than deep) 6-quart slow cooker tends to work best for my recipes. I use one that automatically switches to *warm* after the cook time has elapsed so I don't have to worry about it right away.

In most of these recipes, I will advise you to brown your protein before adding it to the pot. Browning takes extra time, yes. But it's also an invaluable way to add flavor and enrich sauces and gravies. It helps to render some of the fat from large cuts of meat as well. I was always taught that if your meat isn't practically burned after you've browned it, you're not browning it long enough! Of course, you can always skip this step, but I highly encourage you to do it.

To be as efficient as possible, I start to brown the meat, then I chop my vegetables, and measure and mix any sauces, broths, or gravy ingredients. Another option is to brown the meat the night before while you're preparing dinner. Once it's browned, cover it tightly, and store it in the refrigerator overnight. The following day, add the remaining ingredients just before dinner.

From Electric Pressure Cooker to Slow Cooker (and Vice Versa)

A general rule of thumb for converting recipes made in an electric pressure cooker to the slow cooker: Brown the meat in a Dutch oven on the stove top and add the liquid from the recipe after the browning step, scraping any browned bits from the bottom of the pot. Increase the liquid by ½ cup and cook on low for 6 to 8 hours.

When converting recipes made in a slow cooker to the electric pressure cooker: Reduce the liquid by ½ cup (keeping in mind that the machine needs at least 1 cup liquid, including juices that render from the meat as it cooks). Cook on the manual setting at high pressure for 5 to 10 minutes for boneless raw chicken, 15 to 20 minutes for bone-in raw chicken, 20 to 30 minutes for small raw cuts of boneless red meat or pork, 45 to 60 minutes for large roasts, and 60 to 70 minutes for bone-in red meat or pork. If you have the time, letting the pressure release naturally on larger cuts of meat will produce more tender finished products. For frozen meats, add 15 minutes to the above times.

Vegetables overcook quickly in a pressure cooker, so if the cook time is long, quick release the pressure toward the end of cooking, add the vegetables, then seal and cook again for 1 to 3 minutes. Allow the pressure to release naturally after that.

Crispy Chicken with Asparagus-Kale Rice

SERVES 4 TO 6

Prep Time: 10 minutes
Cook Time: 16 minutes

Chicken leg quarters, which come with the drumstick and thigh in one piece, are less expensive than buying the drumsticks and thighs separately, and they stay juicy when cooked at high heat. My two younger kids love digging into a good chicken drumstick, so I just separate the two after cooking. Because the asparagus-kale rice cooks in the chicken juices, it is absolutely delicious. I usually have a bit of it left over and tend to have it for lunch the next day with salmon or shrimp on top.

- 6 chicken leg quarters (drumstick and thigh)
- Fine sea salt
- ½ teaspoon five-spice powder
- 1½ tablespoons avocado oil
- 4 green onions, white and tender green parts, thinly sliced, with white and green separated
- 2 teaspoons peeled and grated fresh ginger
- 4 cloves garlic, thinly sliced
- 1 bunch lacinato (Tuscan) kale, stems and ribs removed and leaves torn into bite-size pieces
- 6 cups Basic Cauli-Rice (page 269)
- 1 bunch asparagus, ends trimmed and cut on the diagonal into ½-inch pieces
- ¼ teaspoon white pepper
- 1 teaspoon toasted sesame oil

Preheat the oven to 450°F.

Pat the chicken dry and season it with ½ teaspoon salt and the five-spice powder. In a Dutch oven large enough to fit all of the chicken in a single layer, heat the oil over medium-high heat. Add the chicken and cook, turning once, for 6 to 8 minutes, until well browned and crispy on both sides. Transfer the chicken to a plate, leaving the rendered fat in the pot.

Add the white parts of the green onions, the ginger, and garlic to the pot and sauté for 30 to 45 seconds, until fragrant and the garlic is golden. Add the kale and a pinch of salt and sauté for 1 to 2 minutes, until wilted. Add the cauli-rice and asparagus, stir well, and remove the pot from the heat. Season the rice with ½ teaspoon salt and the white pepper.

Nestle the chicken, skin side up, into the rice and move the pot to the oven. Roast for 8 to 10 minutes, until the chicken is cooked through and a thermometer inserted into the thickest part of a thigh reads 165°F.

Drizzle the chicken with the sesame oil and sprinkle with the green parts of the green onions. Serve immediately.

Tidbits: **Frozen cauliflower rice speeds this dinner up, or cut it yourself in advance and store it in the fridge for 3 days.**

W30, EF, NF

Arroz con Pollo

SERVES 4 TO 6

Prep Time: 20 minutes
Cook Time: 22 minutes

This Puerto Rican–style arroz con pollo features rice made from plantains; it will completely trick your taste buds into thinking you're eating real rice. Ask your butcher to cut a whole chicken into ten pieces (two breast halves cut into halves, two thighs, two drumsticks, and two wings), and keep the backbone and carcass to make bone broth. Using a whole chicken will appeal to both dark- and white-meat lovers, plus it's much more economical than purchasing boneless, skinless chicken parts.

- 1 (4- to 5-pound) whole chicken, cut up (see headnote)
- 2½ tablespoons Adobo Seasoning (page 31)
- 1 to 2 tablespoons avocado oil
- 4 firm green plantains (about 2 pounds)
- 4 cloves garlic
- 1 small green bell pepper, seeded
- 1 small white onion, quartered
- 1 jalapeño chile, seeded
- ¼ cup firmly packed fresh cilantro leaves and tender stems, plus more for serving
- 1 teaspoon ground cumin
- 1 teaspoon ground coriander
- ¼ teaspoon sweet paprika
- 1 teaspoon fine sea salt
- ⅓ cup chicken Bone Broth (page 42)
- 1 cup tomato puree or strained tomatoes
- 1 cup pitted green olives
- 1 cup fresh or frozen shelled English peas

Pat the chicken dry with paper towels and season all sides and under the skin when possible for maximum flavor with the adobo seasoning. In a Dutch oven, heat 1 tablespoon of the oil over medium-high heat. Add the chicken and sear, turning once, for 4 to 6 minutes per side, until well browned.

Meanwhile, cut off both ends of each plantain and make a shallow cut lengthwise along the peel. Remove the peels and cut the plantains crosswise into thirds. In a food processor fitted with the grater disk, grate the plantains until they resemble long grains of rice. Alternatively, use the large holes on a box grater. Set the plantain rice aside.

Wipe the food processor clean and replace the grater disk with the S-shaped blade. Add the garlic, bell pepper, onion, jalapeño, and cilantro. Process for 5 to 10 seconds, until finely chopped. Alternatively, finely mince with a knife.

Using tongs, transfer the chicken to a plate, leaving the rendered fat in the pot over medium-high heat. If the pot is dry, add the remaining 1 tablespoon oil. Add the chopped vegetables, cumin, coriander, and paprika and sauté for 1 minute, until crisp-tender. Add the plantain rice and salt and sauté for 30 seconds. Add the broth and tomato puree and cook, stirring constantly, for 30 seconds, until most of the liquid has evaporated and any browned bits are released from the bottom.

Stir in the olives, then nestle the chicken, skin side up, into the rice and add any accumulated juices from the plate. Turn the heat to medium-low and simmer for 12 to 15 minutes, until all of the liquid is absorbed, the plantain rice is tender, and a thermometer inserted into the thickest part of a chicken thigh reads 165°F.

Remove the pot from the heat and scatter the peas over the rice. Sprinkle with the cilantro and serve immediately.

Note: **To use cauliflower rice instead of plantains, use 6 cups and cook for half the time.**

Make It Ahead: **Make the sofrito (the pepper, onion, and cilantro mix) and store in the fridge for up to 3 days. Grate the plantains the night before and store in the fridge.**

*omit egg in meatballs

W30, EF*

Meatballs with Creamy Thai-Style Almond Sauce

SERVES 4 TO 6

Prep Time: 12 minutes
Cook Time: 13 minutes

Whenever I make meatballs, I double or triple the mixture and freeze a big batch after they're browned but before they're fully cooked. Then I add them straight from the freezer to marinara sauce, soup, leftover gravy, or a mixture of coconut milk and creamy almond sauce like in this recipe, where they will thaw and finish cooking in the sauce. The browned crust and the fat that renders into the sauce from the meatballs add wonderful depth of flavor.

Meatballs take a little extra time to make, but they're so flavorful and fun for kids to eat (I always enlist mine in the rolling process). Use a cookie scoop for ease in shaping. If you don't have any meatballs in your freezer, grab a bag of gluten-free meatballs from the market. My favorite is Applegate Well Carved Organic Asian Style pork and vegetable meatballs. Of course, shredded meat from a rotisserie chicken would always work as a time-saver.

24 cooked frozen meatballs (page 225)

3 green onions, white and tender green parts, chopped, with white and green separated

2 bunches small white radishes, stemmed and halved (or quartered if large)

2 heads baby bok choy, ends trimmed and leaves separated

1 red bell pepper, seeded and thinly sliced

⅓ cup Creamy Thai-Style Almond Sauce (page 29)

1 (13.5-ounce) can full-fat coconut cream

1½ teaspoons Tagine Seasoning (page 34)

1 teaspoon fine sea salt

¼ cup loosely packed fresh cilantro leaves

1 fresh red chile, thinly sliced

In a Dutch oven, combine the meatballs, white parts of the green onions, the radishes, bok choy, bell pepper, almond sauce, coconut cream, tagine seasoning, and salt. Set over medium-high heat and bring to a boil, then turn down the heat to medium-low, cover, and simmer for 10 minutes. Uncover and continue to simmer for 3 to 5 minutes, until the sauce has thickened and the meatballs are cooked through.

Remove the pot from the heat and top with the green parts of the green onions, the cilantro, and chile. Serve immediately.

Make It Ahead: **Prep and combine all of the ingredients except the cilantro and red chile in a resealable bag or airtight container and store in the freezer for up to 6 months. Thaw overnight in the refrigerator before cooking.**

To Use an Electric Pressure Cooker: **Place all of the ingredients except the cilantro and red chile in the pressure cooker, add ¼ cup chicken Bone Broth (page 42), select the manual button, and cook at high pressure for 5 minutes. Quick release the pressure and serve as directed.**

To Use a Slow Cooker: **Place all of the ingredients except the cilantro and red chile in the slow cooker and cook on low for 8 hours or on high for 4 hours. Serve as directed.**

W30*, EF, NF   *omit bread

Sausages and Pepper in Marinara Sauce

SERVES 6 TO 8

Prep Time: 7 minutes
Cook Time: 3 to 6 hours

I love to make this dish when we have company or on days when my family has different schedules and people are running in and out of the kitchen eating whenever they have a chance. I make it in a slow cooker, and once the cooking time is done, I just let the machine switch to warm and keep it out on the counter for people to graze on as they please. I usually eat mine over sautéed spinach, but Ryan and the kids love theirs over a toasted slice of grain-free bread.

- 12 sweet Italian sausages
- 2 red bell peppers, seeded and thinly sliced
- 1 yellow bell pepper, seeded and thinly sliced
- 1 green bell pepper, seeded and thinly sliced
- 1 yellow onion, halved and thinly sliced
- 2 (24-ounce) jars marinara sauce (such as Rao's)
- 1 teaspoon dried oregano
- 1 teaspoon dried basil
- ⅛ teaspoon ground cinnamon
- Grain-free or gluten-free bread slices, toasted, or sautéed spinach, for serving

In a large skillet, working in batches if necessary, brown the sausages over medium-high heat, turning them as needed, for 5 to 7 minutes, until nicely browned on all sides. Transfer them to a slow cooker and add the peppers, onion, marinara, oregano, basil, and cinnamon. Cover and cook on low for 6 hours or on high for 3 hours.

Serve immediately over slices of the bread.

To Use an Electric Pressure Cooker: Brown the sausages directly in the pot of the pressure cooker using the sauté setting on high. Add the peppers, onion, marinara, ½ cup chicken Bone Broth (page 42), the oregano, basil, and cinnamon, select the manual button, and cook at high pressure for 10 minutes. Let the pressure release naturally and serve as directed.

Tidbits: Applegate offers both a Sweet Italian Sausage made from chicken and a Classic Pork Italian Sausage that are free from sugar and dairy.

Make It Ahead: When I know we're having a big group, I put all of the ingredients in my slow cooker insert and pop it into the fridge the night before. In the morning, I just transfer it to the slow cooker and hit start!

Beef Stroganoff

SERVES 6

Prep Time: 5 minutes
Cook Time: 30 minutes

My mom frequently made the packaged Hamburger Helper stroganoff. She added a tub of sour cream and a can of cream of mushroom soup, which were common ingredients in many of her comforting casseroles and one-pot meals. As a result, I've always had an affinity for beef stroganoff, so my cookbook *Meals Made Simple* has a recipe that has become a favorite among readers. This stroganoff is even easier to make and contains tender chunks of beef. I found using a pressure cooker cuts the cook time drastically, which made this latest version the new favorite in my house.

- 2 tablespoons ghee or avocado oil
- ½ large yellow onion, diced
- 2 teaspoons fine sea salt
- 3 pounds beef stew meat, cut into 1-inch cubes
- ½ teaspoon freshly ground black pepper
- 4 cloves garlic, minced
- ½ teaspoon dried thyme
- 3 tablespoons coconut aminos
- 8 ounces white button mushrooms, chopped
- ¾ cup beef Bone Broth (page 42)
- 2¼ teaspoons freshly squeezed lemon juice
- 1¾ teaspoons apple cider vinegar
- ¼ cup unsweetened raw cashew butter (see Note)
- 1 tablespoon arrowroot
- 1 tablespoon water
- Basic Cauli-Rice (page 269), cooked grain-free noodles, or roasted potatoes, for serving

Heat the ghee in an electric pressure cooker using the sauté setting on high. Add the onion and ½ teaspoon of the salt and sauté for 3 to 4 minutes, until the onion begins to soften. Season the beef all over with the remaining 1½ teaspoons salt and the pepper. Working in batches, add the meat to the pot and cook, stirring occasionally, for about 2 minutes, until evenly browned on all sides. As each batch is done, transfer it to a plate. When all of the meat is browned, select the cancel button.

Return all of the browned meat to the pot and add the garlic, thyme, coconut aminos, mushrooms, broth, lemon juice, and vinegar. Seal the lid, select the manual button, and cook at high pressure for 20 minutes.

Meanwhile, in a small bowl, whisk together the cashew butter, arrowroot, and water.

Quick release the pressure and remove the lid. Stir in the cashew butter mixture, switch the mode back to sauté on high, and bring the sauce to a boil. Cook, stirring frequently, for about 2 minutes, until the sauce has thickened and is creamy. Serve immediately over the cauli-rice.

Note: **If you have any Dairy-Free Heavy Cream (page 38) in the fridge, stir in ⅓ cup in place of the cashew butter and water.**

To Use a Slow Cooker: **Brown the meat and onion on the stove top, then transfer them to the slow cooker. Increase the broth to 1¼ cups, add all of the remaining ingredients except the cashew butter mixture, cover, and cook on low for 8 hours or on high for 4 hours. Stir in the cashew butter mixture and serve as directed.**

Variation

If you tolerate dairy, omit the apple cider vinegar, lemon juice, and cashew butter and stir in ⅓ cup sour cream.

W30, EF, NF, SCD* *omit coconut aminos

Kalua Pork with Pineapple Fried Rice

SERVES 6 TO 8

Prep Time: 20 minutes
Cook Time: 2 hours

My family is partial to slow-cooked, fall-off-the-bone meats like carnitas, pot roast, and beef stew, so it was no surprise when everyone devoured a plate of kalua pork on a family trip to Hawaii. To re-create the dish at home without the hours and hours of cooking time required, I turned to the electric pressure cooker with success. Cooked pineapple and fried cauliflower rice add the perfect hints of sweet and sour to the salty, tender meat.

- 2 tablespoons avocado oil
- 4 pounds boneless pork shoulder or butt, cut into four uniform pieces
- 1½ tablespoons Hawaiian sea salt, kosher salt, or Himalayan pink salt
- ½ yellow onion
- 1 small red bell pepper
- 1 small jalapeño chile
- 2 cloves garlic
- 2 tablespoons coconut aminos
- 1½ teaspoons fish sauce
- Fine sea salt
- ½ cup chicken Bone Broth (page 42)
- 1½ tablespoons natural liquid smoke
- 2 (12-ounce) packages frozen cauliflower rice
- 1 cup fresh pineapple chunks
- ½ teaspoon toasted sesame oil
- Chopped green onions, white and tender green parts, for garnish

Heat 1 tablespoon of the avocado oil in an electric pressure cooker using the sauté setting on high. Season the pork all over with the Hawaiian sea salt, then add to the pot and cook, turning as needed, for about 15 minutes, until well browned on all sides.

Meanwhile, mince the onion, seed and dice the bell pepper and jalapeño, and mince the garlic. In a small bowl, whisk together the coconut aminos, fish sauce, and ¾ teaspoon fine sea salt and set aside.

Pour the broth over the browned pork and stir to release any browned bits from the bottom of the pot. Stir in the liquid smoke, then press the cancel button. Seal the lid, select the manual button, and cook at high pressure for 70 minutes. Let the pressure release naturally. (It will take about 30 minutes.)

Preheat the broiler or preheat the oven to 500°F. Transfer the meat to a sheet pan, discarding the juices. Shred the pork with two forks and spread it into an even layer. Broil for 5 minutes, until the pork is crispy on top.

Return the pot insert to the pressure cooker and select the sauté setting on high. Add the remaining 1 tablespoon avocado oil and the frozen riced cauliflower, onion, bell pepper, jalapeño, garlic, and pineapple and stir-fry for 8 minutes, until the vegetables are crisp-tender. Stir in the coconut aminos mixture and season to taste with salt.

Serve the shredded pork over the cauliflower rice mixture, drizzle the sesame oil over the top, and garnish with the green onions.

To Use a Slow Cooker: Brown the meat on the stove top, then transfer it to the slow cooker. Increase the broth to 1½ cups, stir in the liquid smoke, cover, and cook on low for 8 hours. Just before the pork is ready, cook the cauliflower rice mixture in a large skillet on the stove over medium-high heat and stir in the aminos mixture. Serve as directed.

Make It Ahead: Brown the pork in the pressure cooker as directed and cover and store it in the pot insert in the refrigerator for up to 2 days. Transfer the insert directly from the fridge to the pressure cooker when ready to cook.

*omit cranberry sauce

W30*

Swedish Meatballs

SERVES 4 TO 6

Prep Time: 35 minutes, plus 2 hours to chill

Cook Time: 20 minutes

I've never had real Swedish meatballs, but when IKEA released its prized recipe, I had to develop my own quick version using the pressure cooker. Many traditional recipes call for lingonberry sauce, but homemade cranberry sauce is a nice stand-in. If you're pressed for time, swap in store-bought gluten-free meatballs for the homemade.

- 2 small yellow onions, 1 grated and 1 diced
- 2 eggs
- 2 cloves garlic, minced
- 2 tablespoons coconut flour
- 3 teaspoons fine sea salt
- ½ teaspoon freshly ground black pepper
- ½ teaspoon ground nutmeg
- ½ teaspoon ground allspice
- 2 pounds ground beef
- 1 pound lean ground pork
- 2 to 4 tablespoons ghee or avocado oil
- 3 cups beef Bone Broth (page 42)
- ¼ cup unsweetened raw cashew butter
- 2 tablespoons arrowroot powder
- 4 teaspoons coconut aminos
- 1½ teaspoons Dijon mustard
- Mashed Potatoes (page 266) or Basic Cauli-Rice (page 269), for serving
- ½ cup chopped fresh flat-leaf parsley or dill
- ½ cup cranberry sauce (see page 286), for garnish

In a large bowl, combine the grated onion, eggs, garlic, flour, 2 teaspoons of the salt, the pepper, nutmeg, allspice, beef, and pork. Using your hands, mix everything together gently, but don't overmix. Form into 1½-inch meatballs and place in a single layer on a sheet pan. (If your hands are sticking, dampen them with warm water.) Cover the pan and refrigerate for at least 2 hours or up to 24 hours.

In a Dutch oven, heat 2 tablespoons of the ghee over medium-high heat. Working in batches to avoid crowding, brown the meatballs, turning as needed, for 2 to 3 minutes, until well browned on all sides. As the meatballs are ready, transfer them to a plate. If the pot begins to look dry, add more of the ghee as needed.

When all of the meatballs have been browned, add the diced onion to the pot and sauté for 2 to 3 minutes, until it begins to soften. Pour in the broth and whisk briskly to release any browned bits from the bottom of the pot. Transfer the onion and broth to a blender, add the cashew butter, arrowroot, coconut aminos, mustard, and the remaining 1 teaspoon salt, and blend on high speed for about 1 minute, until a very smooth sauce forms.

Return the meatballs to the pot and add the sauce. Simmer over medium-low heat for 8 to 10 minutes, until the meatballs are cooked through and the sauce has thickened.

To serve, spoon the meatballs over the potatoes, sprinkle with the parsley, and finish with a dollop of the cranberry sauce.

Tidbits: **The cooked meatballs and sauce will keep in the fridge for up to 7 days. Reheat in a covered saucepan over medium heat for 5 to 7 minutes. Or add frozen meatballs to a pot of simmering marinara sauce until warmed through.**

Make It Ahead: **Store the uncooked meatballs in the refrigerator for up to 3 days or in the freezer for up to 6 months. To freeze, arrange them in a single layer on a sheet pan lined with parchment paper and place in the freezer. Once frozen, transfer the meatballs to a resealable bag or airtight container. Thaw the frozen meatballs in the refrigerator overnight, or place the bag in a bowl of warm water until the meatballs have thawed.**

W30*, EF, NF *omit taro and plantain chips

"Skillet" Queso Dip

SERVES 6 TO 8

Prep Time: 10 minutes
Cook Time: 13 minutes

I've been a big fan of chips and queso for as long as I can remember, but after going gluten-free and then grain-free, I learned that most cheesy sauces contain wheat flour to help them stay smooth. Then I went dairy-free, and my beloved queso was completely off the table.

This amazing sauce has all of the flavors I remember but without the cheese. I usually serve this dip with Terra brand taro chips or plantain chips, but it is also delicious when eaten with raw carrot sticks or steamed broccoli.

- 12 ounces white-fleshed sweet potatoes, peeled and cubed (about 1 cup)
- 6 ounces carrots, peeled and diced (about ½ cup)
- 1¼ cups chicken Bone Broth (page 42)
- ⅓ cup ghee (see Tidbits)
- 2 tablespoons nutritional yeast
- 1 tablespoon fine sea salt
- 4 cloves garlic
- ½ cup mild roasted tomatillo salsa
- 2 tablespoons arrowroot powder
- 8 ounces ground beef
- 2 tablespoons Taco Seasoning (page 35)
- 2 teaspoons tomato paste
- Taro chips, plantain chips, carrots, or steamed broccoli, for serving

In an electric pressure cooker, combine the sweet potatoes, carrots, broth, ghee, nutritional yeast, salt, garlic, and salsa. Secure the lid, select the manual button, and cook at high pressure for 5 minutes. Quick release the pressure and transfer the mixture to a blender. Add the arrowroot and blend on high speed for about 1 minute, until very smooth.

Return the mixture to the pressure cooker and switch to the sauté setting on high. Add the beef and taco seasoning and cook, breaking up the meat with a wooden spoon and stirring frequently, for 3 to 5 minutes, until the beef is cooked through. Stir in the tomato paste and sweet potato mixture and whisk constantly for about 5 minutes, until the sauce is bubbling and thickened.

Serve the dip hot with the chips.

Tidbits: Store, tightly covered, in the fridge for up to 1 week or the freezer for up to 6 months. Reheat in a saucepan over low heat for 5 minutes.

If you tolerate russet potatoes, they will work here. Orange-fleshed sweet potatoes will also work but will make the dip a little sweeter.

I use ghee for its buttery flavor, but it does have trace amounts of lactose and casein. To make this completely dairy-free, substitute avocado oil for the ghee.

To Use the Stove Top: Simmer the potatoes, carrots, broth, ghee, nutritional yeast, salt, garlic, and salsa in a covered saucepan for 10 to 12 minutes, until tender, then blend as directed. Brown the meat in the saucepan over medium-high heat for 4 to 6 minutes, then add the pureed mixture to the pan, stir in the tomato paste, and finish and serve as directed.

Variations

Omit the beef and drizzle the queso over Salsa Chicken Tacos (page 98) or chips for nachos. Or omit the beef, tomato paste, and taco seasoning, and drizzle the "cheese" sauce over broccoli.

LE CREUSET

omit plantain chips   W30, EF, NF, SCD

Pork Chile Verde

SERVES 6 TO 8

Prep Time: 10 minutes
Cook Time: 6 to 8 hours

This mildly spiced and somewhat acidic pork stew is my favorite order at Mexican restaurants because it's typically grain- and dairy-free. At home, I serve this over cauliflower rice with a little lime juice and cilantro. I top it with avocado, cilantro, and crushed plantain chips.

- 4 pounds boneless pork shoulder or butt, trimmed of fat and cut into 2-inch cubes
- Fine sea salt and freshly ground black pepper
- 2 tablespoons ghee or avocado oil
- 1 cup chicken Bone Broth (page 42)
- 1 small yellow onion, diced
- 3 cloves garlic, chopped
- 2 cups roasted tomatillo salsa
- 1 tablespoon dried oregano (preferably Mexican)
- 2 teaspoons ground cumin
- 1 teaspoon ground coriander
- 2 bay leaves
- Basic Cauli-Rice (page 269), for serving
- Avocado slices, fresh cilantro leaves, and crushed plantain chips, for serving

Position oven racks in the top and middle slots and preheat to 350°F.

Season the pork well with salt and pepper. In a Dutch oven, heat the ghee over medium-high heat. Add half of the pork and cook, turning as needed, for about 5 minutes, until well browned on all sides. Using a slotted spoon, transfer to a plate. Repeat with the remaining pork. Return all of the pork to the pot.

Add the broth and stir to release any browned bits from the bottom of the pot. Add the onion, garlic, salsa, oregano, cumin, coriander, and bay leaves and stir well. Cover tightly, move the pot to the middle rack in the oven, and braise for about 2 hours, until the pork shreds easily with a fork.

Remove the pot from the oven and turn the oven to broil. Using tongs, transfer the pork to a sheet pan, shaking off any excess liquid. Broil the pork for 3 to 4 minutes, until crispy on top.

Serve the pork over the cauli-rice, adding a ladleful of the brothy sauce from the pot to each serving. Top with the avocado, cilantro, and plantain chips.

Tidbits: Use any leftover pork in Huevos Rancheros (page 54), Wild Mushroom and Zucchini Enchiladas (page 206), or Chilaquiles (page 61).

To Use a Slow Cooker: After browning the pork, transfer it to the slow cooker. While the pot is still warm, quickly pour in the broth and stir to release any browned bits from the bottom. Pour the broth into the slow cooker and add the onion, garlic, salsa, oregano, cumin, coriander, and bay leaves. Cook on low for 8 hours or on high for 4 hours. Broil the meat and serve as directed.

To Use an Electric Pressure Cooker: Brown the pork directly in the pot of the pressure cooker using the sauté setting on high. Add only ½ cup broth, then add the remaining ingredients, secure the lid, select the manual button, and cook at high pressure for 20 minutes. Let the pressure release naturally, then broil the meat and serve as directed.

Make It Ahead: Double the recipe and make meal packets to freeze. First, brown the meat, then divide it and the remaining ingredients among freezer-safe containers. Store in the freezer for up to 6 months. Partially defrost the container in a bowl of warm water for 10 minutes, then place the partially frozen ingredients into an electric pressure cooker, and cook as above for 25 minutes.

W30, EF, NF, V, SCD*

*sub butternut squash for sweet potato and omit coconut aminos

Kabocha, Sweet Potato, Apple, and Bok Choy Curry

SERVES 4 TO 6

Prep Time: 20 minutes
Cook Time: 20 minutes

This curry is a mash-up of two of my favorite meals: the pumpkin curry I order from a local Thai restaurant and the curry soups with squash and apples I always see on restaurant menus in the fall. You can whip up this hearty, meat-free curry quickly in a pressure cooker. And while it's not essential, a dollop of mango chutney on top brings a nice acidity and tartness to the dish. I use Thai Kitchen red curry paste because it's really mild and my kids love it. If you use a spicier brand, use only 1 tablespoon of paste.

- 1 tablespoon avocado oil
- 1 yellow onion, halved and sliced into half-moons
- 4 cloves garlic, minced
- 1 teaspoon peeled and grated fresh ginger
- 2 tablespoons Thai red curry paste
- 2 teaspoons ground turmeric
- 1 teaspoon fine sea salt
- 1 teaspoon ground cumin
- ¾ teaspoon ground coriander
- 1 small kabocha squash, peeled and cubed (see Tidbits)
- 2 apples, cored and grated
- 1 pound sweet potatoes, peeled and diced
- 2 tablespoons coconut aminos
- 1 (13.5-ounce) can full-fat coconut milk
- ½ cup vegetable broth
- Juice of 1 lime (about 2 tablespoons)
- 12 ounces baby bok choy, ends trimmed and halved lengthwise, or spinach, stemmed
- ¼ cup firmly packed fresh cilantro leaves
- ½ cup Mango Chutney (page 24)

In a Dutch oven, heat the oil over medium-high heat. Add the onion, garlic, and ginger and sauté for 1 to 2 minutes, until the onion begins to soften. Add the curry paste, turmeric, salt, cumin, and coriander and sauté for 1 to 2 minutes more, until fragrant.

Add the squash, apples, sweet potatoes, coconut aminos, coconut milk, and broth and bring to a boil, then turn down the heat to medium-low and simmer for 16 to 18 minutes, until the squash is tender and the curry has thickened. Stir in the lime juice and bok choy and simmer for 2 to 3 minutes, until the bok choy is tender.

Remove the pot from the heat and serve immediately. Top each serving with the cilantro and a dollop of chutney.

Tidbits: **Kabocha is a small, round winter squash with mildly sweet, orange flesh and dark green skin. It's similar to a small pie pumpkin. Acorn or butternut squash would be good substitutes.**

To Use an Electric Pressure Cooker: **Place all of the ingredients except the cilantro and chutney in the pressure cooker, secure the lid, select the manual button, and cook at high pressure for 5 minutes. Let the pressure release naturally and serve as directed.**

9

Soups and Stews

Most of these recipes are made in an electric pressure cooker or slow cooker, but there's a few within this chapter where the flavor and depth you can get from browning meats and slow cooking them in a heavy Dutch oven is unmatched. My Le Creuset Dutch (or French) oven is one of my most prized culinary possessions. I've had it since our wedding in 2007, and although Le Creuset or my other favorite, Staub, cookware is not inexpensive, my pot barely shows any wear and tear even though I use it multiple times a week. It's definitely worthwhile to invest in a heavy-duty, cast-iron pot with a well-fitting lid. Le Creuset's enameled inside coating also makes cleanup a dream.

Simply put, I consider having a 4- to 6-quart Dutch oven in your kitchen arsenal essential. Not only is it the ideal pot for all of the recipes in this chapter and for many other recipes in this book, but it's also great for cooking up a huge batch of ground beef for tacos or for browning chicken or steak because its high walls prevent grease from splattering on the stove top. I often choose my Dutch oven over my cast-iron skillet for just this reason.

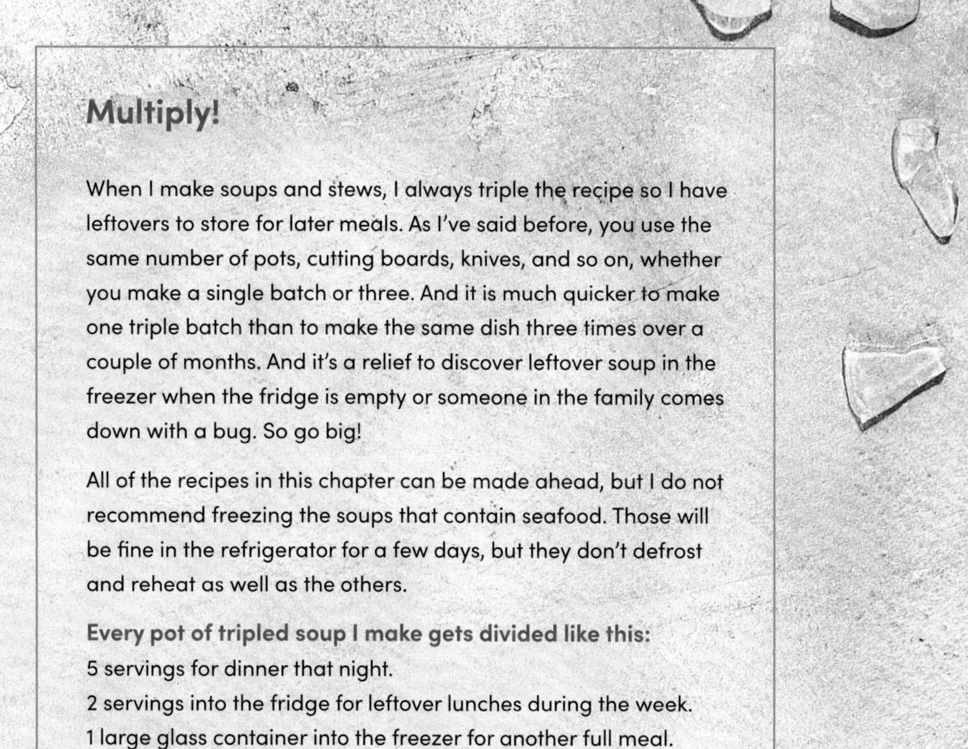

Multiply!

When I make soups and stews, I always triple the recipe so I have leftovers to store for later meals. As I've said before, you use the same number of pots, cutting boards, knives, and so on, whether you make a single batch or three. And it is much quicker to make one triple batch than to make the same dish three times over a couple of months. And it's a relief to discover leftover soup in the freezer when the fridge is empty or someone in the family comes down with a bug. So go big!

All of the recipes in this chapter can be made ahead, but I do not recommend freezing the soups that contain seafood. Those will be fine in the refrigerator for a few days, but they don't defrost and reheat as well as the others.

Every pot of tripled soup I make gets divided like this:
5 servings for dinner that night.
2 servings into the fridge for leftover lunches during the week.
1 large glass container into the freezer for another full meal.
2 to 4 small glass jars (I use old ghee jars!) into the freezer as single servings.

Thai Curry Noodle Soup

SERVES 4

Prep Time: 10 minutes
Cook Time: 8 minutes

This is my spin on Ryan's favorite takeout order, panang curry. When I order it from our local Thai restaurant, I usually repurpose the extra sauce with the addition of vegetables and chicken for lunch the next day!

I took those flavors and created this simple, one-pot soup with chewy noodles similar to the thin glass noodles used in Thai soups. To add that peanut butter taste Ryan loves, I mix in some of my Thai-style almond sauce, and then I finish the soup with a hefty dose of fresh basil.

1½ cups chicken Bone Broth (page 42)

1 (13.5-ounce) can full-fat coconut cream

⅓ cup Creamy Thai-Style Almond Sauce (page 29)

¼ cup Thai red curry paste

3 tablespoons fish sauce

1 teaspoon fine sea salt

1½ pounds bone-in chicken thighs, skinned

1 sweet potato, peeled and cubed

1 red bell pepper, seeded and thinly sliced

1 head baby bok choy, ends trimmed and sliced crosswise

1 (12-ounce) package kelp noodles, or 3 cups zucchini noodles (see Note)

Juice of 1 lime

⅓ cup loosely packed fresh basil leaves, roughly chopped

Chopped cashews or almonds, for serving

In an electric pressure cooker, whisk together the broth, coconut cream, almond sauce, curry paste, fish sauce, and salt. Stir in the chicken, sweet potato, bell pepper, bok choy, and kelp noodles. Secure the lid, select the manual button, and cook at high pressure for 8 minutes.

Quick release the pressure, remove the chicken from the pot, and use two forks to shred it away from the bones, discarding the bones. Return the shredded meat to the pot and stir in the lime juice.

Divide the soup among individual bowls, top with the basil and cashews, and serve immediately.

Note: If using zucchini noodles, do not cook them with the chicken and vegetables, as they will overcook. Stir them into the hot soup at the end with the lime juice.

Tidbits: If you don't have time to make my almond sauce, buy a bottle of Yai's Thai Almond Sauce. Thai Kitchen brand red curry paste (not the roasted red curry paste) is mild enough to use ¼ cup here, but if you use a spicier brand, I suggest halving the amount.

Make It Ahead: Double or triple this recipe. Divide all of the ingredients except the lime juice, basil, and cashews among freezer-safe containers and store in the freezer for up to 6 months. Partially defrost the containers in a bowl of warm water for 10 minutes, then place the partially frozen ingredients in an electric pressure cooker. Secure the lid, select the manual button, and cook at high pressure for 20 minutes. Shred the chicken, stir in the lime juice, and serve as directed.

To Use a Slow Cooker: Place all of the ingredients except the lime juice, basil, and cashews in the slow cooker and cook on low for 6 hours or on high for 3 hours. Shred the chicken, stir in the lime juice, and serve as directed.

EF, NF, SCD*

*omit coconut aminos and use SCD-friendly noodles

Ginger Chicken Noodle Soup

SERVES 4 TO 6

Prep Time: 15 minutes, plus 5 minutes hands-off time

Cook Time: 17 minutes

This Thai-inspired version of the ever-comforting chicken noodle soup is simple yet warming and delicious. In addition to the benefits of the broth, many of the ingredients have anti-inflammatory or antibacterial effects. Instead of the glass noodles or thin rice noodles often used in Thai cooking, I use kelp noodles that have been softened to create the same texture. Thai chicken broth is usually simpler and clearer than the chicken bone broth in this book, so for the most authentic, mild flavor, make or buy a light-colored broth that contains just chicken, water, salt, pepper, and onions. Add some lemongrass, too, if you can find it!

This soup is a favorite of my daughter, Kezia. My memories of her little two-year-old hands holding the long kelp noodles high in the air as she slurped them down will always stay with me!

1 (12-ounce) package kelp noodles

1 tablespoon baking soda

2 teaspoons lemon juice

1 pound ground white-meat chicken

½ teaspoon fine sea salt

¼ teaspoon white pepper

1 tablespoon coconut aminos

2 teaspoons fish sauce

6 cups chicken Bone Broth (page 42)

¼ head napa cabbage, cut into wide slices

1 small yellow onion, halved and thinly sliced

½-inch piece fresh ginger, peeled and chopped

2 cloves garlic, chopped

2 cups firmly packed baby spinach

3 green onions, tender green parts only, sliced ¼ inch thick on the diagonal

¼ cup loosely packed fresh cilantro leaves and tender stems

Break the noodles apart a bit then soak them for 5 minutes in boiling water mixed with 1 tablespoon baking soda and 2 teaspoons lemon juice. Drain and rinse well.

In a bowl, combine the chicken, salt, pepper, coconut aminos, and fish sauce and mix well.

In a stock pot or Dutch oven, bring the broth to a boil over medium-high heat. Turn down the heat until the broth is at a simmer. Add the meat in tablespoonfuls, scattering it around the pot. Then add the cabbage, onion, ginger, garlic, and the rinsed noodles and stir to incorporate. Cover and simmer for 15 minutes, until the cabbage has slightly wilted, the noodles are soft, and the chicken is cooked through.

Stir in the spinach, green onions, and cilantro, ladle into individual bowls, and serve immediately.

Make It Ahead: **Slightly undercook the soup by 5 minutes, so the cabbage is still crisp tender. Stir in the spinach, green onions, and cilantro off heat. Allow the soup to cool to room temperature, then divide into glass containers. Refrigerate for 5 days, or freeze for 6 months. To reheat, defrost overnight in the refrigerator and heat in a saucepan over medium-low heat for 10 minutes.**

*omit biscuits 

Chicken Pot Pie Stew

SERVES 4 TO 6

Prep Time: 17 minutes
Cook Time: 32 minutes

I yearn for the rich flavors of a good pot pie, so I decided to convert it into a stew topped with a biscuit. It's a quick, simple, and flavorful dish with that delicious pastry texture. I brown the chicken with the skin on to add depth of flavor, then remove the skin before cooking the stew so it's not greasy.

- ½ cup raw cashews (see Note)
- 2 tablespoons ghee or extra-virgin olive oil
- 2 pounds bone-in, skin-on chicken thighs
- 2 teaspoons fine sea salt
- ¾ teaspoon freshly ground black pepper
- 4 cups chicken Bone Broth (page 42)
- 2 small yellow onions, quartered
- 3 cloves garlic
- 2 cups peeled and sliced carrots
- 1½ cups sliced celery
- 2 cups halved baby potatoes
- ¼ cup chopped fresh flat-leaf parsley
- 1 teaspoon dried thyme
- ½ cup frozen shelled English peas
- 6 grain-free biscuits, warmed

In a small heatproof bowl, pour boiling water over the cashews and set aside to soak.

On an electric pressure cooker, select the sauté setting on high, then melt the ghee. While the ghee heats, rub the chicken skin all over with 1½ teaspoons of the salt and the pepper. Add the chicken, skin side down, to the pot and brown, turning as needed, for about 10 minutes, until well browned on all sides. Remove the skin from the chicken and discard. Add the broth to the pot and stir to release any browned bits from the bottom of the pot. Select the cancel button.

Add the onions and garlic to the pot, secure the lid, select the manual button, and cook at high pressure for 17 minutes. While the chicken cooks, cut your vegetables.

Quick release the pressure and use tongs to transfer the chicken to a cutting board. Drain and rinse the cashews. Pour the contents of the pot into a stand blender, add the cashews, and blend on high speed for about 30 seconds, until very smooth and creamy, then pour the puree into the pot. Alternatively, add the cashews to the pot and use an immersion blender to puree the soup in the pot.

Select the sauté setting on high. Add the carrots, celery, potatoes, parsley, and thyme and simmer uncovered for 5 to 7 minutes, until the broth has thickened and the vegetables are tender.

Meanwhile, using two forks, shred the chicken away from the bones, discarding the bones. Stir the chicken back into the stew, then select the cancel button and stir in the peas. Season with the remaining ½ teaspoon salt.

To serve, divide the stew among individual bowls and serve with a warm biscuit.

Note: I use raw cashews or cashew butter in place of dairy to make my soups and sauces creamy and thick, but you can substitute ½ cup full-fat coconut cream mixed with 1 tablespoon arrowroot powder. Add it along with the other ingredients to the blender.

Tidbits: Store in the fridge for up to 7 days or the freezer for up to 6 months. Defrost in the fridge overnight before reheating. To reheat in the pressure cooker, use the sauté setting on high for 3 to 5 minutes. To reheat on the stove top, heat over medium heat, stirring frequently, for 5 to 10 minutes, until warmed through.

W30, EF, NF

Creamy Bacon Cheeseburger Soup

SERVES 4 TO 6

Prep Time: 18 minutes
Cook Time: 13 minutes

As I've shared with you before, I grew up eating creamy casseroles and soups—and a cheeseburger soup made with Hamburger Helper and a packet of ranch dressing seasoning was something I learned to cook pretty early on. When I saw a bunch of people on Instagram using my skillet queso recipe (page 226) to make a similar style of soup, I wanted to join the party. This version is just as comforting as my childhood efforts but much, much healthier.

- 1 tablespoon avocado oil or ghee
- 8 ounces ground beef
- 1 yellow onion, minced
- 2 cups "Skillet" Queso Dip (page 226)
- 3 large carrots, peeled and diced
- 3 celery stalks, diced
- 1½ pounds white-fleshed sweet potatoes, peeled and cubed
- 2 cloves garlic, minced
- 4 cups beef Bone Broth (page 42)
- 2 teaspoons dried parsley
- Fine sea salt and freshly ground black pepper
- 1 cup chopped Baked Bacon (page 44)
- ¼ cup chopped fresh chives

In a stockpot or Dutch oven, heat the oil over medium-high heat. Add the beef and onion and cook, breaking up the meat with a wooden spoon and stirring frequently, for 5 to 7 minutes, until the meat is mostly cooked through. Add the queso, carrots, celery, potatoes, garlic, broth, parsley, 2½ teaspoons salt, and ½ teaspoon pepper. Turn down the heat to medium-low, cover, and simmer for 8 to 10 minutes, until the vegetables are tender. Season to taste with salt and pepper.

To serve, divide the soup among individual bowls and top with the bacon and chives.

Tidbits: To use a store-bought option, substitute Siete brand Cashew Queso (spicy blanco) for my homemade queso and increase the ground beef to 1 pound.

To Use a Slow Cooker: After browning the meat and onion, put all of the ingredients except the bacon and chives into a slow cooker and cook on low for 8 hours, then serve as directed.

To Use an Electric Pressure Cooker: Cook the meat and onion in the pressure cooker on the sauté setting on high. Add only 3½ cups broth and the remaining ingredients except the bacon and chives, select the manual button, secure the lid, and cook at high pressure for 5 minutes. Let the pressure release naturally, then serve as directed.

*sub bone broth for wine

30 W30*, EF, NF, SCD

Clams and Mussels in Creamy Turmeric-Coconut Broth

SERVES 4 TO 6

Prep Time: 10 minutes
Cook Time: 12 minutes

Despite what you might think, clams and mussels are actually really easy and affordable to prepare at home. Typically, the clams are already cleaned and the mussels have been debearded, but don't hesitate to ask the fishmonger at your grocery store to help with this. I enjoy pairing this light and quick-to-prepare dish with a simple green salad, but it would also be lovely served over kelp or shirataki noodles (see page 113) or with a few slices of toasted grain-free bread for soaking up any leftover sauce.

- 2 tablespoons ghee or avocado oil
- 1 tablespoon extra-virgin olive oil
- 4 ounces Mexican Chorizo (page 43)
- 10 green onions, white and tender green parts, thinly sliced, with white and green separated
- 8 cloves garlic, thinly sliced
- 1-inch piece fresh ginger, peeled and minced
- ½ teaspoon ground turmeric
- ½ teaspoon red pepper flakes
- ¾ cup dry white wine
- ¾ teaspoon fine sea salt
- ½ teaspoon freshly ground black pepper
- 15 to 20 littleneck clams, scrubbed (about 2 pounds)
- 15 to 20 mussels, scrubbed and debearded (about 2 pounds)
- ½ cup full-fat coconut cream
- 1 tablespoon freshly squeezed lime juice
- Lime wedges, for serving

In a large Dutch oven or stockpot with a tight-fitting lid, heat the ghee and oil over medium-high heat. Add the chorizo, the white parts of the green onions, and the garlic and sauté for 2 to 3 minutes, until the garlic is fragrant and the chorizo is mostly cooked. Stir in the ginger, turmeric, and pepper flakes and cook, stirring constantly, for 30 seconds. Add the wine, salt, and black pepper and bring to a boil.

Stir in the clams and mussels, cover, and cook, stirring once about halfway through, for 8 to 10 minutes, until the clams and mussels open. Discard any clams and mussels that have not opened after 12 minutes.

Stir in the coconut cream and lime juice and top with the green parts of the green onions. Serve immediately with the lime wedges on the side.

W30, EF, NF, SCD* (30)

*sub celeriac for sweet potatoes and omit arrowroot

Shrimp Chowder

SERVES 4 TO 6

Prep Time: 15 minutes
Cook Time: 15 minutes

Creamy seafood chowder is one of my favorite summer foods. In this shrimp and corn chowder, I use jicama, which softens slightly during cooking, as a sweet and crunchy addition. Topped with bacon, chives, and tender shrimp, this is the perfect meal for those late-summer months when the temperature is just starting to change.

If you can't find white-fleshed sweet potatoes, use Yukon gold potatoes. In order to keep this nut-free but still creamy, I puree cauliflower and sweet potatoes with a little arrowroot powder and coconut cream. To make this chowder even creamier (and without the faint taste of coconut), use dairy-free cashew-based cream in place of the coconut cream.

4 slices thick-cut bacon, coarsely chopped

1 bunch green onions, white and tender green parts, thinly sliced, with white and green separated

2 white-fleshed sweet potatoes, peeled and cubed

½ head cauliflower, cut into florets (about 2 cups florets)

4 cups water

1 tablespoon arrowroot powder (optional)

1 cup full-fat coconut cream or Dairy-Free Heavy Cream (page 38)

¼ teaspoon apple cider vinegar

1 teaspoon freshly squeezed lemon juice

Fine sea salt and freshly ground black pepper

1 celery stalk, chopped

1 cup peeled and diced jicama

2 teaspoons seafood seasoning (such as Primal Palate or Simply Organic)

1 sprig thyme, leaves stripped

1 pound medium shrimp, peeled and deveined with tails on

Line a plate with paper towels. In a Dutch oven or stockpot, cook the bacon over medium-high heat, stirring occasionally, for 2 to 3 minutes, until browned and crisp. Using a slotted spoon, transfer the bacon to the paper-lined plate, leaving the rendered fat in the pot.

Add the white parts of the green onions, half of the sweet potatoes, and the cauliflower to the pot and sauté for 30 seconds, until the green onions are fragrant. Add 2 cups of the water, cover, and cook for about 5 minutes, until the potatoes are tender.

Transfer the contents of the pot to a blender, add the arrowroot, coconut cream, vinegar, lemon juice, and 2½ teaspoons salt, and blend on high speed for about 30 seconds, until very smooth. Pour the puree into the pot and add the remaining 2 cups water, the remaining sweet potato, the celery, jicama, seafood seasoning, and thyme. Bring the chowder to a boil, then turn down the heat to medium-low and simmer, stirring occasionally, for 5 to 7 minutes, until the potato and jicama are tender. Stir in the shrimp and the green parts of the green onions and cook for 2 to 3 minutes, until the shrimp turn pink and curl slightly.

Season the chowder to taste with salt and pepper, then top with the bacon and serve immediately.

W30, EF, NF, V, SCD

Butternut Coconut Curry Soup

SERVES 4 TO 6

Prep Time: 10 minutes
Cook Time: 30 minutes

I always think of making curry-flavored dishes during the cooler months of the year because of how they warm my palate in an exciting way. And let me tell you—this soup is packed full of flavor! I often make my own curry paste, but I also absolutely love the flavor of Thai Kitchen's red curry paste, which I use in this recipe. It has a tiny kick, but the heat gets toned down by hearty butternut squash and rich coconut cream. Enjoy this soup on its own or pair it with my Curried Cauliflower and Mango Salad (page 260).

- 1 tablespoon ghee or coconut oil
- 2 cloves garlic, minced
- 1 yellow onion, diced
- ½ teaspoon peeled and grated fresh ginger
- 1 stalk lemongrass, dark green tops and woody base trimmed, tough outer leaves removed, and stalk cut crosswise into thirds
- 1 tablespoon Thai red curry paste (preferably Thai Kitchen brand)
- 4 cups chicken Bone Broth (page 42) or vegetable broth
- 1 medium butternut squash, peeled, halved, seeded, and cut into 1-inch cubes (about 4 cups)
- Fine sea salt and white pepper
- 1 (13.5-ounce) can full-fat coconut cream
- Finely grated zest and juice of 1 lime
- ⅓ cup chopped fresh cilantro
- ¼ cup toasted pepitas or chopped toasted cashews

In a Dutch oven or stockpot, heat the ghee over medium heat. Add the garlic and onion and sauté for about 3 minutes, until fragrant. Stir in the ginger, lemongrass, and curry paste and cook, stirring often, for about 5 minutes, until the onion is soft. Add the broth, squash, 1 teaspoon salt, and ¼ teaspoon white pepper and bring to a boil. Turn down the heat to medium-low, cover, and simmer for about 20 minutes, until the squash is tender. Remove from the heat and remove and discard the lemongrass. Let the soup cool for a few minutes.

Working in batches if necessary, pour the soup into a blender and blend on high speed for 30 to 60 seconds, until very smooth. Return the soup to the pot over medium-low heat and whisk in the coconut cream, reserving a few tablespoons for garnish, and the lime zest and juice. Season to taste with salt and pepper and reheat gently to serving temperature.

To serve, ladle the soup into individual bowls and garnish each bowl with a swirl of the reserved coconut cream and a sprinkle of cilantro and pepitas.

Make It Ahead: **Sauté the vegetables and add the curry paste. Place them in a resealable bag and add the remaining ingredients except the coconut cream, lime zest and juice, cilantro, and pepitas. Store in the fridge for up to 3 days or the freezer for up to 6 months. To cook from frozen in an electric pressure cooker, partially defrost the container in a bowl of warm water for 10 minutes, then place the partially frozen ingredients in the pressure cooker. Following the instructions below, cook at high pressure for 15 minutes (or 3 minutes if thawed from the fridge). For stove top, defrost the ingredients overnight in the refrigerator, transfer to a saucepan, cover, and cook over medium heat for about 20 minutes. Then blend, stir in the coconut cream and lime zest and juice, and serve as directed.**

To Use an Electric Pressure Cooker: **Brown the vegetables using the sauté setting on high. Add the remaining ingredients except the coconut cream, lime zest and juice, cilantro, and pepitas, secure the lid, select the manual or soup button, and cook at high pressure for 3 minutes. Quick release the pressure and remove the lid. Then blend and stir in the remaining ingredients as directed.**

Salads and Sides

Salads

Sides

One of my biggest pet peeves is cookbooks that claim to feature easy meals, then only provide protein dishes with no sides or starches to make the meal complete. It's deceiving because you make the protein in 20 minutes or less, but then have to spend time making a vegetable to go with it. Therefore, I consciously aimed for most of the meals in this book to incorporate vegetables and protein into one dish.

The recipes in this chapter are the ones I use when I've simply grilled, roasted, or braised a piece of fish, chicken, or meat and want something extra (and exciting) to go with it. You'll find a variety of riced-vegetable dishes, oven fries, and mashes that can be made in batches and reheated quickly.

I also find that having polenta and cooked spaghetti squash in the fridge comes in handy for creating super-flavorful meals on the fly. Any of these dishes plus a protein of your choice with a drizzle of one of the sauces you made on a prep day (see pages 22 to 30) combine to make a complete dinner in no time at all.

*use vinaigrette for W30 and SCD, omit nuts for NF

30 | -10 | W30*, EF, NF*, V, SCD*

California Dinner Salad

SERVES 4 TO 6

Prep Time: 15 minutes

This is my simple dinner salad and, truth be told, it may be a little different from what you're expecting. Don't get me wrong, I love a good garden salad with ranch dressing (page 23) and maybe bacon bits. But being a California girl, salad for me has always meant greens with whatever fruit is in season—pears, apples, grapes, Cara Cara oranges, clementines—and lots of avocado, crunchy nuts or seeds, whatever herbs I have on hand, a basic vinaigrette, and sometimes a little soft goat cheese crumbled on top. The crunchy, sweet, and bright combination of these items makes the perfect salad for me, and it gets served alongside dinner at least five out of seven nights per week at my house. My favorite dishes to serve it with are Creamy Sausage, Kale, and Sweet Potato Soup (page 105), Shrimp Chowder (page 246), Cast-Iron Rib-Eye Steaks with Garlic Mushrooms (page 182), all of the meals in the Pasta chapter (page 110), and, of course, any grilled protein.

- 8 cups loosely packed mixed greens
- 1 small head radicchio, leaves torn into bite-size pieces
- 1½ cups fruit (sliced apples, pears, oranges, and/or figs; halved grapes; or clementine segments)
- ½ cup toasted nuts and seeds (lightly salted walnuts, almonds, sunflower seeds, toasted pepitas, and/or pecans)
- ¼ cup chopped fresh flat-leaf parsley, basil, cilantro, chives, or green onions (white and green parts)
- 2 avocados, halved, pitted, peeled, and diced
- ¼ cup Vinaigrette or Maple-Cider Vinaigrette (page 25)

In a large salad bowl, layer the greens, fruit, nuts and/or seeds, herbs, and avocado. Toss gently to combine. Drizzle with the vinaigrette and toss again to coat. Serve immediately.

Make It Ahead: Make the dressing in advance and store in the fridge for up to 3 weeks.

W30*, EF, NF*, V  *omit coconut sugar for W30, omit cashews for NF

Sweet-and-Sour Thai-Style Salad

SERVES 4

Prep Time: 10 minutes

Green papaya salad is one of my favorite side dishes to order at Thai restaurants. I included a recipe for it in my first cookbook, *Against All Grain*, but because I have a hard time finding green papaya in California unless I seek out an Asian market, I've starting using a mix of carrots and kohlrabi in place of the papaya. Shredded jicama will also work here. To save time, purchase preshredded carrots, or process the carrots and kohlrabi in a food processor fitted with the shredding disk. You can also use a julienne peeler or even a spiralizer. I pile this salad on top of Thai Basil Beef (page 189) or alongside any Thai-inspired curry dish, such as Kabocha, Sweet Potato, Apple, and Bok Choy Curry (page 230) or Coconut Chicken Curry (page 101).

- 2 tablespoons coconut sugar
- ¼ cup freshly squeezed lime juice
- 2 cloves garlic, minced
- 3 tablespoons fish sauce
- 1 red chile, seeded and thinly sliced
- ½ cup halved cherry tomatoes
- 1 (12-ounce) package broccoli slaw
- 1 small kohlrabi or jicama, peeled and shredded
- 1 cup mung bean sprouts
- 3 green onions, white and tender green parts, thinly sliced
- ½ cup chopped fresh Thai basil leaves
- 2 tablespoons chopped toasted cashews

In a large bowl, combine the sugar, lime juice, garlic, fish sauce, and chile and mash the ingredients together with the back of a spoon or a muddler. Add the tomatoes and crush slightly to release their juices. Stir in the broccoli slaw, kohlrabi, bean sprouts, green onions, and basil. Top with the cashews and serve.

*omit pecans for NF

W30, EF, NF*, V, SCD

Apple-Butternut Salad with Maple-Cider Vinaigrette

SERVES 6

Prep Time: 15 minutes
Cook Time: 19 minutes

I make a variation of this salad all year round, swapping out the fruits and squash for whatever is in season. Acorn squash, hazelnuts, and dried cranberries are wonderful additions for the fall and winter months, and I love to use stone fruits with toasted walnuts during the summer. The maple-cider dressing is timeless and seems to taste amazing on just about anything I've tried it on. If you tolerate dairy, add ¼ cup crumbled soft goat cheese to the salad.

- 1 small butternut squash, peeled, halved, seeded, and cut into 1-inch cubes
- 1½ tablespoons avocado oil
- 1 tablespoon pure maple syrup
- ½ teaspoon ground cinnamon
- ¼ teaspoon fine sea salt
- ½ cup pecan halves
- ¾ cup Maple-Cider Vinaigrette (page 25)
- 1 small head radicchio, leaves separated and torn into pieces
- 4 cups firmly packed Little Gem lettuce leaves
- 2 cups baby arugula
- ¼ cup dried cherries (preferably sweetened with apple juice)
- 1 tart apple, cored and diced

Preheat the oven to 425°F. Line a sheet pan with parchment paper.

Pile the squash pieces on the prepared pan, drizzle them with the oil and maple syrup, sprinkle with the cinnamon and salt, and toss the squash to coat. Spread in a single layer and roast for 17 to 20 minutes, until golden and tender. Add the pecans to one corner of the pan and toast for 2 minutes, until darkened and fragrant. Remove the pan from the oven and let the squash and pecans cool to room temperature. While they cool, make the vinaigrette.

To assemble the salad, fill a large bowl with the radicchio, lettuce, and arugula. Sprinkle the cherries and apple over the top. Coarsely chop the cooled pecans and scatter them along with the roasted squash on top of the lettuces. Drizzle the salad with ¼ cup of the vinaigrette and toss to coat. Serve the remaining vinaigrette on the side.

Make It Ahead: **Make the dressing ahead of time and store in the fridge for up to 3 weeks.**

W30*, EF, NF, V, SCD*   *omit maple syrup for W30 and SCD

Curried Cauliflower and Mango Salad

SERVES 4 TO 6

Prep Time: 15 minutes
Cook Time: 10 minutes

If you are trying to avoid meat or have committed to eating more vegetables by embracing Meatless Mondays, this salad is for you. I use cauliflower to bulk this up, but you could add any protein of your choice, such as grilled shrimp or rotisserie chicken. I toast the spices I use to coat the cauliflower, which really brings out their flavor. That combined with sweet mango gives the dish a really satisfying complexity. If you have an everything bagel seasoning in your spice drawer (try Everything but the Bagel Sesame Seasoning Blend from Trader Joe's!), sprinkle a teaspoon or two over the top of the finished salad.

1 small head cauliflower, cut into small florets

4 tablespoons avocado oil or ghee

1 teaspoon curry powder

½ teaspoon ground coriander

¼ teaspoon dry mustard powder

¼ teaspoon ground cumin

¼ teaspoon ground turmeric

⅛ teaspoon ground cinnamon

1 yellow onion, thinly sliced

⅓ cup Mediterranean Tahini Dressing (page 29)

1 tablespoon pure maple syrup

2 mangoes (preferably Ataulfo variety), pitted, peeled, and cut into 1-inch pieces

5 ounces baby spinach, stemmed

¼ cup chopped fresh cilantro

Toasted pepitas and everything bagel seasoning, for garnish

Bring a large pot of water to a boil over high heat and add the cauliflower florets. Blanch for 1 minute, then drain the cauliflower into a colander. Transfer the florets to a clean kitchen towel and pat to dry completely.

In a large skillet, heat 3 tablespoons of the oil over medium heat. Add the curry powder, coriander, mustard powder, cumin, turmeric, and cinnamon and toast, stirring constantly, for about 30 seconds, until fragrant. Add the onion and cook, stirring occasionally, for 7 to 10 minutes, until the onion is soft. Add the remaining 1 tablespoon oil and heat for 30 seconds. Add the cauliflower and sauté for 3 to 5 minutes, until just browned on all sides and crisp-tender. Transfer the vegetable mixture to a large serving bowl to cool to room temperature.

In a small bowl, whisk together the dressing and maple syrup. Add 1 teaspoon water at a time if needed to thin the dressing.

Add the mangoes, spinach, cilantro, and 3 tablespoons of the dressing to the serving bowl and toss to combine. Garnish with the pepitas and bagel seasoning and serve the remaining dressing on the side.

Roasted Spring Vegetables with Lemon-Dill Aioli

SERVES 4 TO 6

Prep Time: 15 minutes
Cook Time: 20 minutes

This veggie side takes advantage of a big garden haul or whatever odds and ends remain in my crisper drawer at the end of the week. A drizzle of lemony-herby aioli with a hint of zingy mustard dresses this up nicely. Spring is the start to our grilling season here in California, and this side is my favorite to serve alongside a simple grilled steak or piece of salmon.

- 2 bunches small rainbow carrots, trimmed
- 1 bunch radishes, halved
- 1 fennel bulb, cut into wedges
- 2 to 3 tablespoons ghee or avocado oil
- ¾ teaspoon fine sea salt
- ¼ teaspoon freshly ground black pepper
- 1 bunch asparagus, ends trimmed
- 8 ounces sugar snap peas, trimmed
- ¼ cup Lemon-Dill Aioli (page 24)
- 1 tablespoon grainy mustard
- Finely grated zest and juice of ½ lemon

Preheat the oven to 425°F. Line a large sheet pan with parchment paper.

Pile the carrots, radishes, and fennel on the prepared pan, drizzle with 2 tablespoons of the ghee and toss the vegetables to coat. Spread in a single layer and sprinkle with the salt and pepper. Roast for 15 minutes.

Remove the pan from the oven and toss the asparagus and snap peas with the other vegetables. If the pan is dry, add the remaining 1 tablespoon ghee, then spread the vegetables in a single layer. Roast for 5 to 7 minutes more, until the asparagus is crisp-tender.

In a small bowl, stir together the aioli and mustard. Transfer the vegetables to a platter and drizzle the lemon juice and aioli mixture over the top. Sprinkle with the lemon zest and serve.

W30, EF, SCD  

Creamy Almond-Cauliflower Polenta

SERVES 4 TO 6

Prep Time: 5 minutes
Cook Time: 6 minutes

My grandma Marge used to make polenta all the time to serve under tender meat dishes with tomatoey sauces. Like grits, polenta is made from corn, so it's been some time since I've been able to enjoy it. This dish is inspired by the recipe for grain-free grits in my book *Eat What You Love*. Here, I simmer almond meal until it expands and thickens, then I add riced cauliflower for its nutritional benefits and ground corn–like texture. It's a favorite accompaniment to Cajun Shrimp and Andouille Sausage (page 151), Pork Ragù over Creamy Polenta (page 102), Savory Polenta with Sausage and Blistered Tomatoes (page 57), or Creamy Polenta with Woody Mushroom Sauce (page 205), or I like to pair it simply with a soft-boiled egg and some green onions.

- 2 tablespoons extra-virgin olive oil, plus more for drizzling
- 1 cup fresh or frozen raw riced cauliflower (about 6 ounces)
- 2 cups chicken Bone Broth (page 42) or vegetable broth
- 2 to 2¼ cups almond meal
- ¼ cup Dairy-Free Parmesan Cheese (page 37)
- 2 tablespoons unsweetened raw cashew butter (optional)
- Fine sea salt and freshly ground black pepper

In a saucepan, heat 1 tablespoon of the oil over medium-high heat. Add the cauliflower and sauté for 2 to 3 minutes, until golden. Add the broth and bring to a boil. Turn down the heat to medium-low and whisk in 2 cups of the almond meal a little at a time. Simmer for 3 to 5 minutes, stirring frequently, until the almond meal has absorbed the liquid and the cauliflower is tender. Add the remaining ¼ cup almond meal if needed to absorb any remaining liquid. If you are using a coarse riced cauliflower and want a smoother texture, pulse the mixture a few times with an immersion blender to achieve the desired consistency.

Whisk in the cheese and cashew butter, then remove from the heat and season to taste with salt and pepper. Finish with a drizzle of oil.

Tidbits: **If dairy is tolerated, Parmesan or sheep's milk Pecorino Romano may be used.**

Make It Ahead: **Make the polenta up to 7 days in advance and store in the fridge. Reheat in a covered saucepan over medium-low heat, stirring occasionally, for 10 minutes. Add a tablespoon of water or milk to thin if needed as it heats.**

Basic Root Mash
(page 267)

Mashed Potatoes
(page 266)

Creamy Almond-
Cauliflower Polenta
(opposite)

*sub coconut milk for cashew milk for NF, use vegetable broth for V

Mashed Potatoes

SERVES 8

Prep Time: 15 minutes
Cook Time: 7 minutes

Ryan's favorite food group is mashed potatoes. Not potatoes. Mashed potatoes. If I make them for dinner, you better believe that three-quarters of his plate is filled with them. For this reason, I've been testing ways to cook potatoes more quickly and evenly without having to wait for water to boil (hello, electric pressure cooker!). To make the process even more effortless, sometimes I don't even peel the potatoes. He doesn't mind the rustic-style skin-on mash, and the approach shaves off a ton of time! Yukon gold potatoes tend to work best in this recipe because they're naturally creamy, but russets would also work (Caveat: They are just a bit gritty once mashed).

5 pounds Yukon gold potatoes, peeled or unpeeled and halved if large

2 teaspoons fine sea salt

1 cup chicken Bone Broth (page 42)

½ cup Cashew Milk (page 39)

¼ cup full-fat coconut milk

½ cup ghee, unsalted butter, or dairy-free butter

In an electric pressure cooker, combine the potatoes, 1 teaspoon of the salt, and the broth. Secure the lid, select the manual button, and cook at high pressure for 6 minutes. Quick release the pressure.

Remove the lid and mash the potatoes directly in the pot with a potato masher or handheld electric mixer. Then select the sauté setting on high heat, stir in the cashew milk, coconut milk, and ghee and cook, stirring, for 30 to 60 seconds, until heated through.

Press the cancel button and mix in the remaining 1 teaspoon salt. Serve immediately.

Tidbits: Substitute ¾ cup unsweetened, dairy-free plain coffee creamer, such as NutPods, for the cashew and coconut milks. Miyoko's brand vegan butter can be used in place of the ghee.

Make It Ahead: Make the potatoes and store in the fridge for up to 7 days. Reheat in a covered baking dish in a preheated 400°F oven, stirring occasionally, for 20 minutes, or in the pressure cooker on the sauté setting on high for 5 minutes, stirring frequently.

To Use the Stove Top: Fill a large pot two-thirds full of water and add the potatoes and 1 teaspoon of the salt. Bring to a boil over medium-high heat, then turn down the heat to medium-low and simmer for 10 to 12 minutes, until fork-tender. Drain the potatoes, and add the broth, cashew milk, coconut milk, ghee, and the remaining 1 teaspoon salt to the pot over medium-low heat. Return the potatoes to the pot and mash as directed.

Pictured on page 265.

Basic Root Mash

SERVES 4 TO 6

Prep Time: 8 minutes
Cook Time: 7 minutes

For those of you, like me, who don't tolerate white potatoes (or eat them sparingly), this root mash of mildly sweet sweet potatoes and parsnips is delicious and has the billowy volume and sustenance of mashed potatoes. They're delicious with a roasted chicken or turkey, served under my Swedish Meatballs (page 225) and blanketed in the gravy, or as a hearty accompaniment to any simple roasted or grilled protein. Ryan loves the Jalapeño-Wasabi variation alongside the Meatballs with Creamy Thai-Style Almond Sauce (page 217) or Hawaiian BBQ Chicken with Grilled Bok Choy and Pineapple (page 285).

- 1 pound white-fleshed sweet potatoes, peeled and cut into ¾-inch chunks
- 1 pound parsnips, peeled and cut into ¾-inch chunks
- ½ cup Cashew Milk (page 39) or plain, unsweetened dairy-free coffee creamer
- 3 tablespoons ghee or avocado oil
- ½ teaspoon fine sea salt

Fill a large pot two-thirds full of water, add the potatoes and parsnips, and bring to a boil over medium-high heat. Boil for 7 to 10 minutes, until fork-tender. Drain the vegetables.

Return the pot to medium-high heat, add the cashew milk and ghee and heat for 30 seconds, then return the vegetables to the pot. Mash with a potato masher to your desired consistency. Mix in the salt and serve immediately.

Make It Ahead: **Make the mash up to 7 days in advance and store in the fridge. Reheat in a covered baking dish in a preheated 400°F oven for 20 minutes, stirring occasionally, or in an electric pressure cooker on the sauté setting on high for 5 minutes, stirring frequently.**

Jalapeño-Wasabi Variation

Add 2 jalapeño chiles, seeded and finely minced, and stir in 1½ tablespoons natural wasabi powder with the cashew milk.

Loaded-Up Variation

Stir in 6 slices Baked Bacon (page 44), chopped; ¼ cup chopped fresh chives; and ½ cup shredded dairy-free Cheddar cheese after mashing.

Pictured on page 265.

Rice What?

Making rice from cauliflower is pretty standard practice in the paleo, grain-free, and low-carb communities, but did you know that you can rice many different vegetables? While I use cauliflower rice frequently, it's so nice to change it up now and then.

As a rule of thumb, I choose vegetables that won't get too mushy when cooked and have a slightly chewy bite similar to that of rice. Among my favorite are broccoli, carrot, celery root, kohlrabi, parsnip, plantain, and turnip. Here are some tips on making good rice from vegetables:

- Don't overload your food processor! To get uniform rice-size grains, work in batches and use the grating disk. After processing, switch to the S-shaped blade and pulse three or four times until the pieces are the size of rice. Alternatively, you can use the small holes on a box grater. Just watch those knuckles!
- Remove excess moisture by wrapping the riced vegetable in a clean kitchen towel and gently squeezing to release any water.
- Nowadays, with so many different types of vegetable rice stocked in the freezer or produce section of your grocery store, you can always just buy a riced vegetable. Or you can purchase vegetable noodles and chop them to the size of rice kernels.

*use vegetable broth

W30, EF, NF, V*, SCD

Basic Cauli-Rice

MAKES ABOUT 3 CUPS

Prep Time: 10 minutes
Cook Time: 13 minutes

I serve cauliflower rice with a lot of the dishes in this book because it's the simplest to make and definitely my fallback. I really love the texture of homemade cauliflower rice, and when you grate it, it sautés a little better than store-bought. It's definitely more economical, too.

That said, I often buy bags of frozen cauliflower rice so I have some in the freezer at all times. I keep both the pilaf version filled with herbs and flavor from Whole Foods and the plain version on hand.

- 1 small head cauliflower, cut into florets
- 1 tablespoon ghee or extra-virgin olive oil
- ½ cup diced yellow onion
- 1 clove garlic, minced
- 3 tablespoons chicken Bone Broth (page 42)
- ¾ teaspoon fine sea salt

In a food processor fitted with the grating disk, process the cauliflower into small pieces. Switch to the S-shaped blade and pulse three or four times, until the pieces are the size of rice. Pick out any large fragments that didn't grate and chop them by hand or save for another use. Alternatively, grate the florets by hand on the large holes of a box grater.

In a large skillet, melt the ghee over medium heat. Add the onion and garlic and sauté for 3 to 5 minutes, until the onion has softened. Add the cauliflower rice to the pan and sauté for about 5 minutes, until it begins to soften and brown slightly. Add the broth and salt and raise the heat to medium-high. Continue to cook for 5 to 7 minutes, until the cauliflower is tender and the liquid has been absorbed. Serve immediately.

W30, EF, NF, V, SCD  

Persian-Style Saffron Cauli-Rice with Dried Fruits

SERVES 4 TO 6

Prep Time: 12 minutes
Cook Time: 10 minutes

This flavorful rice dish goes with any fish, poultry, or lamb, but it's an especially amazing partner for my Chicken and Apricot Stew (page 93).

- 2 tablespoons ghee or avocado oil
- 1 yellow onion, finely diced
- 6 cups riced cauliflower
- ¼ teaspoon saffron threads, crumbled and soaked in ¼ cup hot water
- 1 teaspoon fine sea salt
- ¼ teaspoon freshly ground black pepper
- ¼ teaspoon ground cinnamon
- ¼ teaspoon ground cardamom
- ¼ teaspoon ground cumin
- ⅛ teaspoon ground allspice
- ¼ cup chopped dried apricots
- ¼ cup dried currants
- ¼ cup dried cherries or cranberries
- ¼ cup roughly chopped pistachios
- 1 tablespoon chopped fresh mint
- 1 tablespoon chopped fresh cilantro

In a large skillet, heat the ghee over medium heat. Add the onion and sauté for 3 to 5 minutes, until soft. Add the cauliflower and sauté for 2 minutes, until beginning to soften. Stir in the saffron and its soaking water, salt, pepper, cinnamon, cardamom, cumin, allspice, apricots, currants, cherries, and pistachios and sauté for 5 to 7 minutes more, until the liquid has evaporated and the cauliflower is soft.

Sprinkle the cauli-rice with the mint and cilantro and serve immediately.

Tidbits: **Purchase dried fruits that are unsweetened, or sweetened with apple juice, and are unsulphured.**

Persian-Style Saffron
Cauli-Rice with Dried Fruit
(opposite)

Puerto Rican–Style
Plantain Rice
(page 273)

Spanish Cauli-Rice
(page 272)

W30, EF, NF, V*, SCD  *use vegetable broth

Spanish Cauli-Rice

SERVES 4 TO 6

Prep Time: 10 minutes
Cook Time: 7 minutes

Nearly every Sunday when I was growing up, we ate boxed Spanish rice for our family taco day. I looked at the ingredients recently and was surprised to learn that it contains wheat, MSG, and soy! I still love the flavors of Spanish rice, so I developed this version using cauliflower rice simmered with salsa, spices, and chiles.

- 1 tablespoon ghee or extra-virgin olive oil
- ½ cup diced yellow onion
- 6 cups riced cauliflower
- ¼ cup chicken Bone Broth (page 42)
- ½ cup chopped tomatoes with juice
- ¼ cup canned chopped green chiles
- 1 teaspoon fine sea salt
- ¾ teaspoon ground cumin
- ¼ cup loosely packed fresh cilantro leaves and tender stems

In a large skillet, heat the ghee over medium heat. Add the onion and sauté for 3 to 5 minutes, until soft. Add the cauliflower and sauté for 2 minutes, until beginning to soften. Stir in the broth, tomatoes, chiles, salt, and cumin, raise the heat to medium-high, and simmer for 2 to 3 minutes, until the cauliflower rice is tender and the liquid has been absorbed.

Sprinkle the cauli-rice with the cilantro and serve immediately.

Pictured on page 271.

Puerto Rican–Style Plantain Rice

SERVES 4 TO 6

Prep Time: 12 minutes
Cook Time: 7 minutes

This Puerto Rican–inspired rice dish will completely trick your taste buds into thinking you're eating real rice. That's because the high starch content and natural texture of plantains works so well here. If you can't find plantains, you can substitute two 12-ounce packages frozen cauliflower rice and reduce the cook time by half.

- 4 firm green plantains (about 2 pounds)
- 2 cloves garlic
- 1 small green bell pepper, halved and seeded
- 1 small white onion, quartered
- 1 jalapeño chile, halved and seeded
- 1 tablespoon avocado oil
- 1 tablespoon Adobo Seasoning (page 31)
- Fine sea salt and freshly ground black pepper
- ¼ cup chicken Bone Broth (page 42)
- ¼ cup tomato puree or strained tomatoes
- ¼ cup pitted green olives, roughly chopped
- ¼ cup firmly packed cilantro leaves and tender stems, plus more for serving

Cut off both ends of each plantain and make a shallow lengthwise cut along the peel. Remove the peels and cut each plantain crosswise into thirds. In a food processor fitted with the grating disk, grate the plantain chunks until they resemble long grains of rice. Alternatively, use the large holes on a box grater. Set the plantain rice aside.

Remove the grating disk and wipe the processor bowl clean, then fit the processor with the S-shaped blade. Add the garlic, bell pepper, onion, and jalapeño and process for 5 to 10 seconds, until everything is finely chopped. Alternatively, mince vegetables by hand.

In a large skillet, heat the oil over medium-high heat. Add the chopped vegetables and adobo seasoning and sauté for about 1 minute, until the veggies are crisp-tender. Add the plantain rice and ¼ teaspoon salt and sauté for 3 to 5 minutes, until the rice is tender. Add the broth and tomato puree and cook, stirring constantly, for 30 seconds, until any browned bits have released from the bottom of the pan and most of the liquid has evaporated. Turn down the heat to medium-low, cover, and simmer for 2 to 3 minutes, until the rice has absorbed most of the liquid.

Season to taste with salt and pepper, stir in the olives and cilantro, and serve immediately.

Pictured on page 271.

Sweet Chili Sweet Potatoes (page 276)
Rosemary-Garlic Oven Fries (page 277)
Za'atar Fries (opposite)

Za'atar Fries

SERVES 6 TO 8

Prep Time: 15 minutes
Cook Time: 22 minutes

There's an inn near Sonoma, California, that Ryan and I love to visit for lunch because of its amazing Mediterranean-inspired menu with a wine country twist. While I don't tolerate white potatoes well, french fries are my vice, and I always ask Ryan to order them so I can snag a few—especially if they're tossed in a seasoning mix or served with a special dip. It was here that I first had fries tossed in za'atar seasoning and they became a quick favorite. I've always loved za'atar for its woodsy, tangy, nutty, and rich flavors but had never thought to put it on fries! I use Hannah or other white-fleshed sweet potatoes in place of russets so I can eat as many as I like.

- 3 medium white-fleshed sweet potatoes, unpeeled and cut into uniform ¼-inch-thick wedges
- 3 tablespoons extra-virgin olive oil
- 1 tablespoon za'atar
- ½ teaspoon sweet paprika
- Pinch of cayenne pepper
- ½ teaspoon fine sea salt

Preheat the oven to 425°F. Line a large sheet pan with parchment paper. (If the potato wedges won't fit in a single layer without touching, use two pans.)

Put the potato wedges into a large pot, add water to cover, and bring to a boil over high heat. When the water boils, immediately drain the potatoes.

Pat the wedges dry and pile them on the prepared pan. Drizzle with the oil and toss to coat. In a small bowl, stir together the za'atar, paprika, and cayenne. Sprinkle the spice mixture over the wedges and toss to coat. Spread the wedges in a single layer on the pan.

Roast the potatoes, rotating the pan front to back and flipping the wedges halfway through, for 20 to 25 minutes, until crispy on the outside and tender on the inside. Sprinkle the fries with the salt and serve immediately.

EF, NF, V  

Sweet Chili Sweet Potatoes

SERVES 6 TO 8

Prep Time: 10 minutes
Cook Time: 20 minutes

These smoky, tangy sweet potatoes go well with just about anything, but I especially love them with Mexican food or with any of the burgers and skewers in chapter 11. Look for thin sweet potatoes for this dish so you can easily cut them into halves that will bake quickly and evenly.

3 pounds sweet potatoes, unpeeled and halved lengthwise

¼ cup melted ghee or avocado oil

2 tablespoons pure maple syrup or honey

1 teaspoon fine sea salt

½ teaspoon ground coriander

¼ teaspoon cayenne pepper

¼ teaspoon smoked paprika

¼ teaspoon chili powder

¼ cup raw pepitas

¼ cup loosely packed fresh cilantro leaves

Juice of 1 lime

Preheat the oven to 450°F. Line a large sheet pan with parchment paper.

Pile the sweet potatoes on the prepared pan. Top with the ghee, 1 tablespoon of the maple syrup, the salt, coriander, cayenne, paprika, and chili powder and toss to coat. Turn the potatoes cut side down. Roast for 20 to 25 minutes, until tender and browned.

Meanwhile, in a dry small skillet, toast the pepitas over medium-high heat, tossing frequently, for 3 to 5 minutes, until golden brown.

Arrange the sweet potatoes on a platter and top with the pepitas, cilantro, lime juice, and the remaining 1 tablespoon maple syrup. Serve immediately.

Tidbits: **To cut your time and make these especially crispy, use Parboiled Potatoes (page 40) and roast for 12 to 15 minutes.**

Pictured on page 274.

Rosemary-Garlic Oven Fries

SERVES 6 TO 8

Prep Time: 8 minutes
Cook Time: 20 minutes

This has been my go-to side dish since Ryan and I were newlyweds and started hosting family and friends for dinner. It's filling and a sure bet to please a crowd. We have rosemary growing like wildfire on our hillside, so I try to use it whenever I can. I love the slight woody and nutty flavor it gives these roasted potatoes. Of course, the four cloves of garlic help, too!

- 3 pounds baby creamer potatoes, unpeeled and halved, or white-fleshed sweet potatoes, unpeeled and cubed
- 3 tablespoons extra-virgin olive oil
- 1 sprig rosemary, leaves stripped
- 4 cloves garlic, crushed
- ½ teaspoon fine sea salt

Preheat the oven to 425°F. Line a large sheet pan with parchment paper. (If the potatoes won't fit in a single layer without touching, use two pans.)

Pat the potatoes dry and pile them on the prepared pan. In a small bowl, stir together the oil, rosemary, and garlic. Drizzle the oil mixture over the potatoes and toss to coat. Spread the potatoes in a single layer on the pan.

Roast the potatoes, rotating the pan front to back and flipping the wedges halfway through, 20 to 25 minutes, until crispy on the outside and tender on the inside. Sprinkle the fries with the salt and serve immediately.

Pictured on page 274.

W30, EF, NF, V*, SCD  -10

*use olive oil

Burnt Broccoli

SERVES 4

Prep Time: 5 minutes
Cook Time: 25 minutes

The story of my burnt broccoli started with my best friend Hillary's husband, Chris. When I visit Nashville and stay at their house, I start to smell broccoli roasting around ten o'clock on most nights. That's when Chris can be found in the kitchen browning ground turkey meat and roasting broccoli. At first, I was skeptical of his theory that overcooked, crispy broccoli was the way to go, but after tasting it, I can confirm that it is. And now so many others think so, too!

I put my own spin on this dish with a special seasoning and a squeeze of lemon to boost the flavor. And now it has its own hashtag on Instagram (#burntbroccoliisthebestbroccoli). It turns out the seasoning makes every vegetable taste delicious. Even my sister, who hates broccoli, obsesses over this seasoning and now eats broccoli once a week. I keep a quadruple batch of the spice mix on hand so I can quickly boost the flavor of any veggie side dish.

3 heads broccoli, cut into small florets (about 8 cups)

2 tablespoons avocado oil

¾ teaspoon freshly squeezed lemon juice

2½ teaspoons Burnt Broccoli Seasoning (page 31)

1 tablespoon ghee or extra-virgin olive oil

Preheat the oven to 425°F. Line a large sheet pan with parchment paper. (If the broccoli won't fit in a single layer without touching, use two pans.)

Pile the broccoli on the prepared pan, drizzle with the oil and lemon juice, sprinkle with the broccoli seasoning, and toss to coat. Spread the florets in a single layer on the pan.

Drop the ghee onto the center of the sheet pan. Roast the broccoli for 10 minutes. Toss to spread the now-melted ghee throughout. Return the pan to the oven and roast for 15 to 18 minutes more, until the broccoli is browned and crispy. Serve immediately.

11

On the Grill

Every year, I count down the days to grilling season. Thankfully, it happens a lot earlier in California than in many parts of the country. When spring comes around, I cook less and Ryan mans dinner. Well, I marinate, chop, and prep. He cooks.

Plus, grilling requires so much less cleanup, especially when most of the meal is done on the grill—like the recipes in this chapter. Although I usually favor marinating meats and chicken long and slow, I formulated most of these recipes to be quick. They don't have lengthy prep times because I tend to forget I need to prep! Most days, I just want to pull something from my freezer in the morning and defrost it during the day so we can eat something fast and easy for dinner.

Ever since Ryan got a Big Green Egg charcoal grill for Father's Day a decade ago, he has been an avid BBQ guy—and I have zero complaints! In my opinion, a charcoal fire makes every grill recipe taste exponentially better, but using a grill pan on the stove top or a gas-powered grill works just fine, too.

EF, NF

Hawaiian BBQ Chicken with Grilled Bok Choy and Pineapple

SERVES 4 TO 6

Prep Time: 10 minutes, plus 8 hours to marinate

Cook Time: 15 minutes

I was first introduced to huli huli chicken when we lived on the Big Island of Hawaii for a short time. My son Asher, who was a toddler, loved the chicken with its tropical BBQ sauce, and I've been making a version of it ever since. This is one of the dinners my kids ask for again and again. The sweet and tangy sauce is hard to resist, and grilling pineapple brings out the most delicious caramel flavors. You will get the most authentic flavors if you use a charcoal grill here. And might I suggest sticking with the tropical theme and having my Pineapple Whip (page 311) for dessert?

- ½ cup Ketchup (page 22)
- ½ cup unsweetened pineapple juice
- ⅓ cup coconut aminos
- ¼ cup coconut sugar
- 1½ tablespoons balsamic vinegar
- 2 teaspoons peeled and grated fresh ginger
- 3 cloves garlic, grated or pressed
- 4 pounds boneless, skinless chicken thighs
- 2 heads baby bok choy, ends trimmed and halved lengthwise
- 2 teaspoons avocado oil
- Coarse sea salt and freshly ground black pepper
- 1 ripe pineapple, peeled, cored, and cut into rounds
- 2 green onions, white and tender green parts, sliced on the diagonal

In a large bowl, stir together the ketchup, pineapple juice, coconut aminos, sugar, vinegar, ginger, and garlic. Reserve ½ cup of the marinade for basting. Add the chicken to the bowl and stir to coat well. Cover and refrigerate for at least 8 hours or up to 24 hours.

Preheat a grill to medium heat. Lightly oil the grill grate. Using tongs, remove the chicken from the marinade, allowing the excess to drip off, and place on the grate. Discard the marinade. Cover and grill, turning once, for 6 to 8 minutes per side, until a thermometer inserted into the thickest part of a thigh reads 165°F. Brush the chicken with the reserved marinade during the last 5 minutes of cooking. Remove the chicken from the grill and keep warm.

Brush the cut sides of the bok choy with the oil and season with a pinch each of salt and pepper. Place the pineapple and bok choy on the grill rack and grill, uncovered, for 3 to 5 minutes, until the pineapple is golden and the bok choy has wilted slightly.

Transfer the pineapple and bok choy to a platter, top with the chicken, and garnish with the green onions. Serve immediately.

Tidbits: **I use boneless, skinless chicken thighs here because they cook quickly and my kids like them, but bone-in thighs would produce even more flavor. Cook bone-in meat for 20 to 25 minutes, turning the pieces a few times and basting after each turn.**

If you have leftover pineapple fried cauli-rice from my kalua pork (page 222), serve it as a side dish. And if you end up with leftover chicken, dice it for a BBQ chicken salad or stuff it into a roasted sweet potato and drench with Quick BBQ Sauce (page 22) and a drizzle of Herb Ranch Dressing (page 23).

EF, NF 30

Chipotle Cranberry–Sweet Potato Turkey Burgers

SERVES 4 TO 6

Prep Time: 18 minutes
Cook Time: 6 minutes

This is Thanksgiving dinner wrapped up in a burger and grilled so you can enjoy it in the middle of summer or winter. I almost always have a jar of the cranberry sauce from my *Celebrations* cookbook on hand because it keeps for a year if frozen in an airtight container, but I've included a quick homemade version using dried cranberries in this book. It is an especially great recipe to have on hand when fresh cranberries are out of season.

2 pounds ground white-meat turkey

1 small sweet potato, cooked as directed in Pressure Cooker Sweet Potatoes (page 40), then flesh removed from peel and mashed

1 celery stalk

1 small yellow onion

2 sprigs flat-leaf parsley, leaves stripped

6 fresh sage leaves

1 sprig thyme, leaves stripped

1½ teaspoons fine sea salt

½ teaspoon garlic powder

½ teaspoon freshly ground black pepper

½ teaspoon chipotle chile powder

¼ cup Cranberry Sauce (see Tidbits)

6 large Bibb lettuce cups

1 cup loosely packed arugula

¼ cup Garlic Aioli (page 24)

In a large bowl, combine the turkey and sweet potato. In a food processor, combine the celery, onion, parsley, sage, and thyme and process until finely chopped. Add the vegetable mixture, salt, garlic powder, and pepper to the meat mixture and mix just until all of the ingredients are evenly distributed. Be careful not to overmix. Form the mixture into six patties each about 1 inch thick. Do not pack them too tightly.

Preheat a grill or a grill pan on the stove top to medium-high heat. Grill the patties on the hottest part of the grill or grill pan, flipping once halfway through, for 6 to 8 minutes, until the patties are firm and a thermometer inserted into the center of the burger reads 165°F.

While the burgers cook, in a small bowl, stir the chile powder into the cranberry sauce.

To serve, place each burger on a lettuce cup and top with arugula, a large dollop of the spiced cranberry sauce, and a drizzle of garlic aioli.

Tidbits: To make a quick cranberry sauce, simmer 2 cups dried, apple-juice sweetened cranberries with ¼ cup unsweetened cranberry juice, ¼ cup maple syrup, and 2 tablespoon orange juice. Once the berries have rehydrated and absorbed most of the liquid, mash until desired consistency.

Make It Ahead: Mix and shape the patties and store them, tightly wrapped, in the refrigerator for up to 2 days, or double up and store half in the freezer for 6 months for later use. Grill from frozen and add 2 minutes per side.

omit honey | 30 | W30, EF, NF, SCD

California Chicken Sandwiches with Arugula Pear Salad

SERVES 4 TO 6

Prep Time: 20 minutes
Cook Time: 10 minutes

These grilled chicken sandwiches make for a nice summer dinner. And while I've filled them with some of my favorite California-grown produce, they can be enjoyed anywhere and everywhere! I love the smoky flavor that comes from grilling the chicken, but you can also sear it in a cast-iron skillet on the stove top if you want to make these sandwiches during the winter or don't have a grill.

- 6 boneless, skinless chicken breasts (about 2½ pounds)
- Coarse sea salt and freshly ground black pepper
- 6 cups loosely packed arugula
- 2 ripe pears, cored and sliced
- ¼ cup walnut pieces
- 1 teaspoon Dijon mustard
- 2 teaspoons honey
- Finely grated zest and juice of 1 lemon
- ½ cup extra-virgin olive oil
- 12 large leaves green leaf lettuce or other sturdy green
- 6 slices Baked Bacon (page 44)
- 2 ripe tomatoes, cored and sliced
- ½ cup guacamole
- ¼ cup pickle slices
- ¼ cup Herb Ranch Dressing (page 23)

Preheat a grill or a grill pan on the stove top to medium heat. If the chicken breasts are thick, place them between two pieces of parchment paper and flatten them evenly with a rolling pin or heavy pan. Season the chicken generously on both sides with salt and pepper. Grill, turning once halfway through, for 10 to 12 minutes, until a thermometer inserted into the thickest part of a breast reads 165°F.

Meanwhile, in a large bowl, toss together the arugula, pears, and walnuts. In a small bowl, whisk together the mustard, honey, and lemon zest and juice. Slowly whisk in the oil, then season to taste with salt and pepper. Drizzle 3 tablespoons of the dressing on the salad and toss to coat.

To build each sandwich, top a lettuce leaf with a chicken breast, a bacon slice, a couple of tomato slices, a dollop of guacamole, some pickle slices, and a drizzle of ranch dressing. Lay a second piece of lettuce on top and wrap both leaves around the sides and to the bottom to create a lettuce wrap. Serve with the salad and the remaining dressing on the side.

Make It Ahead: This is one of those meals I love to "component prep" like I talked about on page 68. I double up the bacon and chicken and the extra goes into the fridge in separate containers so I can easily put together a quick lunch the next day.

For the guacamole, nestle the avocado pit into the guacamole and use a spoon to flatten the surface and remove any air pockets. Gently pour a thin layer of lime juice so that it covers the guacamole surface completely. Press a piece of plastic wrap directly on the surface of the guacamole, then secure the lid to the container. Refrigerate for up to 2 days.

W30*, EF*, NF, SCD*

*use lettuce cups for W30, EF, and SCD

Curry Chicken Burgers with Mango Chutney and Cucumber Raita

SERVES 4 TO 6

Prep Time: 15 minutes, plus 30 minutes to marinate

Cook Time: 8 minutes

Whenever we order Indian food, I drench most of what I'm eating in cooling cucumber raita to beat the heat. Raita is kind of like the Indian version of Greek tzatziki, so it's no wonder I love it.

These curry-flavored burgers come together easily and get most of their amazing flavor from the toppings. This prep time assumes you have these sauces made up in advance or that store-bought versions are being used, in order to make this recipe come together more quickly. And here's a little tip for making the patties: Wear gloves unless you don't mind having yellow fingernails for a few days from the turmeric-rich curry powder. I love to wrap these in the grain-free naan from my *Eat What You Love* cookbook, but often serve Ryan and the kids on gluten-free store-bought buns.

2-inch piece fresh ginger, peeled

1 large shallot, halved

3 cloves garlic

2 pounds ground dark-meat chicken

Juice of 1 lemon

1½ teaspoons garam masala

1¼ teaspoons mild curry powder

1 teaspoon ground cumin

1½ teaspoons fine sea salt

¼ teaspoon freshly ground black pepper

Grain-free naan or hamburger buns, warmed, or lettuce cups, for serving

Mango Chutney (page 24), for serving

Cucumber Raita (page 25), for serving

2 cups loosely packed arugula

½ cup loosely packed cilantro leaves and tender stems

In a food processor, combine the ginger, shallot, and garlic and process until finely chopped. Remove the processor blade, add the chicken, lemon juice, garam masala, curry powder, cumin, salt, and pepper, and mix gently by hand until all of the ingredients are evenly distributed. Do not overmix. Form the mixture into six patties each about 1 inch thick. Do not pack them too tightly. Cover and refrigerate to marinate for at least 30 minutes or up to 24 hours.

Preheat a grill or a grill pan on the stove top to medium-high heat. Lightly oil the grate or the pan. Grill the patties, flipping once halfway through, for about 8 minutes, until a thermometer inserted into the center of a burger reads 165°F.

Wrap the burgers in the naan, top with the chutney, raita, arugula, and cilantro, and serve immediately.

Tidbits: **There are a few components to these flavorful burgers, so use some store-bought toppings to speed up the process or make the sauce and buns a week in advance on a prep day!**

*omit coconut sugar and use lettuce cups for W30 and SCD, use vegan mayo for EF

W30*, EF*, NF, SCD*

Skirt Steak Tacos with Sriracha Aioli

SERVES 4 TO 6

Prep Time: 12 minutes, plus 1 hour to marinate

Cook Time: 4 minutes

I'm so fortunate to have a lot of amazing and authentic choices for Mexican food here in California. When Ryan and I go out to dinner, we often order street tacos in a handful of different flavors, such as carne asada, al pastor, and carnitas. These spicy skirt steak tacos are my fresh spin on the grilled carne asada tacos Ryan likes to order when we're out. I keep the steak mild so the kids and I can enjoy it with all of the toppings, while Ryan spices his up with a hefty drizzle of the aioli and some jalapeño slices on top for good measure!

2 pounds skirt or flank steak

1 tablespoon avocado oil

1 tablespoon apple cider vinegar

1 tablespoon coconut sugar

1 teaspoon garlic powder

¼ teaspoon red pepper flakes

1 teaspoon fine sea salt

½ teaspoon freshly ground black pepper

2 cups shredded red cabbage

½ cup loosely packed cilantro leaves and tender stems

Mexican-Style Pickled Vegetables (page 44)

2 avocados, halved, pitted, peeled, and sliced

10 grain-free tortillas, warmed, or lettuce cups

Sriracha Aioli

½ cup mayonnaise

2 tablespoons Sriracha sauce

4 teaspoons freshly squeezed lime juice

1 teaspoon fine sea salt

1 teaspoon garlic powder

¾ teaspoon cayenne pepper

½ teaspoon red pepper flakes

Cut the steak against the grain and on the diagonal into three uniform chunks. Place the pieces in a bowl, add the oil, vinegar, sugar, garlic powder, and pepper flakes, and toss to coat. Cover and refrigerate to marinate for at least 1 hour or preferably overnight.

To make the aioli, in a small bowl, stir together the mayonnaise, Sriracha, lime juice, salt, garlic powder, cayenne, and pepper flakes. Cover and refrigerate until ready to serve or for up to 1 month.

Preheat a grill or a grill pan on the stove top to medium-high heat. Remove the steaks from the marinade, shaking off any excess liquid. Discard the marinade. Season the steaks with 1 teaspoon of the salt and the pepper.

Grill the steak, flipping the pieces once, for 2 minutes per side for medium-rare or 3 minutes per side for medium. (A thermometer inserted into the center of the steak should read 140°F for medium-rare and 155°F for medium.) Transfer the meat to a cutting board, tent with aluminum foil, and let rest for 5 minutes.

Slice the meat against the grain into thin strips and transfer to a dish. To serve, set out the steak along with the cabbage, cilantro, pickled vegetables, avocados, aioli, and tortillas. Invite diners to build their own tacos.

Make It Ahead: **Double the meat and marinade, and place one full portion in a freezer-safe bag in the freezer for later use. Store for 6 months, then defrost overnight in the fridge. Bring to room temperature before grilling.**

Steak with Roasted Red Pepper Sauce and Lemon-Charred Beans and Tomatoes

SERVES 6 TO 8

Prep Time: 15 minutes
Cook Time: 8 minutes

This simple grilled salt-and-pepper steak with a flavor-packed sauce is the perfect dinner for the planning impaired. Choosing a high-quality salt, like my favorite fleur de sel, is imperative for getting amazing flavor when you're keeping things so simple. You will want to slurp the roasted red pepper sauce straight from the blender before spooning it over the steak, but don't worry, this makes enough for leftovers.

3 (1-pound) flat-iron steaks

1 tablespoon plus ½ teaspoon coarse sea salt

2 teaspoons freshly ground black pepper

4 tablespoons extra-virgin olive oil or avocado oil

2 cups assorted cherry tomatoes

1 pound green beans or wax beans, trimmed

3 cloves garlic, thinly sliced

Finely grated zest and juice of 1 lemon

Red Pepper Sauce

1 (16-ounce) jar roasted red peppers in oil, drained

3 tablespoons tomato paste

¼ cup extra-virgin olive oil

½ cup toasted natural almonds (about 3 ounces)

3 cloves garlic

3 tablespoons fresh flat-leaf parsley leaves

1 teaspoon balsamic vinegar

1½ teaspoons fine sea salt

¼ teaspoon freshly ground black pepper

½ teaspoon crushed red pepper flakes

2 tablespoons chopped fresh flat-leaf parsley

Preheat a grill or a large cast-iron skillet on the stove top to high heat. If the steaks are thick, place them between pieces of parchment paper and, using a meat mallet or heavy skillet, pound the steaks to ½-inch thickness. Sprinkle the steaks on both sides with 1 tablespoon of the coarse salt and 1 teaspoon of the pepper, then drizzle on both sides with 2 tablespoons of the oil.

Grill the steaks, flipping them once, for 1 to 2 minutes per side for medium-rare or 3 to 4 minutes per side for medium (a thermometer inserted into the center of the steak should read 140°F for medium-rare and 155°F for medium). Transfer the steaks to a cutting board, tent with aluminum foil, and let rest for 10 minutes.

Meanwhile, in a large bowl, toss the tomatoes and beans with the remaining 2 tablespoons oil and ½ teaspoon salt, the garlic, and the lemon zest and juice to coat. If using a grill, transfer the beans to a grilling basket and place on the grate; if using a skillet, transfer the beans directly to the skillet. Grill or sauté, tossing occasionally, for 6 to 8 minutes, until the beans have char marks and the tomatoes begin to burst.

Meanwhile, make the sauce. In a blender or food processor, combine the red peppers, tomato paste, oil, almonds, garlic, parsley, vinegar, fine salt, black pepper, and pepper flakes and process until thick and creamy.

Thinly slice the steaks against the grain. Spoon the sauce over the steaks on the cutting board and arrange the green beans and tomatoes around the sides. Garnish everything with the parsley and serve immediately.

Tidbits: **These steaks reheat nicely to use in recipes such as my Steak Lettuce Wraps with Horseradish Cream Sauce (page 76), Asian-Style Chicken Slaw (page 75), Chilled Sesame Beef, Mango, and "Noodle" Salad (page 80), Thai-Style Shrimp Salad (page 87), or in a steak-and-eggs breakfast.**

Make It Ahead: **Make the red pepper sauce up to 5 days in advance and store in the fridge. Bring it to room temperature before serving. Toss the vegetables with the oil and seasonings, cover, and store in the fridge for up to 2 days.**

Spiced Beef and Lamb Kebabs with Tomato-Cucumber Salad

SERVES 4 TO 6

Prep Time: 20 minutes
Cook Time: 8 minutes

This is my spin on kofta, the Middle Eastern kebabs. The ground onion makes the meat incredibly tender, and the spices and herbs create bold flavors. Pressing and shaping the meat gently on skewers keeps it super delicate and delicious—and is really fun for kids—but forming the meat into patties and grilling them would also work. I serve this with a tahini-based sauce, but if you happen to have any tzatziki or hummus on hand, serve them on the side.

1 yellow onion, quartered

2 cloves garlic

Leaves from 1 small bunch flat-leaf parsley (about 1 cup firmly packed)

1 pound ground beef

12 ounces ground lamb

1 tablespoon avocado oil

1 teaspoon fine sea salt

¼ teaspoon freshly ground black pepper

2 teaspoons Tagine Seasoning (page 34)

1 teaspoon finely grated lemon zest

Salad

1 English cucumber

1 pint cherry tomatoes

¼ cup cilantro leaves and tender stems

½ red onion

2 tablespoons extra-virgin olive oil

Juice of 1 lemon

½ teaspoon fine sea salt

¼ teaspoon freshly ground black pepper

2 tablespoons Mediterranean Tahini Dressing (page 29), optional

Soak twelve bamboo skewers in cold water for 1 hour (or use metal skewers). Line a large sheet pan with parchment paper.

In a food processor, combine the yellow onion, garlic, and parsley and process until a paste forms. Transfer the mixture to a large bowl, add the beef, lamb, avocado oil, salt, pepper, tagine seasoning, and lemon zest, and mix gently with your hands until all of the ingredients are evenly distributed. Do not overmix.

Preheat a grill or a grill pan on the stove top to medium-high heat. Divide the meat mixture into twelve loose balls of equal size. Dampen your hands with water for easier handling and gently shape each ball into an oblong around a skewer. As each skewer is ready, lay it on the prepared sheet pan.

Grill the skewers, turning them once halfway through, for 8 to 10 minutes, until a thermometer inserted into the thickest part of the meat reads 140°F for medium.

While the meat cooks, make the salad. Dice the cucumber, halve the tomatoes, coarsely chop the cilantro, and thinly slice the onion. Transfer them all to a salad bowl, add the olive oil, lemon juice, salt, and pepper, and toss to coat.

Drizzle the warm kebabs with the tahini dressing and serve the salad alongside.

Make it Ahead: **Make and form the kebabs 2 days in advance. Store tightly wrapped in the refrigerator and bring to room temperature for 1 hour prior to grilling.**

W30*, EF, NF, SCD  *omit vinaigrette

BBQ Bacon Burger Bowls with Honey-Mustard Vinaigrette

SERVES 6 TO 8

Prep Time: 15 minutes
Cook Time: 12 minutes

Burger bowls are my jam. I love a good lettuce-wrap sandwich (all hail the #aagwich), but burgers can be messy and end up spritzing juice down your hands and forearms. So loading all of the toppings I would have sandwiched between a bun into a bowl just seems like a smart move. I've been loving ground bison lately for its rich flavor and sustainability, but any ground meat would work here. I dust these bison burgers in my BBQ Rub and then brush them with my Quick BBQ Sauce toward the end of grilling. But the real star here is a tangy and sweet honey-mustard vinaigrette.

3 pounds ground bison or beef
¼ cup grated red onion
3 tablespoons extra-virgin olive oil
½ teaspoon fine sea salt
¼ teaspoon freshly ground black pepper
1½ tablespoons BBQ Rub (page 32)
⅓ cup Quick BBQ Sauce (page 22)

Vinaigrette

¼ cup Dijon mustard
¼ cup honey
1½ teaspoons apple cider vinegar
¼ cup avocado oil
Fine sea salt and freshly ground black pepper

For Serving

10 cups chopped romaine lettuce
1 cup halved cherry tomatoes
¼ cup dill pickle slices
8 slices Baked Bacon (page 44), chopped
3 avocados, halved, pitted, peeled, and sliced

Preheat the grill to medium-high heat for indirect-heat cooking.

In a large bowl, combine the bison, onion, olive oil, salt, and pepper and mix gently with your hands until all of the ingredients are evenly distributed. Do not overmix. Shape the mixture into eight 3-inch patties. Do not pack them too tightly. Sprinkle the rub on both sides of each patty.

Sear the patties over direct heat for 1 minute on each side, then move the patties to indirect heat as far from the coals or gas jets as possible and cook for 5 minutes more per side, until a meat thermometer inserted into the center of a burger reads 160°F for medium. During the final few minutes, brush the top of each burger with the BBQ sauce. Transfer the burgers to a cutting board and tent with aluminum foil to keep warm.

To make the vinaigrette, in a small bowl, whisk together the mustard, honey, vinegar, avocado oil, and a pinch each of salt and pepper.

To serve, set out the burgers, lettuce, tomatoes, pickles, bacon, avocados, and vinaigrette buffet-style so diners can build their bowls how they like. I do the works with a tablespoon or so of the vinaigrette.

Tidbits: For burgers, especially when using bison or grass-fed ground beef, which tends to be leaner, I prefer to give them a good sear to lock in the flavor and fat and then move them away from the heat source to cook slowly afterward. I find that they stay juicier this way and don't tend to char.

Make it Ahead: Double the burger patty ingredients and freeze uncooked patties for later use. Defrost overnight in the refrigerator then grill as directed. The vinaigrette will keep in the fridge for 1 month.

Grilled Shrimp and Asparagus with Cilantro-Kale Pepita Pesto

SERVES 4 TO 6

Prep Time: 10 minutes
Cook Time: 8 minutes

My vibrant and zesty Cilantro-Kale Pepita Pesto is what really shines in this simple dish of grilled shrimp and asparagus. I try always to have a container of the pesto on hand. Every time you scoop some out, add ¼ inch of fresh olive oil to the top of the jar before capping it again and returning it to the fridge. Sealing the pesto under a layer of oil this way will keep it from turning brown for up to 3 weeks in the fridge. My dairy-free version of traditional basil pesto (page 28) also pairs well with the shrimp and asparagus.

- 1½ pounds large shrimp, peeled and deveined with tails on
- 2 tablespoons avocado oil
- ¼ teaspoon cayenne pepper
- ¼ teaspoon ground cumin
- ¾ teaspoon fine sea salt
- ½ teaspoon freshly ground black pepper
- 2 bunches asparagus (about 2 pounds), ends trimmed
- 2 teaspoons freshly squeezed lime juice
- 1 small shallot, minced
- 2 tablespoons toasted pepitas
- 2 tablespoons fresh cilantro leaves
- ¼ cup Cilantro-Kale Pepita Pesto (page 28)

Preheat a grill or a grill pan on the stove top to medium-high heat.

In a medium bowl, toss the shrimp with 1 tablespoon of the oil, the cayenne, cumin, ½ teaspoon of the salt, and ¼ teaspoon of the pepper to coat. In a large bowl, toss the asparagus with the remaining 1 tablespoon oil, the lime juice, and the remaining ¼ teaspoon each salt and pepper.

Add the asparagus to the grill and cook for 5 minutes. Add the shrimp to the grill and turn the asparagus. Cook the shrimp and the asparagus, flipping the shrimp halfway through, for 3 to 5 minutes, until the asparagus is crisp-tender and the shrimp turn pink and curl slightly. If using a grill pan on the stove top, grill the shrimp and asparagus in batches, tenting the finished batches with aluminum foil to keep them warm until everything is cooked.

Transfer the asparagus and shrimp to a platter and top them both with the shallot, pepitas, and cilantro. Serve immediately with the pesto on the side.

Make It Ahead: **Toss the shrimp with its marinade and store in the fridge for 24 hours. Prepare the asparagus with its marinade and store in the fridge for up to 3 days.**

12

Time-Saving Treats

Unless we're celebrating a special occasion, I try to reserve desserts—even paleo ones!—for the weekend, but my meals aren't complete without a little sweet at the end. Although I love to bake with the kids and could easily spend a few very content hours making something unique, sometimes I just want to fulfill my cravings in a few minutes' time.

The treats in this chapter are delicious and decadently guest worthy, but also easy enough to make on a Friday night you plan to spend in sweats with your hair in a topknot. Or for when you just *have* to have something on a weeknight. I suggest the Salted Chocolate Cuties or the Banana-Chocolate Mug Cake because they're both single serve and super quick. Ryan highly suggests the Pineapple Whip. In fact, he doesn't follow my weekend rule and asks me to make that for him at least three nights a week!

Banana-Chocolate Mug Cake

SERVES 1 OR 2

Prep Time: 6 minutes
Cook Time: 1½ minutes

When the craving for dessert strikes, but you don't want an entire cake or batch of cupcakes lying around, this single-serving (or double, depending on whether you want to share!) mug cake is the answer. It tastes like a cross between banana pancakes and a gooey chocolate banana bread and can be made in five minutes flat. When I tested this recipe, I tried to offer my son Easton just one bite, and he ended up sitting down with the rest of the mug, not allowing anyone else to try it!

- ¼ cup mashed ripe banana, plus 2 banana slices, for garnish
- 1 egg
- 2 teaspoons avocado oil if needed (see Note)
- 2 tablespoons pure maple syrup
- 1½ tablespoons unsweetened almond butter
- ½ teaspoon pure vanilla extract
- 1½ tablespoons coconut flour
- 1 tablespoon arrowroot powder
- ½ teaspoon grain-free baking powder
- ⅛ teaspoon fine sea salt
- 2 tablespoons mini chocolate chips or blueberries

This mug cake can be cooked in a microwave or in a conventional oven. If using the latter, preheat the oven to 350°F.

In a large, microwave-safe or oven-safe mug, combine the mashed banana with the egg, oil, maple syrup, and almond butter and mash with a fork until smooth. Still using the fork, whisk in the vanilla, flour, arrowroot, baking powder, and salt until smooth. Stir in the chocolate chips. If the batter reaches higher than halfway up the sides of the mug, divide the batter between two mugs. Gently place the banana slices on top of the batter.

Microwave on high power for 1½ minutes or bake in the oven for 12 to 14 minutes. The cake is ready when it is puffed, feels set to the touch, and spongy. If using the microwave and the cake is not fully cooked, microwave for 30 seconds more.

Let the cake cool for 5 minutes, then grab a spoon!

Note: **If your almond butter is oily, omit the avocado oil.**

Make It Ahead: **Make the cake as directed, let cool completely, cover, and store in the fridge for up to 7 days. Reheat, uncovered, in an oven set to 300°F for 10 minutes or the microwave for 20 seconds.**

EF, NF, V  

Salted Chocolate Cuties

SERVES 5

Prep Time: 10 minutes

Cook Time: 1 minute, plus 15 minutes for cooling

When I want to make something quick and simple for the kids after dinner, these little chocolate-dipped mandarins are my go-to. I make one mandarin per person, which keeps my kids from begging for thirds and fourths because when they're gone, they're gone! The kids sit at the counter and peel and segment the mandarins while I melt the chocolate. Although I don't normally use a microwave, in this case it's the quickest and least messy way to get this done. Of course, a double boiler will work as well. Dried apples, whole fresh strawberries, or pieces of pineapple are also delicious dipped in chocolate.

- ½ cup chopped dark chocolate
- 1½ teaspoons coconut oil
- 5 clementines or other small mandarin oranges, peeled and segmented
- Flaky sea salt or kosher salt

Line a large sheet pan with parchment paper.

In a relatively small, deep microwave-safe bowl, combine the chocolate and oil. Microwave on 50% power in 30-second intervals, stirring after each interval, until the chocolate is mostly melted with just a few chunks remaining. Remove from the microwave and continue to stir the chocolate until completely melted and smooth. Alternatively, melt the chocolate in a double boiler on the stove top.

Dip each mandarin segment into the melted chocolate, leaving about one-fourth of the segment uncoated, and place on the prepared sheet pan. Sprinkle the chocolate coating lightly with salt. Refrigerate the segments for about 15 minutes, until the chocolate has set, before serving.

Tidbits: **I love to use Hu Kitchen gems or Guittard's "Sante" baking chips that are made with coconut sugar.**

Make It Ahead: **Double or triple this recipe and store in an airtight container in the fridge for up to 3 days. The segments start to shrivel after that.**

Pineapple Whip

SERVES 4 TO 6

Prep Time: 5 minutes
Total Time: 8 minutes

I'm turning this one over to Ryan because he has a lot of enthusiasm for this whipped dessert:

"Hi there, Ryan here. I call this recipe 'heaven in a bowl.' I know that sounds like a tall order, but it seriously delivers. I could have had a terrible day—late for school drop-off, kids yelling at one another, botched meeting at work, no time to work out—but if Danielle has made this for me, my troubles melt away. Each bite brings a fresh smile, a new perspective, and literal happiness. The future looks bright after eating this dessert. She will probably tell you that I forced her to make it nearly every night during the second half of our statewide safer-at-home order, but I'm proud to report that I learned how to make it myself and have added it to my list of five recipes I can make."

- 1 banana, peeled, sliced, and frozen
- 3 cups frozen pineapple chunks (about 1½ pounds)
- ½ cup full-fat coconut cream
- ¼ cup unsweetened pineapple juice
- 2 to 3 teaspoons freshly squeezed lemon juice
- ¼ teaspoon pure vanilla extract

In a food processor, combine the banana, 1½ cups of the pineapple, the coconut cream, pineapple juice, 2 teaspoons of the lemon juice, and the vanilla and process for about 5 minutes, until mostly smooth. Add the remaining 1½ cups pineapple and continue to process for 2 to 3 minutes more, until the mixture is very smooth and creamy. If large chunks of pineapple persist, pulse eight to ten times until they break up. Taste and add the remaining 1 teaspoon lemon juice if a tarter soft serve is desired. Serve immediately.

Make It Ahead: **Eating this fresh will give you the best, creamiest texture, but you can store it in an airtight container in the freezer for up to 3 months. Before enjoying it, let it melt a bit on the counter, say 15 to 20 minutes, and then use an immersion blender or handheld electric mixer to smooth it out and make it less icy.**

I suggest keeping frozen bananas in your freezer at all times. When they start to go brown on your counter, just peel, slice, and freeze!

NF, V -10

Lemon Meringue Pie Pudding

SERVES 4

Prep Time: 5 minutes, plus 4 to 6 hours to chill

Cook Time: 5 minutes

These luscious lemon pudding jars are simple to make but taste rich and fancy. They're a cross between lemon curd and lemon meringue pie filling. Crumble my grain-free graham crackers on top (find the recipe on daniellewalker.com) or simply top with fresh berries and/or toasted coconut. You can also spoon the pudding on top of a stack of pancakes or sandwich it between cookies—it's delicious no matter how you serve it.

I use a can of coconut cream for this recipe because the cream can be used straight from the can without refrigerating first. But if you plan ahead, you can refrigerate 2 cans of full-fat coconut milk for 24 hours and then scoop off the thick cream from the top.

½ cup raw honey

Finely grated zest of 1 lemon

½ cup freshly squeezed lemon juice

5 egg yolks

¾ cup full-fat coconut cream

1 tablespoon arrowroot powder

Pinch of fine sea salt

1½ tablespoons ghee or coconut oil

Crumbled grain-free graham crackers, fresh berries, and/or toasted unsweetened coconut flakes, for topping

In a saucepan, whisk together the honey, lemon zest and juice, egg yolks, coconut cream, and arrowroot. Set the pan over medium-low heat and cook, whisking constantly, for 5 to 7 minutes, until the mixture has thickened and coats the back of a spoon. Stir in the ghee.

Divide the pudding evenly among four (6-ounce) widemouthed jars and let them cool on the counter for 15 minutes, until they are no longer steaming. Once cooled, cover and refrigerate for 4 to 6 hours, until set.

Serve the puddings chilled with one or more toppings of your choice.

Tidbits: **If you tolerate grains, Pamela's gluten-free graham crackers would work in place of my homemade version.**

Make It Ahead: **Make the pudding up to 5 days in advance and store in the fridge.**

30 V

Chocolate Coffee Mac Nut Cookie Pie

SERVES 4 TO 6

Prep Time: 10 minutes
Cook Time: 20 minutes

When my parents used to vacation in Hawaii, they always brought back chocolate-covered macadamia nuts for us kids. I have loved the combination ever since. This skillet-baked cookie pie is gooey and chewy and utterly delicious, and it combines those nutty chocolate flavors with just a hint of coffee. My favorite dark chocolate chips are Hu Kitchen brand's dark chocolate gems. The two scoops of dairy-free ice cream on top of this cookie pie are optional but highly recommended. May I suggest coffee or vanilla? You will thank me.

- 3 tablespoons avocado oil or melted ghee
- 1 egg
- 3 tablespoons honey
- ½ cup coconut sugar
- 2 teaspoons finely ground espresso beans or dark-roast coffee beans
- 1 teaspoon pure vanilla extract
- 1 cup blanched almond flour
- ¼ cup arrowroot powder
- 3 tablespoons coconut flour
- ¾ teaspoon grain-free baking powder
- ¼ teaspoon baking soda
- ¼ teaspoon fine sea salt
- ½ cup dark chocolate chips
- ¼ cup chopped salted dry-roasted macadamia nuts
- Dairy-free coffee or vanilla ice cream, for serving (optional)

Preheat the oven to 325°F. Lightly grease an oven-safe 10-inch skillet with ghee.

In a bowl, using a whisk or a handheld electric mixer on medium speed, beat together the oil, egg, honey, sugar, coffee, and vanilla for 1 minute, until smooth and air bubbles have formed on the surface. Add the almond flour, arrowroot, coconut flour, baking powder, baking soda, and salt and mix until well combined.

Transfer the batter to the prepared skillet, spreading it in an even layer. Sprinkle the chocolate and macadamia nuts evenly over the top. Bake for 20 to 22 minutes, until the edges of the cookie are golden brown.

Serve the cookie warm with the ice cream on top and a spoon for everyone.

Tidbits: **Making this for kids? Leave out the coffee and macadamia nuts to turn this into a classic chocolate chip skillet cookie.**

If you measure the honey after measuring the oil, the honey will slip right out of the measuring spoon!

Roasted Peach Crisp Cups

SERVES 4

Prep Time: 15 minutes
Cook Time: 15 minutes

This is like a peach crisp but without all the work of peeling and slicing the peaches. The juices and sugars caramelize while the peaches roast, leaving a delightful sauce at the bottom of the skillet that you spoon over the top before serving.

- ⅓ cup cashew flour or blanched almond flour
- 2 tablespoons coconut flour
- 1½ tablespoons arrowroot powder
- 3 tablespoons maple sugar
- 2 tablespoons coconut sugar
- ⅛ teaspoon fine sea salt
- ¼ cup chilled ghee or coconut oil, plus 1 tablespoon melted ghee or coconut oil
- ¼ cup unsweetened shredded coconut
- 4 peaches
- 2 lemon wedges
- 4 scoops dairy-free vanilla ice cream (optional)

To make the crisp topping, in a bowl, stir together the cashew and coconut flours, arrowroot, 2 tablespoons of the maple sugar, the coconut sugar, and salt. Add the chilled ghee in tablespoon increments, and, using a pastry blender or two knives, cut in the ghee until the flour mixture is the texture of coarse sand. Add the shredded coconut and use your hands to toss and squeeze the mixture until large, moist clumps form. Cover the bowl and place in the freezer to chill while you prepare the peaches.

Preheat the oven to 400°F. Halve and pit the peaches. Rub the cut sides of the peaches with the lemon wedges, then place the peach halves, cut side up, in a cast-iron skillet just large enough to hold them snugly in a single layer. Top each peach half with 1 to 2 tablespoons of the crisp topping. Drizzle the tops of the peaches with the melted ghee and then sprinkle the remaining 1 tablespoon maple sugar evenly over the tops.

Bake the crisps for 15 to 17 minutes, until bubbly and browned on top. Transfer two crisps to each individual bowl and serve warm, topped with a scoop of ice cream.

Tidbits: **Did you know that if you cut in the opposite direction of the seam on a ripe peach, it will halve and reveal the pit more easily? Try it!**

Strawberry-Balsamic Granita

SERVES 4 TO 6

Prep Time: 10 minutes
Total Time: 4 hours

Italian granita is like a cross between shaved ice and sorbet. It's refreshing and easy to make, but you do have to babysit the freezer for a couple of hours to scrape the fragments loose. Otherwise, it'll freeze into a big solid block of fruit juice.

- 2 pounds strawberries, hulled and halved
- ¼ cup maple sugar
- ¼ cup honey
- 1 cup water
- 2 teaspoons freshly squeezed lemon juice
- Pinch of fine sea salt
- Fresh assorted berries and balsamic vinegar, for serving

In a food processor, combine the strawberries, sugar, honey, water, lemon juice, and salt and process for 45 to 60 seconds, until smooth. Pour the mixture into an 8 by 8-inch glass or ceramic baking dish.

Place the dish, uncovered, in the freezer for about 45 minutes, until the mixture barely begins to freeze around the edges. Using a fork, scrape the icy portions into the middle of the dish and stir to incorporate the icy with the still-liquid mixture. Return the dish to the freezer and repeat this step once every hour for 3 to 4 hours, until the granita is light and looks dry and fluffy.

Scrape the granita into individual bowls and serve topped with the berries and a small drizzle of the vinegar.

Make It Ahead: **Store the finished granita in the freezer, covered, for up to 6 months. To serve, let it sit at room temperature for 20 minutes, then fluff it gently with a fork.**

Acknowledgments

This book is dedicated to my readers. During the pandemic, you posted about my recipes more than ever. We were at home all day long, and many of us were trying to work, run our households, be teachers, and manage kids. While initially I saw *a lot* of Banana Bread posts, I took note of what you were cooking consistently: easy meals. Your feedback on my recipes and what you loved during those busy times provided inspiration for the recipes in this book. Thank you for your constant support, buying my cookbooks, gifting them to your friends and family, and visiting my blog. And thank you for always communicating what recipe needs you have or dishes you miss so that I can get into the kitchen and attempt to give you what you hope for! What kind of cookbook do you want to see next?!

Thank you to my crew. My three kids, Asher, Easton, and Kezia—who, at the time of creating these recipes, were ten, five, and three years old—graciously helped me taste everything "to see if other kids would like it." And thank you for being such troopers while posing for photos. These books have become like little albums that we can look back on year to year to see how you, and our family, have grown. To Ryan for helping me brainstorm the idea of this book and the ways that we could support our community, and for handling the techy stuff, like QR codes. Also, Ry, thanks for doing so many dishes while I tested!

A special thank-you to Ryan's parents for testing a few of the recipes when I was short on time, and for coming over for testing buffets while we were in our little family bubble.

To my recipe testers, my books are as foolproof as they are due to those of you who have volunteered. Thank you for so graciously taking these recipes into your own kitchen and providing such valuable feedback! Your efforts give me confidence to put this book out into the world and know that both novice and experienced cooks will be able to re-create and enjoy the recipes.

To my photography Dream Team: Aubrie Pick, Lillian Kang, Glenn Jenkins, and your incredible assistants—I'm thrilled to have the privilege and joy of working with you on these books. I appreciate you allowing me to be so hands-on; you make my recipes come to life on the page.

To Kari Stuart, the best decision I ever made in the book department was choosing to work with you—period. Let's keep creating fun projects together, forever!

To Julie Bennett, Emma Campion, and the entire publishing, design, marketing, and publicity teams at Ten Speed Press. Thank you for always coming along with my vision, and for creating these gorgeous books that are seamless and enjoyable to cook from and beautiful to look at.

To Kelli. I'm launching this book with you in spirit and wishing we were celebrating it together. I'm thankful for everything that I learned from working with you, and for your friendship.

And finally, to my DW team: Nancy, Christina, all our trusted contractors, and my part-time unpaid employee/mother-in-law, Barb, for your behind-the-scenes support on a daily basis in all areas of my business. Your dedication to the work allows me to focus on being creative in the kitchen. Each of you is incredible and I'm so thankful to have you in my corner!

Recipe Index

BREAKFAST

NO-COOK LUNCHES

FREEZE IT

Salsa Chicken Tacos 98
Total time: 17 minutes

Chicken Tortilla Soup 94
Total time: 23 minutes

Turkey Chili Verde 97
Total time: 23 minutes

Chicken and Apricot Stew 93
Total time: 24 minutes

Baked Pepperoni Pizza Spaghetti with Ranch 106
Total time: 57 minutes

Pork Ragu over Creamy Polenta 102
Total time: 60 minutes

PASTA

Chicken Pad Thai Noodles 116
Total time: 17 minutes

Moo Shu Pork Pasta 124
Total time: 17 minutes

One-Pot Beef Pasta with Creamy Tomato-Vodka Sauce 121
Total time: 20 minutes

Roasted Tomato and Pesto Penne 133
Total time: 20 minutes

Cajun Chicken Pasta 115
Total time: 27 minutes

Curry Noodles with Shrimp 126
Total time: 27 minutes

Mac and Cheese 137
Total time: 30 minutes

Smoky Shrimp and Mussels with Crunchy Noodles 129
Total time: 32 minutes

Shrimp Scampi 130
Total time: 35 minutes

Sweet Chili Noodle Stir-Fry 134
Total time: 35 minutes

Creamy Roasted Garlic, Chicken Sausage, and Arugula Pasta 119
Total time: 37 minutes

SHEET PANS

Sweet-and-Sour Pork 152
Total time: 23 minutes

Cajun Shrimp and Andouille Sausage 151
Total time: 26 minutes

Coconut-Crusted Shrimp with Broiled Pineapple-Mint Salad 159
Total time: 27 minutes

Ancho-Citrus Shrimp Tacos with Roasted Pineapple Salsa 160
Total time: 28 minutes

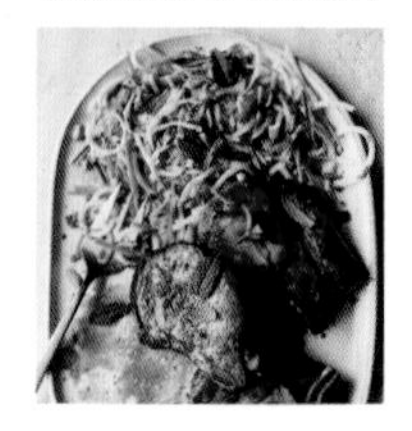

Lemongrass-Ginger Pork Chops with Crunchy Jicama and Mint Salad 155
Total time: 30 minutes

Mediterranean Salmon with Artichokes and Peppers 163
Total time: 30 minutes

Herb-Crusted Black Cod with Harissa Cauliflower 164
Total time: 30 minutes

Mediterranean Meatball Bowl with Spicy Ranch 147
Total time: 33 minutes

Peruvian Steak and French Fries 156
Total time: 33 minutes

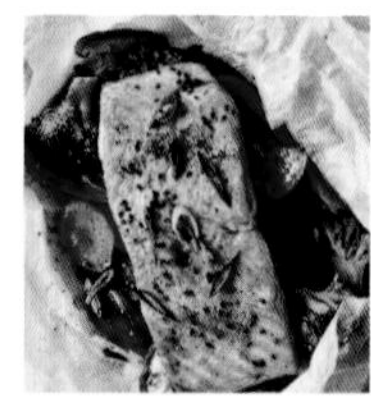

Teriyaki Salmon Packets 167
Total time: 33 minutes

Jerk Chicken Wings and Burnt Broccoli 143
Total time: 34 minutes

Chicken, Bacon, and Ranch Squash Noodles 148
Total time: 37 minutes

Chicken Bruschetta with Tomato Salsa 144
Total time: 48 minutes

STIR-FRIES AND SKILLETS

Cast-Iron Rib-Eye Steaks with Garlic Mushrooms 182
Total time: 15 minutes

Creamy Polenta with Woody Mushroom Sauce 205
Total time: 15 minutes

Thai Basil Beef 189
Total time: 16 minutes

Creamy Sun-Dried Tomato Shrimp 198
Total time: 17 minutes

Kung Pao-Style Chicken 177
Total time: 19 minutes

Chicken Lettuce Wraps 174
Total time: 20 minutes

Spiced Crispy Lamb with Eggplant, Squash, and Hummus 194
Total time: 22 minutes

Cod Florentine 201
Total time: 22 minutes

Lemon-Caper Chicken and Rice 181
Total time: 25 minutes

Philly Cheesesteak Skillet 186
Total time: 25 minutes

Sticky Green Onion Stir-Fried Beef 185
Total time: 26 minutes

Chicken Cordon Bleu with Creamy Dijon Sauce 178
Total time: 27 minutes

Crispy Chicken with Pesto, Charred Romanesco, and Potatoes 173
Total time: 28 minutes

Crispy Salmon and Ginger-Garlic Rice with "Peanut" Sauce 197
Total time: 28 minutes

Veggie Fried Rice 202
Total time: 30 minutes

Mango and Vanilla-Glazed Tenderloin with Spiced Sweet Potatoes 193
Total time: 38 minutes

Wild Mushroom and Zucchini Enchiladas with Mango-Pineapple Salsa 206
Total time: 40 minutes

Brats with Warm Potato Salad and Kraut 190
Total time: 48 minutes

ONE-POT MEALS

Kalua Pork with Pineapple Fried Rice 222
Total time: 22 minutes

"Skillet" Queso Dip 226
Total time: 23 minutes

Meatballs with Creamy Thai-Style Almond Sauce 217
Total time: 25 minutes

Crispy Chicken with Asparagus-Kale Rice 213
Total time: 26 minutes

Beef Stroganoff 221
Total time: 35 minutes

Kabocha, Sweet Potato, Apple, and Bok Choy Curry 230
Total time: 40 minutes

Arroz con Pollo 214
Total time: 42 minutes

Swedish Meatballs 215
Total time: 55 minutes

Pork Chile Verde 229
Total time: 10 minutes prep/6–8 hours cook

Sausages and Pepper in Marinara Sauce 218
Total time: 7 minutes prep/3–6 hours cook

SOUPS AND STEWS

Thai Curry Noodle Soup 237
Total time: 18 minutes

Clams and Mussels in Creamy Turmeric-Coconut Broth 245
Total time: 22 minutes

Shrimp Chowder 246
Total time: 30 minutes

Creamy Bacon Cheeseburger Soup 242
Total time: 31 minutes

Ginger Chicken Noodle Soup 238
Total time: 32 minutes

Butternut Coconut Curry Soup 249
Total time: 40 minutes

Chicken Potpie Stew 241
Total time: 49 minutes

SALADS AND SIDES

Sweet-and-Sour Thai-Style Salad 256
Total time: 10 minutes

Creamy Almond-Cauliflower Polenta 264
Total time: 11 minutes

California Dinner Salad 255
Total time: 15 minutes

Basic Root Mash 267
Total time: 15 minutes

Spanish Cauli-Rice 272
Total time: 17 minutes

Puerto Rican-Style Plantain Rice 273
Total time: 19 minutes

Mashed Potatoes 266
Total time: 22 minutes

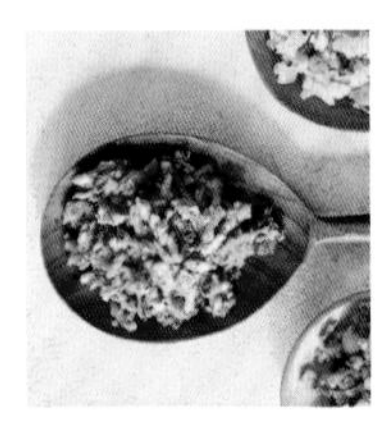

Persian-Style Saffron Cauli-Rice with Dried Fruits 270
Total time: 22 minutes

Basic Cauli-Rice 269
Total time: 23 minutes

Curried Cauliflower and Mango Salad 260
Total time: 25 minutes

Rosemary-Garlic Oven Fries 277
Total time: 28 minutes

Sweet Chili Sweet Potatoes 276
Total time: 30 minutes

Burnt Broccoli 278
Total time: 30 minutes

Apple-Butternut Salad with Maple-Cider Vinaigrette 259
Total time: 34 minutes

Roasted Spring Vegetables with Lemon-Dill Aioli 263
Total time: 35 minutes

Za'atar Fries 275
Total time: 37 minutes

ON THE GRILL

Skirt Steak Tacos with Sriracha Aioli 293
Total time: 16 minutes

Grilled Shrimp and Asparagus with Cilantro-Kale Pepita Pesto 301
Total time: 18 minutes

TIME-SAVING TREATS

Index

T

V

Y

Z

Published in the United States by Ten Speed Press, an imprint of Random House, a division of Penguin Random House LLC, New York.
Tenspeed.com
RandomHouseBooks.com

Typefaces: Mostardesign's Sofia Pro, Alberto Romanos' BW Beto and Beto Grande, and Latinotype's Águila

Library of Congress Cataloging-in-Publication Data is on file with the publisher.

Hardcover ISBN: 978-1-9848-5766-8
eBook ISBN: 978-1-9848-5767-5

Printed in China

Editor: Julie Bennett | Production editor: Kimmy Tejasindhu
Art director and designer: Emma Campion
Production designers: Mari Gill and Faith Hague
Production manager: Serena Sigona | Prepress color manager: Jane Chinn
Food stylist: Lillian Kang | Food stylist assistant: Paige Arnett
Prop stylist: Glenn Jenkins
Hair and make-up: Megan Ray and Sherrie Long
Photo assistant: Patrick Aguilar
Copyeditor: Sharon Silva | Proofreader: Hope Clarke
Indexer: Ken DellaPenta
Publicist: Lauren Kretzschmar | Marketer: Brianne Sperber

10 9 8 7 6 5 4 3 2 1

First Edition